Lorca's Drawings
and Poems

Lorca's Drawings and Poems

Forming the Eye of the Reader

Cecelia J. Cavanaugh, SSJ

Lewisburg
Bucknell University Press
London: Associated University Presses

Associated University Presses
440 Forsgate Drive
Cranbury, NJ 08512

Associated University Presses
25 Sicilian Avenue
London WC1A 2QH, England

Associated University Presses
P.O. Box 338, Port Credit
Mississauga, Ontario
Canada L5G 4L8

The paper used in this publication meets the requirements
of the American National Standard for Permanence of Paper
for Printed Library Materials Z39.48-1984.

Library of Congress Cataloging-in-Publication Data

Cavanaugh, Cecelia J., 1956–
    Lorca's drawings and poems : forming the eye of the reader /
Cecelia J. Cavanaugh.
        p.   cm.
    Based on the author's thesis (doctoral)—University of North
Carolina.
    Includes bibliographical references (p.   ) and index.
    ISBN 0-8387-5302-7 (alk. paper)
    1. García Lorca, Federico, 1898–1936—Criticism and
interpretation.   2. Art and literature.   3. Authors as artists.
I. Title.
PQ6613.A763Z582   1995
861'.62—dc20   95-4099
                                                                              CIP

PRINTED IN THE UNITED STATES OF AMERICA

For my parents
and grandparents

Contents

Illustrations

Color reproductions

The color illustrations appear as a group between pages 64 and 65.

Acknowledgments

My interest in Federico García Lorca's drawings began in 1987, when I came across and purchased the just-published catalog in a bookstore in Granada. That fall the drawings were my focus of research in a Lorca seminar at the University of North Carolina at Chapel Hill, where I was pursuing the doctorate. From that beginning, I encountered what was to be my consistent experience throughout the years: the exhilaration and trepidation of researching a topic of great interest to many yet scarcely explored. Eventually the drawings and their influence on the writing and reading of Lorca's poetry became the subject of my dissertation. Many persons have contributed to my study of García Lorca, to the completion of the dissertation and of this book. My gratitude is first extended to Dr. José Manuel Polo de Bernabé, my dissertation director, in whose classes my interest in Lorca and especially in the drawings was first nurtured, for his encouragement and guidance. Mr. Manuel Fernández Montesinos García of the Fundación García Lorca has been most gracious in his answering countless questions, by collaborating in the reproductions of the drawings in this book, and in providing me with photocopies of those original manuscripts available of the texts analyzed in my study. Dr. Michael Mezzatesta, director of the Duke University Museum of Art, has been of immeasurable assistance since the spring of 1991, when Lorca's drawings were on exhibit at Duke. Among his contributions were special arrangements that allowed me to study the drawings firsthand. Many of the insights I gained would not have been possible without the kind of access he so generously provided. His encouragement and belief in my project continue to provide important support. Other Lorca scholars have offered me their support, in particular Dr. Andrew Anderson, with his wealth of invaluable bibliographic information, and Dr. Candelas Newton in ongoing conversations about our work. Dr. William Ilgen engaged the complexities of many library searches and citations; José Ignacio Badenes, SJ, proofread all the translations I prepared for the book; and Christine Doyle's artist's eye affirmed my readings on many occasions. My thanks to all of them.

11

Personal support has been offered by my family, religious community, friends, colleagues and students at the University of North Carolina at Chapel Hill and Chestnut Hill College in Philadelphia. Their interest in my work, and generous patience with me throughout the preparation of the manuscript infinitely advanced the cause of its completion.

* * *

Permission to reprint the following is gratefully acknowledged:

Quotations from Federico García Lorca's *Obras Completas* (© 1989), and the reproductions of his drawings, © heirs of Federico García Lorca, by permission of Manuel Fernández Montesinos García.

From Maurice Blanchot's "Mallarmé and Literary Space," *The Siren's Song: Selected Essays by Maurice Blanchot*, © 1982, by permission of Harvester Wheatsheaf.

From Mary Ann Caws's *The Eye in the Text: Essays on Perception, Mannerist to Modern*, © 1981, by permission of Princeton University Press.

From Christopher Flint's "Flesh of the Body: Representations of the Body in *Romancero gitano* and *Poeta en Nueva York*," *Papers on Language and Literature*, © 1988, by permission of Southern Illinois University at Edwardsville.

From Lucia Garcia de Carpi's "Bajo el astro de la noche," *Dibujos*, © 1986, by permission of Lucia García de Carpi.

From Sebastià Gasch's "Del cubismo al superrealismo," "El arte poético y plástico del pintor Domingo," "La Exposición en Dalmau," "Lorca, dibujante," "Obras recientes de Dalí," "El pintor Joan Miró," "Salvador Dalí," and "Pintura y cinema," *La Gaceta Literaria* 1 (1927–1929), © 1980 by Topos Verlag Ag.

From Mario Hernández's "Catalogación y comentario" and "Ronda de los autorretratos con animal fabuloso y análisis de dos dibujos neoyorquinos," *Dibujos*, © 1986, by permission of Mario Hernández; and *Line of Light and Shadow: The Drawings of Federico García Lorca*, © 1991, by permission of Duke University Press and Tabapress.

From Richard Klein's "Straight Lines and Arabesques: Metaphors of Metaphor," *Yale French Studies*, © 1970, by permission of *Yale French Studies*.

From David K. Loughran's *Federico García Lorca: The Poetry of Limits*, © 1978, by permission of Boydell and Brewer, Ltd.

From Terence McMullan's "Federico García Lorca's 'Santa Lucía y San Lázaro' and the Aesthetics of Transition," *Bulletin of Hispanic Studies*, © 1990, by permission of Liverpool University Press.

All translations of Spanish and French citations are mine.

Introduction

Federico García Lorca has been recognized for years as a master of visual imagery in his poems and plays. His writing possesses a rich visual quality, characterized by a vibrant use of color, unusual descriptions, and insightful juxtapositions of imagery. His ability to paint with words enables his readers to visualize persons, scenes, and images. But Lorca's descriptive talent did not merely reside in the realm of the written word. From as early as 1923 when he painted theater sets for his production of "La niña que riega la albahaca" [The girl who waters the basil] and drew caricatures on café tables for the amusement of his friends in the *Rinconcillo* in Granada, the poet consistently engaged in drawing.

Lorca's own declarations about his work establish drawing as an intrinsic element in his creative process, and critics have noted its importance.[1] Yet, little has been written about correspondences between Lorca's writing and his drawings, resulting in a lack of integration in the study of these two important facets of Lorca's work. This gap in scholarship is due primarily to a lack of familiarity with Lorca's drawings and to critical suspicion about the validity of discussing the two expressions together.

This study begins the task of bringing Lorca's drawing and his poetry together, reading the drawings as texts for new insights into his poetry. Experience of the structures of meaning present in Lorca's graphic work will naturally affect the reading of his poems. In the past, the drawings familiar to students of Lorca were considered secondary, companion texts to Lorca's poetry and theater and have been interpreted largely by way of the literature. However, Lorca's writing reveals that in his mind a more basic connection exists between his two forms of expression.

In Chapter 1, I shall first discuss the phenomenon of drawing and its role in the human creative purpose. This will be accompanied by excerpts of Lorca's writing, which affirm his experience of drawing along these lines. Next, I shall present Lorca's own statements about drawing and writing poems, establishing in the specific context of his work an intrinsic connection between the two means of expression.

13

Comparing statements made by Lorca about his drawing as well as those he made about writing poetry and then studying his drawings and poems together creates a dialogue between the two media that integrates our vision and understanding of the poet's work.

Furthermore, Lorca's own efforts in drawing, his interest in the plastic arts, and his insistence that they were integral to his work must be considered not only as a manifestation of his innate multiple talent but also as the result of his living and participating in his times, as Carmona observes, a period when poetry was being stripped of its hierarchical superiority over the plastic arts.[2] To that end, I shall examine the artistic currents of his time through Lorca's writing and the writing of Sebastià Gasch, an art critic who influenced Lorca's aesthetic development.

Since one of my goals is to explore various means by which to discuss Lorca's drawings and poetry together, I shall not limit myself to one reading in this work. The following three chapters approach the poem-drawing relationship from three different perspectives. For the purposes of my analysis, I shall consider his poetry and drawing as equals, although I shall begin with the reading of the drawings and proceed to the poems.

In Chapter 2, the focus will be on the drawings and poems done by Lorca in 1927–1928. This was a time of intense exposure to leading currents in modern art for Lorca, and since a major thrust in the art world was the coexistence and the interpenetration of verbal and visual art, it is appropriate first to discuss some of the aesthetics of the era. Specifically, I shall read these principles as they are articulated in the writing of Gasch. His theory of *totalismo* provided a critical space in which Lorca could experiment—indeed, in which he was able to "dibujar poemas" [draw poems]. Adhering to the concept of the union of the poetic and plastic arts, my study looks at Lorca's attempts to implement the tenets of plastic art first in his own drawings and then in subsequent poems. Since, for a brief period, Lorca was drawing instead of writing, the drawings of this period are especially significant.

In Chapter 3, I consider work throughout each stage of Lorca's career, and analyze Lorca's presentation of both space- and place-setting, especially as they relate to the portrayal of the human figure, at times, to the poetic self. Observing the expression of these elements in drawing enlightens the reading of poems in which Lorca portrays persons and setting. This is a logical and appropriate approach for an overview of Lorca's production, since the phenomenon of space and its portrayal as well as its perception lies at the heart of the interart polemic. Several critics' work shall be considered, specifically those who have analyzed Lorca's treatment of space and figure in poetry.

Chapter 4 returns to a limited chronological focus and studies the phenomenon of the arabesque, a late development in Lorca's style and corresponding expression in his late poems found in the *Diván del Tamarit*. This phenomenon in drawings as well as in a series of embellished signatures shows the interpenetration of writing and drawing, a fitting subject to end the study.

This new reading further facilitates the integration of the drawings into Lorca criticism and will prompt recognition of the drawings as an essential component of Lorca's literary production.

Lorca's Drawings
and Poems

1

The Place of the Drawings in Reading Lorca

Drawing in the Creative Context

Federico García Lorca's career was marked by a consistent refusal to distinguish between the different forms of artistic expression. As many scholars have noted, Lorca described his work with terms that referred to other arts: the play *Mariana Pineda* as a series of lithographs, poems entitled "Panorama" or "Paisaje" [Landscape]. In all his efforts in literature, music, and drawing, Lorca was, in Manuel Fernández Montesinos' words, "a poet opposed to duality." Montesinos asserts that Lorca, in his life and in his work

> searches for a totality that would end with the duality of everyday reality, searches for a plentitude, a communion with every thing in all its aspects, a communion that is capable of procuring a peaceful state for the individual as well as the collective soul and for social coexistence itself.[1]

In his practice of drawing, Lorca is a perfect example of a person whose creative talent is both manifested and empowered by that practice. Drawing is natural to small children, and when it is not abandoned with the approach of adolescence, as it often is, it has immense value in human creativity. Drawing can stretch the imagination into the abstract or the fantastic, or it can serve the purpose of pinning down an idea into concrete terms. In either case, the act of drawing greatly expands the creative potential of those who draw. Hanks and Belliston's study of the practice of drawing includes a survey of successful, creative people (such as Thomas Edison) for whom the practice of drawing increased creative potential and ultimately contributed to great accomplishments.[2] A project visualized and articulated is more easily or more successfully realized: "drawing provides vision" (18).

This conventional wisdom surrounding drawing and creativity is apparent when we read Lorca's statements about his drawing. The

19

poet affirms the place of drawing in his work in an important series of letters to Sebastià Gasch, a friend and art critic. He specifically links his drawings to his poems when he says in a letter dated 8 September 1928, "Si te gustan los dibujos, dime cuál o cuáles piensas publicar, y te mandaré sus poemas correspondientes" [If you like the drawings, tell me which you plan to publish, and I'll send you their corresponding poems] (*O.C.* 3:963).[3] Lorca explains drawing's role in his thinking process by stating:

> Ahora empiezo a escribir y a dibujar poesías como ésta que le envío dedicada. Cuando un asunto es demasiado largo o tiene poéticamente una emoción manida, lo resuelvo con los lápices. Esto me alegra y divierte de manera extraordinaria.

> [Now, I'm beginning to write and to draw poems like this one that I am sending dedicated to you. When a subject is too lengthy or contains a poetically stale emotion, I resolve it with the pencils. This makes me happy and amuses me extraordinarily.] (*O.C.* 3:953)

These words provide important insights for the purpose of this study. The striking juncture of *"dibujar poesías"* [to draw poems] has not gone unnoticed by readers of Lorca. Not only are some drawings connected directly to poems, but in fact, others are, in Lorca's mind, poems in their own right. This assertion validates our approaching Lorca's drawings as poetic texts. Secondly, the poet reveals in this letter that the practice of drawing is intrinsic to his creative practice. It would seem that drawing allows him a direct access to feelings and to poetic intuition that expression in language tends to complicate.

Drawing is a means not only to the expression of reality, but also to its experience. In addition to enjoying drawing's enhancement of creativity and its problem-solving capabilities, the person who draws regularly is able to perceive reality with greater insight than the one who does not.[4] The habit of transferring perceptions and experiences to paper or canvas develops the individual's ability to appreciate more fully detail, harmony, form—all of the elements in visual experience. Anyone who has read Lorca knows of his talent for observation, and for retaining what he observed, to be transformed in subsequent writing. It seems logical that Lorca should be attracted to the practice of drawing. In the introduction to *Line of Light and Shadow*, the more recent catalog of Lorca's drawings, Mario Hernández says that drawing "became an integral part of the way he [Lorca] interpreted reality."[5]

The reality perceived by the artist is not limited to the visual or the external. This concept may be further expanded, both theoretically and in reference to Lorca's expressed experience. In his instructions to his students, Kimon Nicholaïdes, the renowned teacher of drawing, broadens the field of their observing:

> There is only one right way to draw and that is a perfectly natural way. It has nothing to do with artifice or technique. It has nothing to do with aesthetics or conception. It has only to do with the act of correct observation and by that I mean *a physical contact with all sorts of objects through all the senses* [my italics].[6]

Beyond the realm of external sensual experience, Philip Rawson observes that "genuine intuition in drawing has as much to do with reading one's own bodily sensations as it has to do with recording external likeness."[7] Similarly, during his lecture on Góngora, Lorca illustrated this reading of bodily sensations when he described the encounter with the blank page, and the way in which he conquered that empty space:

> El poeta que va a hacer un poema (lo sé por experiencia propia) tiene la sensación vaga de que va a una cacería nocturna en un bosque lejanísimo. Un miedo inexplicable rumorea en el corazón. Para serenarse, siempre es conveniente beber un vaso de agua fresca y hacer con la pluma negros rasgos sin sentido.

> [The poet who is going to make a poem (I know this from personal experience) has the vague sensation that he is embarking on a nocturnal hunt in a far-off wood. An inexplicable fear rumbles in his heart. To calm himself, it's advantageous to drink a glass of cold water and make some senseless black strokes with the pen.] (*O.C.* 3:235)

This rich quote not only verifies Lorca's presence to bodily sensations, it also provides one more reference to drawing as a creative constant in his process. The action of drinking fresh water suggests purifying. It is fascinating to note that the very act of drawing, of putting pen or pencil to paper even just to make *"negros rasgos sin sentido"* [black meaningless strokes], provides reassurance, grounding, an anchor. Both purity and grounding are named by Lorca as essential to his creative state.

This body-mind-hand connection experienced by Lorca is reflected in drawing's unique qualities among the plastic arts. Drawings can provide insights into their creator, for example, in psychological evaluation and in handwriting analysis. In a way that is intrinsic to no other plastic art, drawing (and this would include handwriting), provides a link between the mind, the idea that it engenders, and the expression of that idea—a shorthand of thinking. Perhaps this is why Lorca resolved poetic problems with his drawing pencils. This is because of the direct connection of hand through point to paper. This connection has implications for the role of drawing in Lorca's experience. Philip Rawson explains that "drawing is direct because it can reflect immediately the impulses of your imagination as your arm and hand respond to them."[8] Joan Snitzer, an art historian at Barnard College who worked as a technical adviser to the 1991 New York exhibit of Lorca's drawings, observed:

> His creative genius extended to his hands, his art . . . particularly with the medium of drawing which is tied to his thinking; they're a direct diagram of his thought. His art is very immediate and his drawings very spontaneous; they do give you a sense of his person and his poetry.[9]

Such a bodily experience accounts for drawings' intimate nature. Lorca further reveals to Gasch that his drawings are an expression of something very personal by his care in sending them to others: "Te mando dibujos. Tú eres la única persona con quien hago esto porque me siento muy comprendido por tí" [I'm sending you drawings. You are the only person with whom I do this, because I feel very understood by you] (O.C. 3:963). It is a fact that Lorca gave away many drawings to many people; Gasch was not the only person to whom he gave drawings, but the importance here is not in his exaggeration but rather in the identification of the poet with the drawings he created.

Parallels in Creativity: Writing and Drawing

Lorca felt and expressed an intrinsic connection between his drawing and writing, affirmed by such critics as Mario Hernández, who notes that in Lorca's work, "both graphic and literary expression are born from the same unitary intuition."[10] Manuel Fernández Montesinos has said that Lorca "conceived the submission of all different artistic manifestations to the same aesthetic principles."[11]

For Lorca, then, drawing and poetry share more than themes and images. Deeper correspondences between the two media are evident in parallels between statements Lorca made about drawing and poetry. In the Góngora lecture cited above, Lorca referred to writing poetry as embarking on a hunt; writing to Gasch, Lorca described drawing in analogous terms, as a fishing expedition:

Unos dibujos salen así, como las metáforas más bellas, y otros buscándolos en el sitio *donde se sabe de seguro* que están. Es una pesca. Unas veces entra el pez en el cestillo y otras se busca la mejor agua y se lanza al mejor anzuelo a propósito para conseguir. El anzuelo se llama *realidad*.

[Some drawings come out like that, like the most beautiful metaphors, and others by searching for them in the spot where you know for sure they are. It's like going fishing. Sometimes the fish jumps in the basket, and other times you look for the best water, and you throw your best fishhook to catch it. The fishhook is called reality.] (*O.C.* 3:969)

In a lecture given in 1928 entitled "Imaginación, inspiración, evasión," Lorca speaks of the process of writing poetry in terms that echo these observations: "La hija directa de la imaginación es la <<metáfora>>, nacida a veces al golpe rápido de la intuición, alumbrada por la lenta angustia del presentimiento" [The direct daughter of the imagination is the metaphor, born sometimes in the rapid jump of the intuition illumined by the slow anguish of premonition] (*O.C.* 3:259). The casting of a fishing net and the seeking out of prey are repeated when in the lecture on the poet Góngora, Lorca describes the poet as shooting arrows, to protect himself perhaps, but also to capture:

Debe tapar sus oídos como Ulises frente a las sirenas, y debe lanzar sus flechas sobre las metáforas vivas, y no figuradas o falsas que le van acompañando.

[He must cover his ears as did Ulysses faced by the sirens and must launch his arrows over the living metaphors, not the imagined or false ones that accompany him]. (*O.C.* 3:236)

Not only the activity of casting or hunting about for images, but also the place in which this activity occurs is shared by the artist involved in either expression. For Lorca, the artistic experience involves both entering the creative space ("el poeta . . . va a una cacería nocturna") and leaving it. Lorca continues the hunting image, speaking of the forest or poetic realm:

Hay que salir. Y éste es el momento peligroso para el poeta. El poeta debe llevar un plano de los sitios que va a recorrer y debe estar sereno frente a las mil bellezas y las mil fealdades disfrazadas de belleza que han de pasar ante sus ojos.

[One must leave, and this is the dangerous moment for the poet. The poet must carry a map of the spots which he's going to come across and must be serene in front of a thousand beauties and ugly things disguised as beautiful which must pass before his eyes.] (*O.C.* 3:235)

The "map of the places" that "the poet must carry" suggests here that writing or drawing serves as a guide; on other occasions Lorca suggests that this map is the fruit of his excursions. He wrote to Gasch of his creative adventures: "Yo nunca me atrevo en terrenos que no son de hombre porque vuelvo tierras atrás en seguida y rompo casi siempre *el producto de mi viaje*" [italics mine] [I never venture into territories alien to man, because I quickly wander back and almost always rip up the fruits of my voyage] (*O.C.* 3:967).

Another of Lorca's conferences, in which he explored the richness of the Spanish lullaby, provides yet another reading of Lorca's creative experience. In this conference, it is the child who is the artist, for in another creative venture, he or she must transform the sounds and words being sung to him into images. The night forest encountered in the above references resembles the frightening realm occupied by this listening child:

Está dentro de un mundo poético inaccesible, donde ni la retórica ni la alcahueta imaginación, ni la fantasía tienen entrada; planicie con los centros nerviosos al aire de horror y de belleza aguda donde un caballo blanquísimo, mitad de níquel, mitad de humo, cae herido de repente con un enjambre de abejas clavadas de furiosa manera sobre sus ojos.

[He is within an inaccessible poetic world, where neither rhetoric nor the busybody imagination nor fantasy can enter, a plain with nerve centers exposed to the air, of horror and of sharp beauty, where a very white horse, half nickel half smoke falls suddenly wounded with a swarm of bees holding on furiously to its eyes.] (*O.C.* 3:291–92)

Venturing into unknown space is an inherent and consistent part of the creative act. The anticipation that accompanies such an excursion is derived from the artist's acquaintance with the beauty and the terror that await in this creative space.

In spite of the terrifying aspects of this poetic plane, one detects in Lorca's words a sense of optimism, the serenity that he regards as essential to the poetic process. In this process, drawing plays a key role for Lorca. It allows him to concretize the abstract as well as to stay in touch with inner sensations. Lorca states:

Cuando hago una cosa de pura abstracción, siempre tiene (creo yo) un salvoconducto de sonrisas y equilibrio bastante humano. Mi estado es siempre alegre, y este soñar mío no tiene peligro en mí, que llevo defensas; es peligroso para el que se deje fascinar por los grandes espejos oscuros que la poesía y la locura ponen en el fondo de sus barrancos. Yo ESTOY Y ME SIENTO CON PIES DE PLOMO EN ARTE.

[When I do a purely abstract thing, it always has (I believe) a safe conduct pass of smiles and a rather human equilibrium. My state is always happy, and this dreaming of mine is not dangerous for me, because I have defenses; it is dangerous for one who lets himself be fascinated by the great dark mirrors that poetry and madness wield at the bottom of their chasms. I HAVE AND I FEEL I HAVE MY FEET FIRMLY ON THE GROUND IN ART.] (*O.C.* 3:967)[12]

The groundedness described by Lorca is akin to the sensation of putting a point to paper—"making [senseless] black marks" in order to calm himself—just as the images of wandering and casting that he employs are paralleled in the meandering of that same point and of the line it creates. This description of himself while he draws is echoed in the way in which he describes the poet: "El poeta debe ir a su cacería limpio y sereno, hasta disfrazado" [The poet should embark on his hunt clean and serene, even disguised] (236). How can this cleanness, and serenity be achieved? One way is by drawing. Lorca tells Gasch:

Pero sin tortura ni sueño (abomino del arte de los sueños) ni complicaciones. Estos dibujos son poesía pura o plástica a la vez. Me siento limpio, confortado, alegre, *niño*, cuando los hago.

[But without torture or dream (I hate the art of dreams) or complications. These drawings are pure poetry or pure plasticity at once. I feel clean, comforted, happy, a child when I do them.] (*O.C.* 3:970)

The direct, economical nature of drawing may explain its attraction for Lorca. By avoiding the tired path of language and the "trite emotion" that he faced at times in his writing, the poet was able to record his sensations in a way that was fresh. For Lorca drawing provided many benefits to his poetic activity. It accessed and maintained contact with his creative center; it enabled him to express in economical terms the images, feelings, and insights he derived from his incursions into the realm of creativity; finally, it provided him with a defense against being overwhelmed or overpowered, an anchor to reality, to the human. Personal encounter with Lorca's drawings reaffirms their vital quality. They *do* carry an emotion, first hand, what Mario Hernández characterizes as "their suggestiveness and unending fragrance."[13] Lorca was aware of this; his concern for their exact reproduction is clear in instructions he gave in 1928 pertaining to three drawings to be reproduced: "Los dibujos debes cuidarlos para que, al ser reproducidos, las líneas no pierdan la *emoción*, que es lo único que tienen. Deben salir exactos. Recomienda esto mucho a los grabadores" [You must be very careful with the drawings so that, upon being reproduced, the lines don't lose their emotion, which is all they have. They must come out exactly. Recommend this a great deal to the printers] (*O.C.* 3:947).

Lorca believed that the sense of sight is crucial to the poetic transformation of reality. Many of his images in poetry and in drawing are rooted in an initial visual experience. For example, some of Lorca's drawings are inspired by drawings of nerve cells he saw in the press of his day. These were based on the work of Santiago Ramón y Cajal, the recipient of the 1906 Nobel Prize for medicine.[14] Variations of the images contained in Ramón y Cajal's sketches and those of his students, with whom Lorca was familiar, occur throughout the poet's work, as in the drawing *La Vista y el tacto* [Sight and touch] drawn in 1929–1930. They may also have inspired the phrase "planicie con los centros nerviosos al aire de horror y de belleza aguda" [a plain with nerve centers exposed to the air, of horror and of sharp beauty], already quoted from the lecture on the lullaby (*O.C.* 3:291–92). Lorca drew many costumbristic drawings throughout his career, especially in the earlier twenties. These include drawings of Andalusian ladies, Holy Week processions, Gypsies, churches—all familiar sights to the poet. These visual experiences inspired his poetry and drama as well.

Seizing such images and then lending himself to the play of drawing empowered Lorca to continue the poetic journey, to transform the reality he perceived, and to create signs from his perceptions. Lorca speaks of this interplay in "Imaginación, inspiración, evasión:"

Pero la imaginación está limitada por la realidad: no se puede imaginar lo que no existe; necesita de objetos, paisajes, números, planetas, y se hacen precisas las relaciones entre ellos dentro de la lógica más pura. No se puede saltar al abismo ni prescindir de los términos reales. La imaginación tiene horizontes, quiere dibujar y concretar todo lo que abarca. La imaginación poética viaja y transforma las cosas, les da su sentido más puro y define relaciones que no se sospechaban; pero siempre, siempre, siempre opera sobre hechos de la realidad más neta y precisa.

[But the imagination is limited by reality: what doesn't exist cannot be imagined, it needs objects, landscapes, numbers, planets, and the relationships between them are made precise within the most pure logic. It cannot jump to the abyss or avoid real terms. The imagination has horizons, it wants to draw and concretize all which it embraces. Poetic imagination travels and transforms things, it gives them their most pure sense and defines relationships that hadn't been suspected; but always, always, always, it operates on facts of the most precise and neat reality.] (*O.C.* 3:259)

Lorca himself notes how his reading of reality is expressed in poetry and drawing and how those "readings" may be read in light of each other.

The process of visualization offers the reader new interpretations of images viewed in Lorca's drawings and found in his writing. By visualizing a counterpart in drawing to an image inscribed verbally in Lorca's poetry—that is, by asking oneself how that image might look drawn—Lorca's reader facilitates the comprehension of otherwise inaccessible significance, provides a starting point for the unraveling of Lorca's imagery, and often opens further connections between texts. This kind of reading will be practiced throughout this study.

The aim of this study is to create, in Tim Mathews's words, a "space where reading and seeing are confronted with one another."[15] It seeks to relate the bodily experience Lorca expresses in his drawings and his poems to the bodily experience evoked in the viewing of his drawings, the hearing of his words, the reading of his poetry, the sensing of the shape of the poetry. This entails reading Lorca's plastic works, drawing words from them. This reading will not seek to force artificial correspondences between texts, but rather to complement, contrast, and frame drawings and poems in such a way that reading does not violate the intuitive, impalpable beauty of his work, but rather serves to fill in the gaps so that, in Lorca's words, readers may "better understand" (*O.C.* 3:969).

The Place of the Drawings in Lorca Scholarship

Since it is apparent from Lorca's own writings and, as I shall discuss later, in much of his imagery, that drawing is part of his poetic process, one wonders why these connections have been neglected in the study of his work. Several reasons are immediately apparent. First, Lorca's drawings were not published comprehensively until 1986. Second, the field of interdisciplinary comparative theory has long debated the existence of an instrument for such a study. Third, in addition to the complexities of dealing with more than one medium, Lorca's work in poetry and theater as well as in music and drawing has been consistently accompanied by biographical details, anecdotes, personal remembrances and the like. Many of these stories are extraneous to the work, and some are less than accurate, embellished over time. Thus, the student must grapple not only with the demands of scholarship in the medium or genre in which he or she is focused, but also with the task of sifting through the legend, the myth that has arisen around Lorca. In the case of the drawings, for example, the fascination with the mere fact that Lorca drew, the status derived from familiarity with this lesser-known aspect of his creativity and/or the possession of a Lorca drawing or drawings resulted in presentations of his drawings as merely interesting phenomena, as an addendum to more scholarly studies of his writing.

Lorca's drawings received some critical attention during his lifetime, essentially in reviews of the only exhibit of his work, in Barcelona in 1927. In the years since his death, few books devoted entirely to Lorca's drawings have been published. Jean Gebser, Gregorio Prieto, and most recently, Helen Oppenheimer have focused directly on the drawings themselves, providing at least a starting point for a study of Lorca that integrates his literary accomplishments with his achievements in the plastic arts.[16]

Gregorio Prieto, an acquaintance of Lorca, was the first to publish on the subject of the drawings. His study "García Lorca as a Painter" (1946) is republished both in *Los Dibujos de García Lorca* and in *Lorca y la generación del 27*. His other books, *Lorca en color* and *Lorca y su mundo angélico* are best classified as books of tribute and are less an analysis of drawings or poems. Prieto, a recognized painter in his own right, and a friend and associate of Lorca from his days in the Residencia de estudiantes [the Students' Residence] in Madrid, brought his technical knowledge of art to the study of the drawings. Prieto insists that Lorca's visual productions must be considered as drawings because Lorca drew in ink and pencil. When he added color, particularly in the early days of his career, he did so with the colored pencils that were his constant companions.[17] Prieto analyzes technical and thematic patterns and the artistic influences present in Lorca's drawings; he relates these observations to the poems. According to Prieto, Lorca's mastery of poetry eclipsed his talent for drawing, a conclusion with which most critics agree. Prieto's analysis of the relation between the drawings and the poetry, however, does not go beyond similarities in theme and/or color.

In *Lorca, poète-dessinateur*, Jean Gebser introduces and analyzes thirteen drawings given to him by Lorca. As an early work studying the drawings, Gebser's book contains many elements common to the studies that would follow it: a biographical and literary sketch of Lorca, a presentation and description of the pieces to be considered, and an attempt to consider the phenomenon of drawing as part of Lorca's production. Gebser concentrates specifically on a spatial division in each drawing to which he assigns psychological values: the coexistence of and sometimes confrontation between (1) the rational and the irrational, (2) the conscious and unconscious; as well as the corresponding images of father and mother. Gebser has been criticized for basing so many of his conclusions, especially those of a psychological nature, on his relationship with Lorca, a relationship that is difficult to document beyond Gebser's claims.[18] It must be noted, nevertheless, that however superficial Gebser's linking of Lorca's poetry to his drawings may have been, it opens the way for subsequent integrating studies.

Helen Oppenheimer observes similar relationships in *Lorca: The Drawings: Their Relation to the Poet's Life and Work*. This work, hailed inaccurately by some as the first of such studies, makes several largely organizational contributions to the field. First, Oppenheimer divides the drawings thematically and chronologically into five categories: (1) works related to Andalusia, (2) works related to personal identity, (3) experimental drawings, (4) what she terms "literary" drawings, and (5) theater sketches. In each of the first four divisions, the author relates the drawings to Lorca's life, for which purpose she adheres faithfully to Ian Gibson's biography of the poet. She presents not only the biographical context for the drawings but also the artistic milieu in which Lorca conceived and produced them. She summarizes well the influences on his work: Cubism and Surrealism, for example, and artists such as Dalí and Miró.

Oppenheimer offers a detailed study of several leitmotivs that appear in the drawings. In her view each image is to some degree a representation of Lorca's search for identity. She shows some parallels between themes, images and techniques in each division of the drawings. Her thesis, that recurrent images and the technique of doubling in Lorca's drawings reveal the poet's inner conflicts, resonates with Gebser's psychological perspective. Her attribution of these inner conflicts to Lorca's homosexuality agrees with the position of Ian Gibson.[19] Although Oppenheimer convincingly relates images and themes to the idea of identity, specifically sexual identity, she finds only limited correspondences between specific poems and drawings. She asserts that some of the drawings represent characters from Lorca's earlier poetry. Oppenheimer had originally proposed to demonstrate that specific drawings executed during Lorca's stay in New York illustrate poems from *Poeta en Nueva York*, but she concludes less ambitiously by saying that some drawings are illustrations of one or two lines from certain poems in that collection.

Despite her fine expository study of Lorca's drawings, in the final analysis, Oppenheimer's discussion of the direct relationship between Lorca's writing and drawing is restricted in its treatment. She appears to accept the historical-biographical approach to Lorca's work as the most authoritative, critical method. This restricts the reading of his texts and impoverishes the interpretation and analysis of the poet's works.

Actually, the limited correspondence Oppenheimer draws between images in the drawings and single lines in the poems suggests the reverse of her thesis. Why not consider the drawings as first drafts, as a visual grasping of a feeling, then its image, or of a character or an idea on the part of Lorca, and his setting down of these abstractions as a first step in their subsequent development in the written word? Why not consider the drawings' role in Lorca's work in terms of possibilities rather than limitations?

Other critics have included Lorca's pictorial production in investigations into his work. The drawings were featured in Marie Laffranque's study of Lorca's writing, a well-rounded presentation of his aesthetic system. David K. Loughran dedicates a chapter of his book, *Federico García Lorca: The Poetry of Limits*, to the drawings. His comments, written in 1978, are still true today:

> It is strange that Lorca's graphic art has received so little critical attention, given its deep and vital connection with his poetry. In fact, the one very much helps explain the other in a mutual correspondence that has been mentioned but never pursued in depth in order to demonstrate just *how* they are related. (197)[20]

In the chapter of his book entitled "To Draw Poems," Loughran comments on the work done by Gebser and Prieto and underlines the key role Lorca's letters to Sebastià Gasch play in understanding the drawings. Loughran analyzes twenty-four of Lorca's drawings, focusing on subject matter and the use of line, and linking them with many of the observations he had made about Lorca's poetry in the book's previous chapters.[21] At the time of Loughran's writing (1978), twenty-four drawings "represent[ed] a very large percentage of those available."[22] More recently, Felicia Londré dedicated a chapter of her book *Federico García Lorca* to the drawings, operating on the premise that only 150 of the drawings were known. Like Loughran, but less thoroughly, she analyzes them in light of the imagery at work in the poetry and Lorca's plays and film script.[23] She refers to Loughran's work as "the best study to date [1984] of the correspondences that exist between Lorca's poetry and his drawings."[24] Estelle Irizarry includes Lorca in her book *Painter-Poets of Contemporary Spain* in a chapter that summarizes previous research and makes a general analysis of the drawings in relation to Lorca's work and what she calls his iconology.[25] These studies trace the resemblances between the poetry and drawings, but while they may have alluded to a more vital relation between the two, they do not explore it satisfactorily.

Although there has been scanty attention paid to Lorca's drawing on the part of scholars over the years, a look at recent bibliography reveals a surge of interest in this topic. Mario Hernández, who had already written extensively on the subject, made a momentous contribution in 1986, when he edited the first catalog of the drawings.[26] After fifty years of attempts to gather and publish the drawings, an immense number of the drawings, many never seen before, were introduced to the public. The book also includes a collection of critical essays by Hernández and others on the subject of Lorca's drawings and his aesthetics.

After the publication of this catalog in 1986, a number of articles focusing on the drawings have appeared. However, few consider thoroughly the "mutual correspondence" of which Loughran speaks. There is great potential for research in the large number of previously unknown or unanalyzed drawings. The unavailability of such material for so long has resulted in a lack of thorough studies of the interrelatedness of the drawings, poems, and Lorca's poetics. Recent articles reveal a search for a more developed theoretical approach to the problem. Again, even when theories are proposed, direct application to specific texts is notably absent.

Mario Hernández's *Line of Light and Shadow: The Drawings of Federico García Lorca* (1991), translated by Christopher Maurer, is the latest and most complete catalog of Lorca's graphic work. In this collection, Hernández increases the number of drawings catalogued from 352 to 383, he corrects and updates the information surrounding them, and he provides more accurate dating. In his words: "The book has a double objective: the cataloguing and reproduction of all of the known material in chronological order and also the detailed interpretation of the principal sequences" (13).

The introduction to the catalog furnishes a history of Lorca's efforts in drawing, from the caricatures of the early 1920s to the later more abstract, stylized expression; this study neither separates the drawings from Lorca's work in poetry and theater nor from the cultural, literary, and artistic milieu in which they were created. The influence of the Cubists, of Miró, of Salvador Dalí, and of Surrealism is documented and contextualized by Hernández, weaving Lorca's declarations about the place of these movements in his aesthetics with the observations made about the poet's work by others.

Hernández places Lorca's graphic expression in a more comprehensive context when he refers specifically to Lorca's writing and how the two media reflect each other. He reads, for example, in the "Oda a Salvador Dalí" [Ode to Salvador Dalí] how Lorca seeks to "define Cubism in painting and Dalí's attitude as a painter," whereas he reads the maturation of style evident in the "Oda al santísimo sacramento del altar" [Ode to the most holy sacrament of the altar] as mirrored in Lorca's final drawings (19).

Hernández's presentation of the drawings also reflects the development of Lorca's worldview, from the happiness and innocence of childhood to the awareness of coexistent sides of reality, life's contradictions, and its use to create "a world of terrifying presences," and works in which "precision blends mysteriously with grace and a wounding, impalpable 'graphism' is fragrant with lyricism" (31). Hernández divides the drawings into eight thematic or chronological sequences in which he discusses the interplay of the biographical, literary, and artistic factors that figure in Lorca's execution of these works. He also analyzes representative drawings: from early illustrations of Granada, to drawings of women, clowns, saints, Gypsies, and sailors. The sequences represent both an evolution in Lorca's mastery of technique as well as in the significance of their images. The practical application of drawing in the service of theatrical productions reveals the preoccupation of Lorca with the human figure and shows how drawing enriched Lorca's plays and poems with a wealth of "plastic detail" (87–88).

In the two sequences in which Hernández analyzes the series of drawings from 1927 to 1928, to which Lorca himself refers as poems, and the self-portraits and other drawings associated with New York, Hernández notes an analogous development in drawing and poetry. In the series of line drawings, he finds evidence of Lorca's "instinct" and his striving for "lyrical abstraction" (148). In the New York series, he notes the presence of a "negative apocalyptic vision" (111) of "deep terror" and of "figures from beyond the grave" (112). Hernández's scholarship is based on years of firsthand work with the drawings. Not only the accomplishment of compiling them from literally hundreds of private collections and editing them (including sorting through apocryphal work), but also his investigations into possible sources for Lorca's graphic imagery provides the kind of background that greatly facilitates further exploration of Lorca's drawings and their rightful place as texts in his work.

The Challenge of a New Reading

The development traced above in the study of Lorca's drawings is only partly explained by the recent availability of the drawings. Another crucial factor is the state of literary theory as concerns the interart relationship. The challenge to establish a common language between these texts demands reading texts in both media for the correspondences already in existence between them. My intention is not to make direct comparisons, hence the reading produced here will be of correspondences, commonalities that are neither entirely verbal nor visual. How can Lorca's plastic and verbal texts be discussed together? What is their common ground?

Lorca's experience and his observations, influenced by his consistent drawing and by his association with the visual arts of others, richly endowed Lorca's poetry with many levels of significance and interpretation. And, in like terms, readers of Lorca who know his drawings and their relation to twentieth-century art are even further opened to possibilities of meaning in his writing than those who are not.

Such familiarity provides momentum for a second reading of the text. This second reading is intrinsic to the perception of either literature or the plastic arts, according to Rudolf Arnheim:

> In vision . . . we have the primary presence of the total scene, the unselected raw material that hits us when we open our eyes. It is passive reception. This raw material, however, is immediately subjected to the active perception of searching for the organization of the sight, the tracing of its constituent features, the discovery of the underlying theme, which is the clue to meaning. Works of art cannot be said to be seen unless they are received in this active manner—an effort that requires a determined concentration similar to the one we ascribe to the evocation of mental images in literature.[27]

Just as the reader of a poem must first read it in its entirety, then consider the images, figures and relationships that it portrays, so the viewer of the picture derives meaning by a sweeping gaze followed by a second viewing, which considers the picture's components singly and then in relationship to each other. Such seeing and reading is a path to analyzing Lorca's work in poetry and drawing in conjunction with one another.

I intend to explore what Susan Langer calls the "ensemble of relations between the two media" as it can be applied specifically to Lorca's work. Such an approach keeps the two media separate insofar as their surface or "primary apparition" while it searches for deeper correspondences, for example, how one medium's "primary apparition" (space in a drawing and time in a poem) might be secondary in the other.[28]

The reader of any poem or drawing must rely on the conjunction of impressions received from the text in order to fully understand or appreciate it. So, too, as readers of Lorca, we read best when we employ this holding operation, allowing our impressions of both drawing and poetry to occupy a common space and mutually inform our perception. This is my first step in reading both drawing and poem: to consider how my reading moves within a text from element to element, or from word to word, from point to point along a line, and so forth. This prepares a reading from one text to another. Because I am interested in the mutual influence between the two, any poems and drawings considered together will be from the same period. I will also consider any theoretical statements made by Lorca, thereby including him not only as an artist but also as a reader of his work and experience.

Reading implies a diversity of interpretations dependent on the perspective and preparedness of the reader. There is a new reader of Lorca evolving in the aftermath of the revelation of his drawings. This new reader approaches Lorca's written texts from a new perspective, with new information, with new eyes, at least new in our day. The kinds of statements Lorca makes about writing and drawing suggest that seventy years ago he realized the dynamic of cross-fertilization, of intertextuality, an ongoing production of meaning among all his texts. Such cross-fertilization is contained in the very relationship between drawing and writing. Not only the nature of Lorca's work, its richness of inspiration and influence, but also the very act of bringing multiple texts to one reading provide a fecundity of interpretation. Such integration is expressed by Susan Langer:

> But if you trace the differences among the arts as far and as minutely as possible, there comes a point beyond which no more distinctions can be made. It is the point where the deeper structural devices—ambivalent images, intersecting forces, great rhythms and their analogues in detail, variations, congruences, in short: all the organizing devices—reveal the principles of dynamic form. . . . these principles appear, in one art after

another, as the guiding ones in every work that achieves organic unity, vitality of form or expressiveness, which is what we mean by the significance of art.[29]

Lorca's drawings provide maps of his thought, and records of the inner reality he transferred to the written word. Lorca's drawings put us in touch with his inner world as well as with the creative power with which he expressed it, and they convey the presence of play, energy, and motion. In addition to being maps of Lorca's thought with potential for revealing insights into their creator, the drawings must be considered as autonomous works of art. Lorca's stated intention to exhibit and to publish the drawings, and the evaluation of his peers as well as of subsequent critics affirms that the drawings are worthwhile plastic works.[30] Studying the drawings, looking at them, reading about them, searching for their counterparts in Lorca's writing and in the work of artists who were his contemporaries, provide new insight into Lorca's poems, creating a space in which they may dialogue with one another and allowing this dialogue to inform our perception and interpretation.

2

Reading Poetry and Plasticity

We have established the appropriateness of bringing together poetry and the plastic arts in this study of Lorca's work by virtue of his talent as well as by the times in which he wrote and drew.[1] Lorca's activity as a literary critic and his lectures on music and art provide added support to the analysis of his multidimensional participation in and contribution to the artistic and literary movements of his day. Between 1925 and 1928 Lorca was involved in drawing, writing, and criticism while immersed in what Soria Olmedo refers to as the "aesthetic debate of the avante-garde." Such was the extent of Lorca's participation in this debate that Soria Olmedo insists that "the plot of the texts—lectures, letters, poems, drawings—thickens in such a way that one is obliged to follow closely the chronology."[2] The principles that Lorca expounds in his critical/theoretical texts have not been applied rigorously to his drawings from this period, and certainly not to the conjunction of poetry and drawing in his work (62). Critics who influenced Lorca—Sebastià Gasch is a prime example—have only recently been studied. Analyzing selected poems and drawings from these years in light of the principles of Lorca's theoretical work illuminates the correspondences between poetry and drawing for the poet.

The avante-garde movement of Ultraism had placed new value on painting, evidenced, for example, by the placing of paintings and other plastic texts in its journals, paving the way for similar treatment of Cubism and Surrealism. Carmona observes:

> In its journals and public acts Ultraism established something that would have to be a point of indispensable definition in all the cultural circuits created around 1927 until the Civil War: that of the "natural" and necessary confluence between painting and literature always under the common belief in working in favor and in defense of "young art" or of "new art."[3]

This fertile aesthetic environment shaped what Lorca read, wrote, and drew. The results of his activity and the presence of artistic influences will be explored in both his drawings and poems.

Dalí in Drawing and Poetry

It is impossible to speak of Lorca in the early twenties without considering the influence of Salvador Dalí. From their days at the Residencia de estudiantes, the Catalán painter was a force in Lorca's life and work. Through Dalí, among others, Lorca came to know the art and artists of his day. Most significantly, it was Dalí who introduced Lorca to the artistic circles active in Barcelona. This made possible Lorca's relationship with Gasch and Josep Dalmau, who would arrange the exhibition of Lorca's drawings in his gallery in 1927. Lorca's poetry and drawings show the presence of Dalí through allusions and imitations. At times the painter is himself the subject of Lorca's work.[4] Lorca articulates his artistic theory and applies that theory in three drawings and in the "Oda a Salvador Dalí" [Ode to Salvador Dalí], in which he treats the subject of Salvador Dalí.

Lorca's first and second portraits of Dalí were both drawn in 1925, the same year that Lorca wrote the "Oda a Salvador Dalí." In both drawings, Lorca draws Dalí as a solid figure, dressed in clothing recognizable to those who knew the painter. The painter's face is drawn as an oval, his nose a long thin line, and his eyes empty ovals—the first appearance of a motif soon to become predominant in Lorca's drawings. Dalí is presented in the first drawing in relation to a foreground, and, in the second, a background indicative of some attribute of Dalí: the café environment invoked by the table, glass, and pipe before the subject in the first drawing and the artist's easel behind him in the second. In each of the two drawings, Lorca uses words as well as visual images to convey meaning.

The title of the first *Retrato de Dalí* [Portrait of Dalí] is printed in large letters of varying texture, solid and stippled. The names of the colors on the artist's palette are also written out, and *gris* [gray] is stylized, the final *s* written over *gri*, turned in much the same way that the bowl of a pipe held by Dalí and the palette superimposed onto his left cheek are turned along a plane to face out toward the spectator. The stipple of the title is repeated in the smoke that emanates from the bowl of the pipe Dalí holds and travels, guiding the viewer's eye over his head and to his mouth. Dalí appears to be inhaling the smoke from the bowl, not from the mouthpiece. Circum-

"Slavdor Adil" © 1994 Artists Rights Society (ARS), New York/VEGAP, Madrid

venting the conventional piques the attention of the viewer and demands interpretation, or at least speculation. Smoke is a product of a process, here we see a connection between Dalí's mouth and the pipe's bowl. Smoke emanating from both link the artist's mouth, not his hand, to productivity. Perhaps Lorca wishes to focus not on Dalí's works in themselves but rather on the artist's goals and aesthetic principles.

In the second portrait, Lorca continues to experiment with modes of depiction that challenge his viewer. He writes the title of the drawing in inverted anagram form, calling the painter "Slavdor Adil." Dalí is named "peintre" [painter] at first glance, superfluous information, given that he is depicted in front of a canvas with brush and palette in his hands. Again, the colors on his palette are represented by blotches of paint and also named—this time the color blue is named in French and Spanish, and the letters for *gris* [gray] are out of order, "srgi." Lorca is certainly being playful here, and his innovations echo anecdotes of the kinds of word games he and Dalí were known to have invented. The use of French may refer to Dalí's Paris connections. However, such departure from straightforward wording to inversion of Spanish words and use of foreign phrases exemplifies the tenets of Dalí's art. Lorca distorts language within the bounds of recognition: the viewer does not require letters in order, or in Spanish, to understand meaning. This is a renaming or reclaiming on the part of Lorca, exercising control over his subject, making art of the portrait of an artist. The viewer of the portrait looks first on the foregrounded plane at the figure of Dalí and then beyond him, over his shoulder toward the canvas on which one may assume he has been working. In fact, the body of Dalí blocks our viewing the whole of the canvas. The viewer is left with the task of divining what the representation hides. The text provides information, makes connections, and raises questions for the viewer.

In this second drawing, Dalí is represented both outside the canvas on the easel and inside it. Lorca has, in effect, repeated a Cubist practice. He manipulates his subject matter so as to offer more than one view of it. Multiple languages, inverted words, and so on do not impede the comprehension of his drawing, but, as in synthetic Cubism, call on the viewer to reorder the images to construct the reality on which the drawing is based (if that is the goal of the viewer). But such manipulation also invites a consideration of the relationships implied between painting and language, representation and reality, the artist and his art. The canvas on the easel in the second drawing contains images of a human figure—perhaps another image of Dalí with a pipe in his mouth. This abstract depiction is surrounded by heavy black strokes, and is in sharp contrast stylistically to the window or painting in the upper right of the canvas. Through that frame a scene similar to more traditional seascapes executed by Dalí is viewed. Several surfaces, depicted by a change in color or stroke of the pen are present. It seems that Lorca has removed Dalí from his painting, while simultaneously representing his work. When one turns to the "Oda a Salvador Dalí," one finds that in the written text Lorca similarly considers the subject of his friend, his physical surroundings in Cadaqués, and the work he was doing in art.

The "Oda a Salvador Dalí" has been analyzed by critics, usually along the lines of the relationship between Dalí and Lorca, and/or Lorca's efforts at art criticism. The poem was written in 1925, at a time when Dalí was painting in the Cubist mode, and has been seen as Lorca's articulation and emulation of the Cubist aesthetic.[5] Certainly, the form that Lorca employed (alexandrine cuartets) imitates Cubist rigidity, and his language reflects and celebrates the newness and excitement generated in the art world by the Cubists and their work. One notes in critical comments about the text a tension between its nature as a "Cubist text" and what other critics read as allusions to Surrealism found in its verses. However, the "Oda a Salvador Dalí" is not so simply delineated. As is the case with Lorca's work in drawing, there is evidence of contact with other artists, art critics and aesthetic movements (such as Dalí and the aesthetics he espoused), and their integration into the poet's creative activity. This is consistent throughout Lorca's career. In addition to Cubism and Surrealism, then, other forces are at work in this poem. For example, Hernández cites many examples of Dalí's influence on Lorca: the technique of doubling, the motif of severed body parts, and so forth.[6] Although in the "Oda a Salvador Dalí" Lorca does extol the achievements of Dalí and explores the artist's attempts to portray an objective reality, devoid of emotions, Lorca himself does not wholeheartedly espouse such an aesthetic, in this poem or in general, throughout his work.

One expression of the dynamic between Lorca and Dalí and an opening into the reading of this poem may be found in a third portrait drawn by Lorca of Dalí in 1927. In this portrait, Dalí appears in a fashion distinct from the two already analyzed. He stands in front of a tower and a waning moon. His right hand is submerged in a fishbowl; its fingers are each bitten or eaten by a fish. Similarly, a larger fish is attached at Dalí's throat. Lorca may be using the figure of the fish as a pointer, as a sexual symbol, also linked to creativity. His left hand holds a palette, passively waiting for the brush, but the painting hand, trapped by the fish, is unable to execute. The presence of a fish at his throat occupies the space of a necktie, but also perhaps implies a cutting off of the voice. This reading of the portrait draws attention to Dalí's expressive powers and suggests possible impediment to that expression. Recalling the image of fishing, which Lorca employed to describe his own drawing activity, these fish would be metaphors, some sought out, some discovered spontaneously.

In contrast to the other portraits, the eyes are filled in. Dalí is not dressed in contemporary clothing, but rather, he wears a helmet. Dalí himself ascribes interesting significance to this portrayal in his description of the drawing: "Lorca saw me as incarnating life, wearing the headgear of one of the Dioscuri."[7] The Dioscuri are Castor and Pollox, the inseparable twin sons of Jupiter, hatched from an egg laid by Leda. If, in fact, Lorca is depicting Dalí as one of these twins, where and who is the other? The absence of the twin leads the viewer to conclude that Lorca is expressing the incompleteness of one school of art without dialogue to complement and complete it. This assumption provides another reading of the text as Lorca's reading of Dalí's painting and as his dialogue with its principles. At the end of the ode, Lorca states "Digo lo que me dicen tu persona y tus cuadros" [I tell what your person and your paintings tell me] (O.C. 1:956). He acknowledges Dalí's (read Cubism's) technique, goals, and accomplishments but simultaneously and consistently evokes the very elements, values, and materials that Dalí has rejected. By acknowledging their absence in Dalí's work, Lorca fills in the gaps they leave. Lorca highlights the Dalian perspective—his aims and his work in the Cubist mode—all the while presenting another mode (one that may be seen as a precursor of both men's Surrealist stages) by means of negation. That is, Lorca offers the "other side" of Dalí's images by countering what Dalí seeks with what he rejects, what he values with what he disdains. The missing twin is portrayed through the establishing of a polarity. At times, Lorca is explicit: "una ausencia de bosques, biombos, y entrecejos yerra por los tejados de las casas antiguas" [An absence of forests, screens and brows errs among the roofs of the ancient houses]. Usually the absent concepts are evoked in negative terms: "ignoran el vino y la penumbra" [ignore wine and shadow]; "no elogio tu pincel adolescente ni tu color que ronda la color de tu tiempo" [I do not praise your adolescent brush or your color, which hovers around the color of your age]; "El mundo tiene sordas penumbras y desorden en los primeros términos que el humano frecuenta" [the world has deaf shadows and disorder in the limits that humanity frequent]; "donde no cabe el sueño ni su flora inexacta" [where neither sleep nor its inexact flower fit], and many other examples. Mario Hernández acknowledges the presence of two dynamics in the poem, and refers, not to the portrait, but to a photograph taken of Dalí and Lorca in which he reads the symbols of their opposing views of art, the Dionysian and the Apollonian:

> This anecdote seems to cast light on the "Ode." In opposition to the beloved grapevines and the disorder of curving water, cold marble and architectures raise their rational, mathematical edifice. The vague, menacing flora of dreams and the corruption of mildew linger outside, warning against the coming kingdom of Surrealism (which will produce the "soft forms" of Dalí) and against all the disorder which the painter has willed out of existence.[8]

The construction and placement of images present in the poem, recall another drawing by Lorca. *El Beso* [The kiss], drawn in 1927, resembles Dalí's *Still Life: Invitation to Dream* (1925). In both works, heads that appear to be Lorca's and Dalí's are superimposed. The doubling evidenced in both is a motif repeated many times in Lorca's drawings, which Hernández refers to as a "plastic suggestion that Lorca has taken from the painting of Dalí."[9] One might imagine this drawing's technique present in the last portrait of Dalí. Lorca, the other twin, is positing his portrait behind Dalí's. Just as in *El Beso* one face is clearly foregrounded and delineated and the second merely a solid form distinguished by a change of color, a shadow so to speak in suggestion but not in shape, so too in the "Oda a Salvador Dalí" the absent images are backgrounded through negation.

The drawing of limits and the containment of subjective expression resonates with images consistent in this poem and in the lecture on Góngora, given by Lorca a year later in 1926. The image in the poem of the horizon as an aqueduct, channeling the force of water, is analogous to the description of the poet's activity Lorca offered in the lecture:

> Como lleva la imaginación atada, la detiene cuando quiere y no se deja arrastrar por las oscuras fuerzas naturales de la ley de inercia ni por los fugaces espejismos donde mueren los poetas incautos como mariposas en el farol.

> [Since he has imagination tied up, he detains it when he wants and does not allow himself to be dragged by the dark natural forces of the law of inertia nor by fleeting mirages where heedless poets die like butterflies in a lantern.] (*O.C.* 3:232)

These and other images refer to the presence of a force that threatens what Dalí termed "Holy Objectivity," a force that in order to be

"El Beso" © 1994 Artists Rights Society (ARS), New York/VEGAP, Madrid

expressed must be controlled. In his lecture "Imaginación, inspiración, evasión," given in 1928, Lorca repeated this concept: "La imaginación tiene horizontes, quiere dibujar y concretar todo lo que abarca" [The imagination has horizons, it wants to draw and concretize all that it embraces] (*O.C.* 3:299).

In the last seven stanzas the poet insists on the expression of emotion. Whereas throughout the poem Lorca had consistently reflected Dalí's pursuit of control in form, he now extols his human content, awarding primacy to feeling over art itself: "no es el Arte la luz que nos ciega los ojos. Es primero el amor, la amistad o la esgrima" [Art is not the light that blinds our eyes. It is first love, friendship, or fencing].

In addition to the doubling phenomena noted, images invoked in the poem are seen in the three portraits of Dalí, suggesting a greater coherence between these works and the poem than has previously been acknowledged. The second portrait suggests "el soneto del mar en tu ventana" [the sonnet of the sea in your window]. The foreground and background images of the third are suggested in "los grandes vidrios del pez y de la luna" [the great glasses of the fish and the moon] and the image of the fish prolonging Dalí's fingers in "tu fantasía llega donde llegan tus manos" [your fantasy goes as far as your hands]. Lorca's repeated references to stars—"Pero ya las estrellas, ocultando paisajes, señalan el esquema perfecto de sus órbitas" [But already the stars, hiding landscapes, signal the perfect plan of their orbits]; "estrellas como puños sin halcón te relumbran, mientras que tu pintura y tu vida florecen" [stars like fists without a falcon glare at you, while your painting and your life flower]; "canto tu corazón astronómico y tierno" [I sing your astronomic and tender heart]—could be explained by accepting the symbol of the Dioscuri, figured in myth by the Gemini constellation.[10] Also, the playing card seen in the second portrait recalls what remains of the verse: " . . . de baraja francesa, y sin ninguna herida" [made of a French deck of cards and without any wound]. The posing of opposites or doubles cited throughout the poem and drawings is reflected in "astronómico y tierno" as well as in the expression "jugar con dos barajas" [to act with duplicity] invoked in the reader.

Lorca endorses Dalí's art as the result of an act of seeing: "Estilizas o copias después de haber mirado con honestas pupilas sus cuerpecillos ágiles" [You stylize or copy after having looked with honest pupils at their agile little bodies]. The force of vision that Lorca extols in Dalí's work links the poem with the Góngora lecture and places both in the context of the artistic milieu of the early twentieth century. In his lecture on this poet, whom he named the father of modern poetry, Lorca repeatedly emphasized the primacy of the sense of sight in the poetic process. He defined the poetic image as "una traslación de sentido" [a transporting of meaning] and when he drew analogies between the plasticity of images in popular sayings, he aligned both plastic and poetic image with the sense of sight:

> Buey de agua y lengua de río son dos imágenes
> hechas por el pueblo y que responden a una manera de ver ya muy cerca
> de don Luis de Góngora.

> [A water ox and a river tongue are two images created by the people and which correspond to a way of seeing very close to don Luis de Góngora.]
> (*O.C.* 3:224)

He refers to himself and others interested in the Baroque poet as "los ojos nuevos que venían a comprenderlo" [the new eyes that were coming to understand him] (227). Finally, he describes the process by which he understands Góngora's creation of the poetic image:

> Naturalmente, Góngora no crea sus imágenes sobre la misma Naturaleza, sino que lleva el objeto, cosa o acto a la cámara oscura de su cerebro y de allí salen transformados para dar el gran salto sobre el otro mundo con que se funden. Por eso, su poesía, como no es directa, es imposible de leer ante los objetos de que habla.

> [Naturally, Góngora does not create his images on Nature itself, but rather takes the object, thing, or act to the dark chamber of his brain and they come out from there transformed in order to take the great leap toward the other world with which they are fused. For this reason, it is impossible to read his poetry, which is not direct, while facing the objects of which he speaks.] (*O.C.* 3:235)

This developing of the image emphasizes its transformation once it is received by the artist/poet. It explains Lorca's description of the poet's "obscure chamber," by no accident also the Spanish for the camera, as the place where images enter, are stored and subsecuently revealed.

The primacy of visual experience and its subsequent transformation into images explains more coherently than any aesthetic classification, what empowers Lorca's work. Thus, the images he creates are well considered first in light of his experience, in a personal, cultural context. Lorca's correspondence, interviews and lectures contain statements affirming that images he employs often have their origin in his visual experience. As noted above, Lorca insists that the sense of sight is key to the poetic process:

El poeta tiene que ser profesor en los cinco sentidos corporales . . . en
este orden: vista, tacto, oído, olfato y gusto."

[The poet must be a professor of the five physical senses . . . in this
order: sight, touch, hearing, smell, and taste.] (O.C. 3:229)

Beginning the analysis of an image with an understanding of his visual
experience permits a study of how he transforms such images. Lorca's
work and the recollection of his contemporaries testify to the poet's
extraordinary capacity to take in and remember—persons, writing,
art, experiences. Both the lecture on Góngora and the "Oda a Salvador Dalí" contain numerous examples of Lorca's powers of observation, retention and transformation of images. These powers would
continue to empower his work, and the trajectory of his aesthetics,
evidenced in his drawing and poetry, would continue to demonstrate
an integration of influences and impressions. In the next phase of
Lorca's work, he himself will attempt in his drawings what he has
praised in others.

Drawing Poems in 1927: Gasch and *Totalismo*

The summer of 1927 was a critical time in Lorca's life and work
and invites close study by students of his poetic evolution. The dynamics at work in Lorca's drawing: his choice of theme, of elements,
and manner of execution will next be compared to his writing during
the same period. Lorca's letters to Gasch, to Jorge Zalamea, his drawings of 1927, and the poetry he wrote in 1927–1928 all share a similar
focus, and to varying degrees, similar creative processses.

As early as January 1927, Lorca expressed an increasing dissatisfac-
tion with his work and especially with what Terence McMullan cites
as "a widespread misunderstanding of his poetic intentions and . . .
a distorted public perception of his creative personality."[11] This dis-
content and an outburst of immense creative energy caused him to
focus the following summer on his creative process, both in the practice of drawing and writing. He also gave voice to his poetics/aesthet-
ics in an important series of letters to Sebastià Gasch. According to
Fourneret, this period is

the apogee of the drawing activity and at the same time of his greatest
theoretical reflection on art. . . . this phase will have to be considered as
the crucial point of reference for any critical analysis.[12]

Mario Hernández affirms this judgment:

But is would be in 1927–1928 when his rich correspondence with the art critic Sebastián Gasch denotes the blending of his surrender to drawing and his parallel aesthetic reflection on his creations and the principles which uphold them.[13]

Mariana Pineda had made a successful debut in Barcelona in June, and in July an exhibition of twenty-four of the poet's drawings took place in the Dalmau Gallery in the same city. Ian Gibson relates that during his stay in Granada in August, "Lorca found himself possessed of a creative frenzy that compelled him above all to draw. . . . The poet was in a state of hypersensitivity."[14] Lorca's own words confirm this experience. In a letter to Gasch, he wrote of engaging in creative activity:

> Ahora empiezo a escribir y a dibujar poesías como ésta que le envío dedicada.

> [Now I'm beginning to write and to draw poems like this one which I'm sending dedicated to you.] (*O.C.* 3:953)

He also wrote of the creative state in which he found himself:

> Te agradezco extraordinariamente tus elogios, pero éstos me ayudan a dibujar como no tienes idea, y verdaderamente disfruto con los dibujos. Yo me voy *proponiendo* temas antes de dibujar y consigo el mismo efecto que cuando no pienso en nada. Desde luego me encuentro en estos momentos con una sensibilidad ya casi física que me lleva a planos donde es difícil tenerse de pie y donde casi se vuela sobre el abismo. Me cuesta un trabajo ímprobo sostener una conversación normal con estas gentes del balneario porque mis ojos y mis palabras están en otro sitio. Están en la inmensa biblioteca que no ha leído nadie, en un aire fresquísimo, país donde las cosas bailan con un solo pie.

> [I thank you profusely for your praise, but it helps me to draw like you have no idea, and I really enjoy myself with the drawings. I propose themes to myself before drawing, and achieve the same effects as when I'm not thinking about anything. Naturally, on these occasions I find myself with an almost physical sensation that carries me to levels where it's difficult to find one's footing and where one almost flies over the abyss. It takes a lot out of me to keep up a normal conversation with these people at the spa because my eyes and my words are someplace else. They are in the immense library that no one has read, in the freshest air, a country where things dance on one foot.] (*O.C.* 3:968)

Creativity appears to have been effortless at this time, and one must ask if the drawing is a result of or in fact a contributing factor to such a state. Both are reasonable conclusions, since the reference to his "sensibilidad ya casi física" [almost physical sensitivity] indicates that Lorca was tapping deep, intuitive energy, accessible through drawing.

An interesting series of drawings is the result of this creative period. Accepting Lorca's explanation of the role of drawing in his creative process produces a reading of this series as an important bridge between the poetics of the *Romancero gitano* and *Poeta en Nueva York*. Significantly, Lorca wrote little if any poetry at this time. For a brief time, the drawings were the only product of Lorca's focused creative energy. In a letter to Fernández Almagro in July 1927, Lorca wrote:

> He trabajado bastante en nuevos y originales poemas, ya una vez terminado el *Romancero gitano*, a otra clase de cosas.

> [I've worked a good bit on new and original poems, now that *Gypsy Ballads* is finished, on another type of thing.] (*O.C.* 3:764)

This statement, along with Lorca's contention that he was "drawing poems," suggests that he considered the drawings to be poems and invites exploration into his vision of them.

The confluence of painting, drawing, and poetic texts in Lorca's day has already been noted. Many who worked in one genre were experimenting in the other.[15] The discussions of art and literary critics show a consistent attempt to bring the two expressions together. Sebastià Gasch's articles, published in *L'Amic de las Arts* and in *La Gaceta Literaria*, articulate a search for artistic expression that would draw from the advantages enjoyed by such media in expression as well as from the various aesthetic currents within each. For Gasch, this hybrid expression was what he called *"Totalismo."*[16] In the articles Gasch wrote at this time, he provides a history of art trends up to his moment and evaluates current work in the light of these trends and of his own perspective. In these texts, Gasch uses the terms *plástico* [plastic] and *poético* [poetic] consistently, and when Lorca uses them, it is in obvious dialogue with the critic.[17] One must take care to understand these terms in the way in which the two men employed them. Like so many theorists, Gasch was eminently aware of the dangers of inappropriate comparisons. When asked to write a poetry-cinema comparison, he declared:

> I think involuntarily of the confusion of genres, of hybrid solutions, of adulterous and unnaturalized mixtures.[18]

However, Gasch consistently insisted in the interrelations and mutual influence between poetry and painting.

Along with other writers of the time, specifically those in the *Gaceta Literaria*, Gasch consistently lamented Cubism's development away from the fresh perspective of its early stages toward lifeless expression. He faulted painters like Dalí, who, as Gasch saw it, was allowing his intelligence to prevent the free expression of his "instinct and his lyricism,"[19] and he praised the work of Joan Miró for expressing artistic reality, independent of imitation:

> works of pure imagination, of pure instinct, refuse the criticism of the dissection laboratory, and accept only poetic criticism, that criticism of poets.[20]

Poetic criticism reflects on the artistic reality expressed in a work, not only its surface, technique, or material. Thus, it refuses to employ the "criticism of the dissection laboratory." It acknowledges and accommodates the dual nature Gasch sought in art—technique and form united with intuition and emotion. In the article on Dalí, Gasch described Surrealism as a

> tendency based on the total expulsion of intelligence from artistic domains, and the most absolute establishment of unbridled instinct. (84)

and defined what he sought in *totalismo* when he referred to recent exhibition of Picasso's work. In Picasso, Gasch saw

> a dosage of the findings of reason and of the findings of instinct . . . as far away from the cerebral Cubism that came immediately after the war as from completely instinctive Surrealism. To opposite poles, as much from one as from the others is, however, its wise fusion, and toward this fusion the most select spirits of this generation seem to be leaning. *Plasticity and poetry* at the same time. (84) [my italics]

Gasch connects reason with Cubism, cerebral with plastic; likewise he groups instinct with Surrealism, instinctive with poetry. This defines his subsequent use of the terms plastic and poetic. At the end of the Dalí review, he calls for "works totally offspring of the fusion of reason and of instinct" (84). This is a concept that appears consistently in his writing, in which he lauds the presence of both dynamics in some artists, and laments their absence in others. These artists include Rafael Barradas, whom Gasch criticized for allowing the poetic element to overcome the plastic in some of his paintings:

his paintings have reflected also, at every moment, this lyricism that animates it. This poetry, however, has dominated painting many times. Plastic values have been put aside many times in favor of pictorial values, the lyric wave sweeping away everything in its wake.

Gasch praises the balance in other works of Barradas:

Plasticity and poetry, we could say of these paintings of Rafael Barradas. Plasticity and poetry fraternally united in these intense, pathetic canvasses.[21]

These and other examples of Gasch's discourse have been manipulated by critics to support the position that paintings are literally to be considered poems and vice versa in order to justify their analysis. It is clear from this reading that Gasch is speaking in very definite terms about the best of Cubist technique and abstraction and the force of instinct and spontaneous feeling that he saw in Surrealism. It is interesting to note that Gasch did not believe Surrealism's objectives to be completely relevant to the plastic arts. He refers to the movement as the orphan of plastic values, shipwrecked from pure literature.[22] On numerous occasions, he defines art as the resonances of his (the artist's) interior world that run into the exterior world.[23] Reviewing the work of Domingo, whom he considered a success, Gasch praised his technical/plastic mastery and the quality of the poetic, or spiritual in his art: To summarize: the soul of things and the soul of the artist equals Poetry (310).

In an important article, "Del cubismo al superrealismo," Gasch defined the characteristics of *totalista* art in these terms:

Avidly we await the ingenious work that takes advantage of the technical conquests of Cubism, that enriches these with the poetry of Surrealism, that fuses, finally, abstraction and reality, that unites, finally, intelligence and sensitivity. Avidly we await the new Picasso who channels the disordered waters of the river of this moment's painting, [the aqueduct of the "Oda a Dalí"?] who pilots finally, into safe harbor the pictorial vessel that floats adrift over the agitated sea of current plasticity.[24]

Gasch's comments testify to the rapidity and intensity with which influence, reaction and change were sweeping the art world. Furthermore, although we can only surmise the extent to which his observations formed Lorca's art, they most certainly describe it. In this context we turn our attention to Lorca's drawing, reading both his drawings as well as his own interpretation of those drawings in light of Gasch's challenge.

It is no coincidence that, to date, the drawings that Lorca produced in 1927 have been studied more than most of the others. This is due largely to the fact that Lorca himself wrote specifically about their creation and their significance. These statements have been applied by other critics to the whole of Lorca's plastic work. In fact, the very same statements made by Lorca about his work have been used by critics to validate opposing positions, especially as regards Lorca's participation in the Surrealist movement. For our purposes, Lorca's declaration to Gasch and others will introduce and guide our analysis of the specific drawings to which we know Lorca refers. These explications constitute a reading on Lorca's part of others (Gasch and Dalí) and of his own work.

This suite of drawings is unique in that they are among the few that Lorca provided with titles. The drawings of which Lorca speaks in his letters to Gasch were further distinguished from other drawings by being marked by him with a small cross near the title. They are: *San Sebastián* [St. Sebastian], *Pavo Real* [Peacock] (no cross, but specifically included in the series by Lorca's statements), *Torero sevillano* [Sevillian bullfighter], *Sirena* [Mermaid], *Poema del anzuelo* [Poem of the fishhook], *Arlequín ahogado* [Drowned harlequin], *¡Ecce homo!* [Behold the man!], *Melodía de violín* [Violin melody], *Canción* [Song], *Suplicio del patriarca San José,* [Torture of St. Joseph the patriarch], *Epitalamio* [Epithalamium], and *Venus* [Venus]. In addition to this group, other drawings that are not marked by Lorca's little cross but which are both contemporary and similar to the drawings so indicated will also be treated in this chapter or mentioned in the analysis of the drawings they closely resemble.

Lorca's remarks to Gasch about executing the drawings highlight two important characteristics of the drawing process: the spontaneity of the process and the vital connection between the hand and the creative center. He states:

Estos últimos dibujos que he hecho me han costado un trabajo de elaboración grande. Abandonaba la mano a la tierra virgen y la mano junto con mi corazón me traía los elementos milagrosos. Y los descubría y los anotaba. Volvía a lanzar mi mano, y así, con muchos elementos, escogía las características del asunto o los más bellos e inexplicables, y componía mi dibujo. Así he compuesto el <<Torero sevillano>>, la <<Sirena>>, el <<San Sebastián>>, y casi todos los que tienen una crucecita. Hay milagros puros, como <<Cleopatra,>> que tuve verdadero escalofrío cuando salió esa armonía de lineas que no *había pensado, ni soñado, ni querido, ni estaba inspirado,* y yo dije ¡Cleopatra! al verlo, ¡y es verdad! Luego me lo corroboró mi hermano. Aquellas líneas eran *el retrato exacto, la emoción pura* de la reina de Egipto. Unos dibujos salen así, como las metáforas más bellas, y otros buscándolos en el sitio *donde se sabe de seguro* que están.

[These last drawings I've done cost me a great deal of time and effort. I'd abandon my heart to virgin territory and my hand together with my heart would bring to light the miraculous elements. I'd discover them and take them down. I'd cast my hand again, and so, out of many elements, would choose the characteristics of the subject or the most beautiful and the most inexplicable ones, and I'd compose my drawing. Thus I composed the "Sevillian bullfighter," "the Siren," "Saint Sebastian," and almost all the ones that have a little cross. There are pure miracles, like "Cleopatra," I really got a chill when that harmony of lines came forth, which I hadn't thought of or dreamed, or wanted or been inspired to, and I said, "Cleopatra!" on seeing it, and it's true! Later my brother corroborated it for me. Those lines were the exact portrait, the pure emotion of the queen 'of Egypt. Some drawings come out like that, like the most beautiful metaphors, and others by searching for them in the spot where you know for sure they are.] (*O.C.* 3:969)

Lorca's language in this letter raises the question of automatic writing, a crucial component of Surrealist activity. In fact, some critics read these statements as contradictions of Lorca's denial, on other occasions, of the influence of Surrealism in his work.[25] But the text of Lorca's letter presents, as in the "Oda a Salvador Dalí," the tension between the forces of reason and imagination, of intellectual control and intuition and notes Lorca's use of terms that express a balance between the two poles. Lorca speaks of abandonment, of the vision of elements that are "milagrosos, bellos, inexplicables" [miraculous, beautiful, inexplicable.][26] He counters this with verbs that indicate conscious control, judgment—"escogía las características"; "componía mi dibujo." [I would choose the characteristics; I would compose my drawing.] He expresses the cooperation between "mano y corazón" [hand and heart] and stresses that spontaneity and hard work go hand in hand in this process: "unos dibujos salen así . . . y otros buscándolos en el sitio donde se sabe de seguro que están" [some drawings come out like that . . . and others by searching for them in the spot where you know for sure they are].

Moreover, Lorca insists that this description of his sensitive creative state, especially his mention of "planos donde es difícil tenerse de pie y donde casi se vuela sobre el abismo" [levels where it's difficult to find one's footing and where one almost flies over the abyss] (*O.C.* 3:968), need not be interpreted as a statement of haphazardness or even of automatism as he executes his drawings. Indeed,

Gasch seems to have responded to Lorca's statement with just such concern, for in a subsequent letter, Lorca reassures the critic:

Pero mi estado no es de <<perpetuo sueño>>. Me he expresado mal. He cercado algunos días al sueño, pero sin caer del todo en él, y teniendo desde luego un atadero de risa y un seguro andamio de madera. Yo nunca me aventuro en terrenos que no son del hombre, porque vuelvo tierras atrás en seguida y rompo casi siempre el producto de mi viaje. Cuando hago una cosa de pura abstracción, siempre tiene (creo yo) un salvoconducto de sonrisas y equilibrio bastante humano. Mi estado es siempre alegre, y este soñar mío no tiene peligro en mí, que llevo defensas; es peligroso para el que se deje fascinar por los grandes espejos oscuros que la poesía y la locura ponen en el fondo de sus barrancos. Yo ESTOY Y ME SIENTO CON PIES DE PLOMO EN ARTE.

[But my state is not one of "perpetual dream." I've expressed myself badly. Some days, I've skirted the dream, but haven't fallen totally into it, possessing, of course, a tether of laughter to hang onto and a secure wooden scaffold. I never venture into territories alien to man, because I quickly wander back and almost always rip up the fruits of my voyage. When I do a purely abstract thing, it always has (I believe) a safe conduct pass of smiles and a rather human equilibrium. My state is always happy, and this dreaming of mine is not dangerous for me, because I have defenses; it is dangerous for one who lets himself be fascinated by the great dark mirrors that poetry and madness wield at the bottom of their chasms. I HAVE AND I FEEL I HAVE MY FEET FIRMLY ON THE GROUND IN ART.] (*O.C.* 3:967)

Lorca's reference in this text to the "products of my voyage" recalls the poet's statement in his conference on Góngora that the poem (or, we surmise, the drawing) is the result of just such a voyage: "Se vuelve de la inspiración como se vuelve de un país extranjero. El poema es la narración del viaje" [One returns from inspiration as one returns from a foreign land. The poem is the narration of the voyage] (*O.C.* 3:237). The description of the poetic space—"el abismo," "los grandes espejos oscuros" [the abyss, the great dark mirrors]—and Lorca's reference to needing defenses are also present in the lecture on Góngora:

[El poeta] se mantendrá firme contra los espejismos y acechará cautelosamente las carnes palpitantes y reales que armonicen con el plano del poema que lleva entrevisto. Hay a veces que dar grandes gritos en la soledad poética para ahuyentar los malos espíritus fáciles que quieren llevarnos a los halagos populares sin sentido estético y sin orden ni belleza.

[The poet will hold firm against the mirages and will ambush prudently the real and palpitating flesh that harmonizes with the already seen map of the poem that he carries. Sometimes one must give great shouts in poetic solitude in order to drive away the evil, easy spirits that want to carry us off to popular flattery that lacks aesthetic sense and order or beauty.] (*O.C.* 3:236)

Even before he describes his drawings, then, Lorca proposes a basic tenet of his poetics, that his work always pertains to the human realm and that even work that might be considered abstract is based on what he calls human balance, "su fantasía cuenta con sus cinco sentidos corporales" [his fantasy counts on his five physical senses] (*O.C.* 3:236). Fourneret reiterates:

> However, the series of letters sent by Lorca to his friend the art critic gather aspects that are esssential to approaching the creative process and the aesthetic ideas of the poet. In them, he affirms his desire to flee from pure and dehumanized art as much as his rejection of the art of dreams.[27]

Much has been written about Surrealism in Lorca's work, resulting in a range of contradictory conclusions. To make a definitive judgment in that regard at this point in my analysis would both deny the polemical nature of the question and, more importantly, limit the reading of the texts to follow. Like Carmona, I prefer not to "measure the degree of Lorca's Surrealism" but rather "to consider his struggles with it and evidently his contagion."[28] When both letters and drawings are read in light of Gasch's writing at this time and his call for a *totalismo* in art, one appreciates Lorca's struggle and begins to discern a consistent process, already articulated in the Góngora lecture and the Dalí text.

Lorca's letter to Gasch may also be read as a powerful statement of the creative process at its most instinctive, innate level of experience, so characteristic of spontaneous drawing. Lorca's describes a process striking in its lack of self-censure. If he operated in the way in which he describes the process here, he responded to creative, almost bodily urges without the need to express them in words. His hand ("Volvía a lanzar mi mano") [I would cast my hand again] has become what he had described as the *anzuelo de realidad* [the fishhook of reality]. The drawings came first, diagrams of the thought or feeling that inspired them. Words, descriptions, and titles followed. Such spontaneity and the giving over of self to the creative moment are described by Carl Jung, who, in terms analogous to Lorca's, describes the poet seized by the creative impulse and the resultant works:

These works positively force themselves upon the author; his hand is seized, his pen writes things down that his mind contemplates with amazement. While his conscious mind stands amazed and empty before this phenomena, he is overwhelmed by a flood of thoughts and images which he never intended to create and which his own will could never have brought into being. Yet in spite of himself he is forced to admit that it is his own self speaking, his own inner nature revealing itself and uttering things which he would never have entrusted to his tongue.[29]

Lorca did not fear such an experience; he trusted it. In a letter dated 20 January 1928, he asserted his confidence in his own intuition: "Yo me equivoco dificilmente en estas cosas de intuición" [It's difficult for me to err in these matters of intuition] (*O.C.* 3:957). The result of such a creative experience is the same for both Jung and for Lorca. The "own self," the "own inner nature" of which Jung speaks is the "terreno humano" and the "salvoconducto de equilibrio bastante humano" [the human terrain and the safe conduct pass of rather human equilibrium] that Lorca says is the foundation of his work.

One general characteristic of the majority of Lorca's drawings, is that, at least in subject, they pertain to real life, to familiar people, places, things. A survey of the titles listed above confirms this. Even those subjects that might be considered less than ordinary—a harlequin, St. Joseph, a siren—are familiar to literature, art, religion, and culture. However, in the process of drawing, Lorca views these subjects in a new light, opening himself, and consequently his viewer, to a new understanding of their meaning. The means to this new reading is the freedom of which Dalí speaks in his article "Surrealismo," a freedom that leads to a reading of reality independent of intellectual baggage:

> far from the sterotyped, anti-real image that our intellect has artificially forged, endowing it with cognitive, false attributes, annulled by poetic reason and which are possible to avoid only by means of the absence of our intellectual control.[30]

If Lorca is allowing himself to read reality in its immediate experience, in a moment, without background, context, or censorship, seizing images as they arise in his consciousness and putting them down in his drawings, then how are we to read the works? Perhaps that is the appeal of this particular suite of drawings to the viewer. By their very nature they allow for a free response, since they are the very free, spontaneous capturing of a moment of experience, the seizing of what Lorca called the "*rasgos esenciales*" [the essential characteristics] of his subject (*O.C.* 3:969). Lorca says that these drawings are the product of two steps: (1) the free abandonment of hand to sensation and perception and (2) the selective choice of the images/aspects gathered in the first stage that will be retained. What he chooses can be surprising, or it can resonate with the viewer's apprehension of the image. In either case, the viewer's judgment is exercised. Lorca says he has elected specific characteristics, that he is applying criteria. This exercise of intelligence, of artistic control is one characteristic that distinguished Spanish Surrealism from French Surrealism.[31]

In his choice of subject and of specifics within each subject, Lorca demonstrates a consistent power of selective observation. As early as 1918, in his book *Impresiones y paisajes* [Impressions and landscapes], we see this power at work. Settings such as the monasteries and cathedrals visited by Lorca "stimulate Lorca's eye for the significant detail that can suddenly and provocatively epitomize a whole environment."[32] Ten years later, Lorca further elaborates the nature of his drawings, providing even more insight into what he considers their content and his achievement:

> Yo he pensado y hecho estos dibujitos con un criterio poético-plástico o plástico-poético en justa unión. Y muchos son metáforas lineales o tópicos sublimados, como el <<San Sebastián>> y el <<Pavo Real>>. He procurado escoger los rasgos esenciales de emoción y de forma, o de super-realidad y super-forma, para hacer de ellos un signo que, como llave mágica, nos lleve a comprender mejor la realidad que tienen en el mundo.

> [I have thought and have made these little drawings with a poetic-plastic or plastic-poetic criterion, in fitting union. And many are linear metaphors or sublimated topics like St. Sebastian or the Peacock. I've strived to choose the essential characteristics of emotion and of form, or of super-reality and super-form, in order to make of them a sign that, like a magic key will help us understand better the reality that they have in the world.] (*O.C.* 3:969)[33]

In his statement of purpose, Lorca identifies his artistic role as one who highlights aspects of reality, bringing them to his own and to the viewer's attention in order to form associations that will consequently provide new meaning. Lorca employs terminology here, specifically "super-realidad" and "super-forma," that indicate an awareness of artistic discourse. Gasch notes, however, that although these terms have been coined by the Surrealists, the purpose is not unique to their movement.[34]

How does Lorca attain the expression of reality, of emotion and form for which he strives? How does he choose the "essential characteristics" of his subjects that portray this form and feeling? How does he meet his *"criterio poético-plástico o plástico-poético"* [poetic-plastic or plastic-poetic criterion]? Considering some general characteristics of this series of drawings will help elucidate these questions. These are all line drawings, most executed with ink on paper. Technically, the majority of these pieces is marked by an austerity of color and of solidity of form. But for all their sparseness, these drawings are by no means simple. Fourneret observes:

> In them, Lorca makes exclusive use of pen and ink, without exception, contrasting the fantastic plastic and emotional richness of these drawings with the poverty of the graphic means employed.[35]

The richness of which Fourneret speaks is the result of Lorca's use of line. The poet was aware of this; we have read above that he considers these drawings "metáforas lineales" [lineal metaphors] and that for him, the lines alone were capable of capturing the subject, the "retrato exacto, la emoción pura de Cleopatra" [the exact portrait, the pure emotion of Cleopatra], for example. He strives for an "armonía de líneas" [a harmony of lines]. Lorca's observation that emotion is the only content of the line offers an explanation of his earlier statements (*O.C.* 3:947). One of the most striking characteristics of this series of drawings is the power and directness of Lorca's lines by which he fuses the plastic (form) and the poetic (emotion) principle. They are carefully executed to convey meaning. By an abstraction or by the reduction of the subject's appearance through the use of one predominant element—line—Lorca limits the drawings to the essential. This phenomenon is explained by Fourneret who states:

> The poverty of the graphic means employed is also the expression of a choice and of a discipline The exact line needs a perfect control of the hand and a spiritual discipline at the same time. (81)

Rather than poverty of means, one might well use the artistic term economy of means. Furthermore, Lorca's technique parallels the figures of metaphor and metonym. Lorca makes use of the most basic elements of his subject. Thus, he is able to focus the eye of his viewer on the "reality" he wishes to portray. This is the process he would laud in 1928 in his "Sketch de la nueva pintura" [Sketch of new painting]. Speaking of the Cubists, whom he characterized as "una escuela franciscana" [a Franciscan school]. Lorca said:

> Se ha partido de la realidad para llegar a esta creación. Lo mismo que el poeta crea la imagen que define, el pintor crea la imagen plástica que fija

y orienta la emoción. Con unos cuantos objetos le basta. Parte de ellos y
los crea de nuevo, mejor.

[He has separated himself from reality in order to reach this creation.
Just as the poet creates an image that defines, so the painter creates the
plastic image that fixes and orients emotion. Just a few objects suffice.
He separates from them and makes them over, better.] (*O.C.* 3:275)

Simultaneously, Lorca is identifying the process with Surrealism in
which "lyrical deformation would emphasize reality's potential for
expressing surreality."[36] It is this "super reality" and/or "super form"
that will accentuate, or, in Lorca's words, "serve as a sign of" meaning. Considered in the light of the reading or perceiving process,
these words highlight as well the role of the reader. By offering only
the minimum of detail, these drawings demand completion by the
one who views them. Indeed, in many cases the viewer has a choice
in understanding meaning: each of this particular suite of drawings
could be completed—"filled in" as a mimetic reflection of its model,
or the viewer might, instead of looking back to the the model, "look
forward to surreality prefigured in the painted image."[37] This choice
would affirm the nature of these particular drawings, in Gasch's
words, as "works (that are) totally offspring of the union of reason
and instinct."[38]

The page itself on which he draws is an important component in
Lorca's masterful execution of line in these drawings. Instead of
being a negative value in the drawings, the whiteness of the page is
a positive force. The expanse of the white page against which lie the
lines of the drawing provides a contrast and gives the eye of the
viewer a place, a space in which to roam and rest and experience "el
abismo." This space, then, must be seen as a player in the game, a
partner in dialogue with the lines of the drawing and with the viewer.

The "essential characteristics" that Lorca chooses to highlight in
each drawing and then the depiction of such elements are revealed
through the study of Lorca's use of line in the drawings: its direction,
length, weight, distribution on the page, and the emotion it portrays.
This was not unique to Lorca's drawing; in February 1928, Gasch
wrote a review in *La Gaceta Literaria* describing the work of Ernesto
Giménez Caballero as

posters, of acuity, of formidable power to evoke, of the admirable apti-
tudes of their author to synthesize, in a meeting of primary elements, a
complete personality; to summarize: by means of summary allusions,
the essential traits, the physical or psychic characteristics of a personality.
[my italics][39]

Chronologically, Gasch's comments postdate Lorca's work in these line drawings. One wonders if Gasch or Lorca first coined the phrase *rasgos essenciales* [essential traits] in this context. What we may have here is yet another example of intertextuality—in this instance, of Lorca influencing the art criticism of his day.

The first drawing cited by Lorca as a "metáfora lineal" [linear metaphor], *San Sebastián*, portrays the martyred saint, who is often depicted as tied to a tree, his body pierced by arrows. Lorca and Dalí were fascinated by the figure of this saint; each created plastic images of him, and Dalí wrote a long prose poem entitled "San Sebastián," which Lorca greatly admired.[40] Mario Hernández refers to St. Sebastian as a "motivo de discusiones estéticas y vitales entre Dalí y Lorca" [a point of aesthetic and vital discussions between Dalí and Lorca].[41] Lorca completed more conventional drawings of the saint and with a pen, superimposed symbols of the saint on a now famous photo of himself. In *San Sebastián* both the depiction of arrows and of the saint are reduced. Fourneret states that

> different elements are charged with a concrete meaning and are easily identifiable . . . these "magic keys" evoke the reality of martyrdom in the viewer and carry him to the center of the tragedy.[42]

The body of St. Sebastian is represented by one eye, off to the left of the drawing, and by a circle enclosing a point, a mouth that could serve also as a "bull's eye." The heavy circles (made by bleeding the penpoint into the paper) in which all the arrows terminate form a sort of half circle that helps to suggest the shape of a face. The simplicity of the eye/mouth configuration is as gripping and eloquent as any other painting of this suffering victim.

The six straight lines that represent the arrows have feathers or fletching at one end, the drawing's lower section, but are missing arrowheads. This may insinuate that they have pierced the saint's body and are no longer visible, but the highly stylized points that Lorca places at the end of the lines indicate an artistic purpose. A set of six other lines appear in the upper third of the drawing. These have no fletching but rather begin and end in the heavy points that finish the arrow lines. One notes, however, that of the two ends the points that meet in the center of the drawing are heavier. The effect of this technique is the guidance of the viewer's eye to the drawing's center where we find that small "bull's eye" that serves a double purpose, as a reference to his execution as well as part of the portrait of the saint himself.

While five of the six arrows point upward vertically, one of them

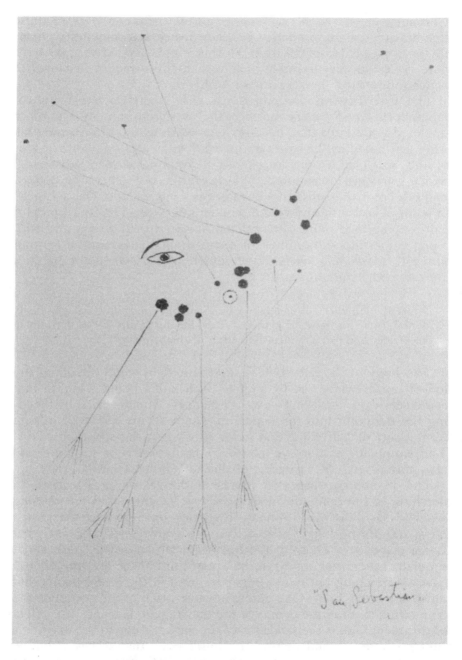

points on the diagonal, crossing over the others. This diagonal is on a plane with two of the upper lines, and guides the eye toward the upper right of the drawing. Meeting the upper lines are two more moving in the opposite direction. The result is the creation of a *V* under which Lorca has drawn the saint's eye and mouth. Thus, the viewer who begins to gaze at the lower left follows an arrow up to a heavy point, encounters the eye, follows the shape of the points to the mouth or bulls-eye, then moves up and over to the upper right-hand corner of the piece. Lorca, in addition to expressing suffering and the instrument of that suffering, seems to invite a transcendent view of his subject. We are urged by means of the visual components of this drawing to move onward and upward from this scene of suffering. In *Line of Light and Shadow*, Mario Hernández quotes a letter from Lorca to Dalí on the subject of St. Sebastian. The poet's words are as eloquent as his lines:

> I am moved by his grace in the midst of torture and by the complete lack of resignation shown by his Hellenic face, for he is not resigned, but triumphant, a man who has triumphed, full of elegance and full of gray tones, like a faithful oarsman who knows nothing of the boulevards of the city. . . . Everyone else constructs a prayer from their martyrdom, but St. Sebastian is different. He poses, he constructs his body, giving eternity to what is fleeting and managing to give visible form to an abstract aesthetic idea. That is why I love him.[43]

By "giving eternity to what is fleeting" and "managing to give visible form to an abstract aesthetic idea," Lorca has created a linear metaphor from the image of St. Sebastian that is true to the nature of the subject as Lorca perceives it. Lorca's portrayal of the saint in this drawing transcends the conventional depictions that emphasize his youth and beauty and/or the torturingly slowness of his agony—qualities that have resulted in the saint's evolution into a favored figure among homosexuals—and captures these intrinsic qualities by means of what he calls a metaphor.

Lorca's naming of these drawings as linear metaphors is especially intriguing and invites the reader to further exploration of how they function as a metaphor As noted, his technique suggests the dynamic of metonymy, the part representing the whole. In this linear metaphor, Sebastian's open eye and mouth represent his entire body—both are open, drawn in tight lines which show his alertness and strength. The arrows (or oars, if we apply Lorca's comments from the letter) represent his suffering and have come to stand for St. Sebastian in art. He is known not for his life but in his death. He has a second life, for he was, according to tradition, rescued half dead after his first "execution," nursed back to health, and then ultimately caught again and killed. Lorca's metaphors of mouth as target, eye as person, arrows as part of a portrait show how qualities and anecdotes form such an intrinsic part of the perception of a subject that they merely have to be suggested to be appreciated.

Two drawings that have much in common with *San Sebastián* are *Arlequín ahogado* [Drowned harlequin] and *¡Ecce homo!* In both of these drawings, the subject of suffering is represented by the bare essentials of a human face and some depiction of the instrument of that suffering. *¡Ecce homo!* is, of course, an illustration of the suffering of another victim, Christ. This drawing will be discussed at a later point in relation to a written depiction of the Passion in "Santa Lucía y San Lázaro."

Arlequín ahogado, a drawing whose style strongly resembles the geometric Cubist style, is composed of seven lines, five that traverse the surface of the drawing, either forming right angles or bending slightly as they cross the drawing's center. The result is twelve lines leading out from the center, ending in the same sort of point observed in *San Sebastián*. In this drawing, the result is a sense of being pulled apart, away from the center. The configurations of the angles, together with the presence of four different eyes and three mouths produces a possible total of eight different facial structures. The central face, whose nose is formed by one of the angles already described, possesses the same silent, almost tragic gaze observed in *San Sebastián*. In addition to the vertical lines of the drawing, Lorca adds horizontal joinings around the outer section, achieving texture in the spaces created in this way by means of various types of dotted lines and stipple.

Once again this drawing contains the essence of the subject, both the suggestion of the harlequin's face and of its multiplications. By nature the harlequin figure is divided, usually into halves of black and white, and its identity is often further divided by means of masks. Both of these attributes are represented here. In addition, the fracturing of the facial image into geometric pieces suggests the effect of viewing an object through water, the multifaceted view one attains through the rippled surface, and finally, the destruction of identity that is death, all of which refer to the word *ahogado*, or drowned.

Like *San Sebastián*, *Pavo Real* [Peacock] is called "una metáfora lineal, un tópico sublimado" [a linear metaphor, a sublimated topic] by its author. This representation captures the nature of the peacock. More precisely, in the words of Fourneret:

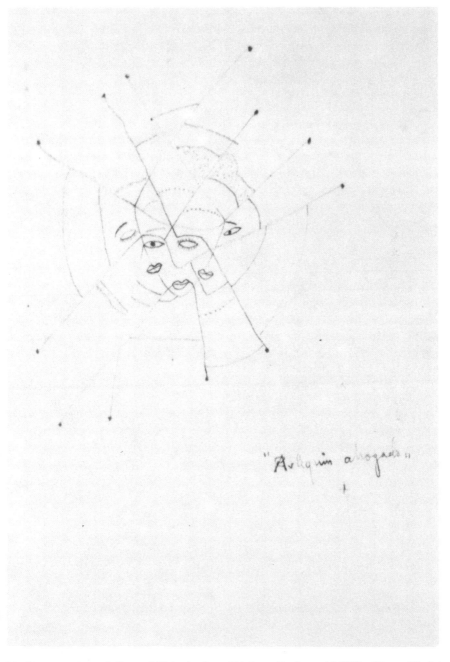

"Arlequín ahogado" © 1994 Artists Rights Society (ARS), New York/
VEGAP, Madrid

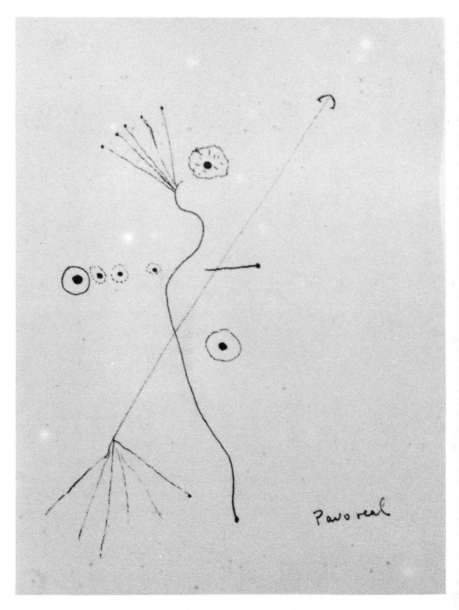

"Pavo Real" © 1994 Artists Rights Society (ARS), New York/VEGAP, Madrid

"Sueño del marinero" © 1994 Artists Rights Society (ARS), New York/
VEGAP, Madrid

"Sala de casa aristocrática" © 1994 Artists Rights Society (ARS), New York/ VEGAP, Madrid

"Jardín con el arbol del sol y arbol de la luna" © 1994 Artists Rights Society (ARS), New York/VEGAP, Madrid

"Muchacha granadina en un jardín" © 1994 Artists Rights Society (ARS),
New York/VEGAP, Madrid

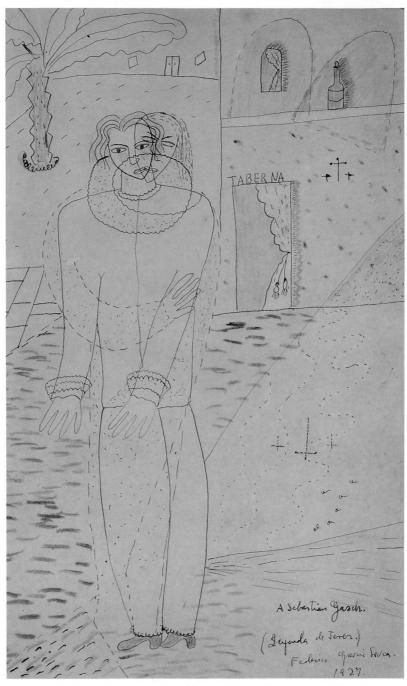

"Leyenda de Jerez" © 1994 Artists Rights Society (ARS), New York/
VEGAP, Madrid

"*Florero sobre tejado*" © 1994 Artists Rights Society (ARS), New York/
VEGAP, Madrid

"Bailarina española" © 1994 Artists Rights Society (ARS), New York/
VEGAP, Madrid

"Hombre muerto" © 1994 Artists Rights Society (ARS), New York/
VEGAP, Madrid

"Puta y luna" © 1994 Artists Rights Society (ARS), New York/VEGAP,
Madrid

That is, that which the drawing loses as a representation or copy of reality, it regains as its essence.(80)

A central vertical line is complemented by a diagonal arrow; both have on one end a set of plumes. Those on the top of the center line suggest the plumes of the peacock's head; those on the arrow, the fletching of the arrow and/or the bird's tail. The upward movement of the arrow may allude to the piercing cry of the peacock. Five dots within circles suggest, by virtue of their positions, the bird's eye and the "eyes" on its tail. A sixth such detail in the front half of the drawing balances the piece and may serve to represent gender. This interpretation would be in keeping with the role of the magnificent tail feathers as well as the cry of the male peacock in its courtship strutting. These are the delineation of the "rasgos esenciales" of the peacock. As in each of the other drawings, Lorca constantly varies the elements of his drawing by means of different types of line, size, and texture. Some of the circles here are empty, others filled in. Some are larger than others; some are outlined in solid, others in dotted lines. This attention to variety and detail underlines the conscious effort invested by Lorca in the drawings as well as enhances the viewer's experience. Fourneret notes the activity of the viewer facing this and all the "little cross" drawings:

> The viewer interiorizes the architecture and reality of the peacock beginning with these essential signs in order to reconstruct (the peacock) mentally and emotionally. The line's force of expression is independent of its functional role, to permit the recognition of an object. Without delimiting the contours of the peacock, it suggests his haughtiness and elegance. (80)

The emotion contained in Lorca's line is an essential element in each of these drawings. It is what first attracts the eye of the viewer and what fills in the gaps created by Lorca's deliberate economy of expression. The reader of each of these drawings is at best an informed reader who knows the subject and himself or herself well enough to, as Fourneret says, "reconstruct it mentally and emotionally." Thus, just as the act of drawing requires attention both to the subject and to the artist's reaction to that subject, so the reader of these drawings must be in touch with external and internal experience.

Another reading of the drawings just analyzed, as well as *¡Ecce Homo!* and *Poema del anzuelo* [Poem of the fishook], is to see them as a whole—a treatment of various symbols of Christ, different aspects of the Christian mystery. This would explain how Lorca sees them as "tópicos sublimados" [sublimated topics]. As symbols, these topics are already one step removed from their origin; they are already abstractions. The peacock, sign of eternal life, the martyr who through his suffering becomes another Christ, the image of Christ's suffering on the white page, the fishhook, a reference to Gospel imagery—each assumes a different relationship to the central theme. Each drawing highlights one aspect of this subject, while it simultaneously opens its symbols to the viewer's consideration. We shall see that this religious theme is later repeated in "Santa Lucia y San Lázaro" and in the "Oda al santísimo sacramento del altar" ["Ode to the most holy sacrament of the altar"].

Yet another reading considers these texts as self-portrayal—a prelude to the self-portraits of 1929. The image of the fishhook is explicitly linked by Lorca to poetic activity. His popularity in social and artistic circles and his consciousness of his private and public identities are expressed in the portrait of the peacock and the fragmentation of the drowned harlequin. The suffering tied to these identity struggles, especially in his coming to terms with his homosexuality, surely led Lorca to identify with the agony of St. Sebastian. This reading of the drawings marked by a little cross leads the reader to consider a text which, on first glance, seems distanced in style and execution from those just analyzed.

Lorca not only titled the drawing *Arlequín* [Harlequin], drawn in 1927, but also subtitled it a poem. *Arlequín* features a mask, divided in halves in black and white. Its one head has long flowing hair, and Lorca suggests ribs, this time by means of four dotted vertical lines on either side of the central vertical. A three-pronged crow's foot is encircled and placed in a location suggesting the genital area. Although there is no doubling of this figure, Lorca plays with space and representation by drawing the head, arms, and legs off-center from the figure's spine. He divides it at the top of the spine into a continuation of the original line rising from the bottom on the right and, off toward the left, a depiction of spine and rib cage. In addition to feet, Lorca adds a base from which the spinal column of the figure rises, and which, instead of the feet, supports the figure. One is reminded of a puppet on a stick in precarious balance by the base and by the position of the arms and legs in relation to the supporting horizontal lines.

Thus one reads another manipulation of the "rasgos esenciales" of the subject of the harlequin in which Lorca extends his portrayal to suggest various interpretations, or seizings of the meaning of his theme. As seen previously in the portraits of Dalí, Lorca introduces letters into the drawing. Here he writes "a b c d" on a banner that rises from the base and takes the position of the head on the other side. These letters, along with the subtitle *Poema* suggest that *Ar-*

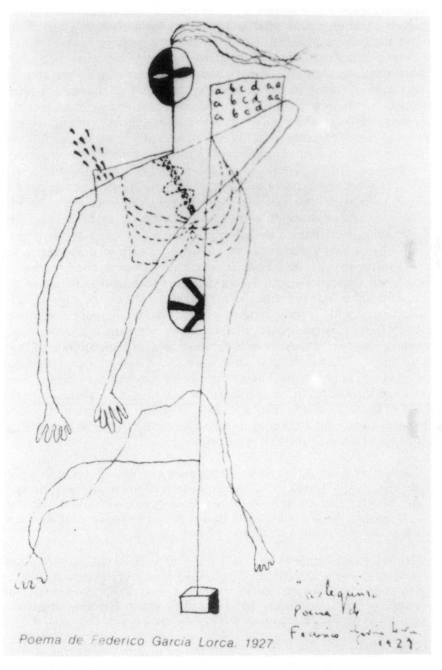

Poema de Federico García Lorca. 1927.

lequín represents the fusion of drawing and writing. This drawing poses a question about what is needed to support such a fusion and about identifying oneself or at least one's artistic persona. Its lines are less defined than those of the drawings already discussed, and the entire drawing does not, in my reading, measure up to the forceful expression of others in this series. Perhaps the fact that Lorca called it a poem indicates that he was more self-conscious in executing this drawing. It lacks the vitality of the others, their spontaneity and intrinsic power of expression. The inclusion of language may indicate that this drawing is not strong enough to speak for itself. If we accept the premise that drawing can be a recording of innate bodily sensations, this text may also belie Lorca's sense of himself at the time at which he executed it. The other drawings in the suite are linked by a common shared strength of line; this drawing may be read as part of the suite in its nature as self-expression.

Of all of Lorca's drawings, this 1927 suite of line drawings is the most impressive group. This effect results from a combination of factors. In these drawings, Lorca achieves technical mastery of the elements of his drawing, line, form, and space. Even their positioning on the page and Lorca's generous use of negative space contribute to their beauty. Furthermore, the simplicity with which Lorca invokes meaning in these drawings makes them easy to look at, not so busy or detailed, not so charged with movement and emotion that the viewer's eye is repelled. Their very nature invokes meditation, and, as I have shown, invites a multitude of readings. Lorca's limiting the focus of these drawings results in control and in expression. Looking at them, I am reminded of an image Lorca employed to describe the activity of Góngora and the poem he crafted:

> Tanto deseo tiene de dominarlo y redondearlo, que ama inconcientemente las islas, porque piensa y con mucha razón, que un hombre puede gobernar y poseer, mejor que ninguna otra tierra, el orbe definido y visible de la redonda. Tierra limitada por las aguas. Su mecánica imaginativa es perfecta. Cada imagen a veces es un mito creado.

> [He has such a desire to dominate it and to round it out that he unconsciously loves the islands, because he thinks, and very rightly, that a man can govern and possess, better than any other land, the defined and visible world of the region. Land bound by water. His imaginative machinery is perfect. Each image is at times a created myth.] (*O.C.* 3:231)

Lorca's talent for isolating a line or image in order to charge it with meaning is obvious in these texts, whether one views them individually or hung together. Each of these drawings is an island, "un mito

creado" [a created myth]. This image of the island, conquerable because of its size and limited delineation, recalls the image of the
surface. The metaphor as island is what rises above the surface. It
is what is seen and consequently remembered by the viewer. So too,
whether we are viewing Lorca's drawings or reading his writing, it is
the captured image, the joining of images in metaphor that attracts
our eye, guides our reading, remains in our memory. The "essential
characteristics" have risen to the surface of the page; we know that
the island consists of much more than what we observe on the surface
of the water. The thoughtful reader/viewer of Lorca moves on to
probe the depths in order to experience the reality implied by such
a configuration of presence and absence.

Sebastià Gasch's appraisal of Lorca's work was enthusiastic, and
the critic applauded Lorca in the same language with which he described the "plastic-poetic" dynamic in other work. In reading
Gasch's review, it is important to remember that the critic is referring
not only to the drawings and letters that are available today for analysis but to others, as well as to conversations he had with Lorca that
are not available. His words provide still another window into Lorca's
creative process and the role that drawing played in that process.

In his review, which appeared first in *L'Amic des Arts* and months
later in *La Gaceta Literaria* in March 1928, Gasch evaluated Lorca's
drawings as no mere pastime of a poet, but of value in and of themselves as works of art, acknowledging Lorca's greatest formal success
in the expression of emotion through the lines in his drawings. This
would indicate not only that Lorca is in control of his pen, but also
that he is simultaneously in touch with what Gasch described in his
review as "the resonances of his interior world upon colliding with
the exterior world." Gasch listed the plastic accomplishments of
Lorca in terms of technique: "equilibrium of lines, dimension, relation of tones" but emphasized that Lorca's talent appeared to be
effortless, "an instinctive plastic sense".[44] This quality, observed and
articulated by Gasch, and evident to the viewer of Lorca today, is
the result of the spontaneity of the drawings. They have a freshness
about them that indicates that they are not exercises nor are they
reworked. The sense of playfulness articulated by Lorca when he
spoke about them and the mind-hand connection of drawing are the
driving force behind their success. They are first drafts—not of a
specific poem per se, but of the unconscious images and energy first
felt by the poet. Gasch attributed this role to the drawings:

Federico García Lorca, the poet, the authentic poet, the most eminent
poet, often feels the need, like Jean Cocteau, like Max Jacob, to mold

his dreams in a plastic mode, to fix the relationships that unite his soul
with the exterior world by essentially plastic means. Pre-sensed drawings,
divined drawings, drawings seen in a moment of inspiration, and which
pass directly from the deepest part of the poet's being to his hand. (4)

Gasch related Lorca's drawings to techniques employed by Picasso
and by Miró as a first step in setting down images:

We also think of the drawings of Miró, who lives attentive to the visions
of his interior world, and who quickly puts them down on paper when
they present themselves, in the same manner that the poet notes in his
notebook the metaphor which he has just created. (4)

Finally, Gasch provided the formula against which, as I have indicated, he measured art: "a plastic-poetic tendency . . . that is, the
translation of a state of being by means of the rhythm of lines and
colors." According to his review, Gasch evaluated Lorca's drawings
as successfully meeting this criterion.

In September 1927, Lorca responded to Gasch's article in another
letter to the critic, referring to his experience of drawing the very
same texts as the springboard for his further reflections on his art:

Pero sin tortura ni sueño (abomino del arte de los sueños) ni complicaciones. Estos dibujos son poesía pura o plástica a la vez. . . . Y me da
horror la palabra que tengo que usar para llamarlos. Y me da horror la
pintura que llaman directa, que no es sino una angustiosa lucha con las
formas en las que el pintor sale siempre vencido y con la obra muerta.

[But without torture or dream (I hate the art of dreams) or complications.
These drawings are pure poetry or pure plasticity at once. . . . And the
word that I have to use to name them horrifies me. And the painting they
call "direct" horrifies me, since it is nothing but an anguished fight with
the forms in which the painter always comes out vanquished and with
the work dead.] (O.C. 3:970)

This letter may be read as an effort on Lorca's part to further balance
his earlier description of the poet's state of "flying over the abyss."
Carmona refers to it as a rectifying of Lorca's relationship with Surrealism.[45] The poet maintains his artistic freedom as well as the freedom of interpretation offered by his texts. This posture is consistent
with the aesthetics that Lorca had been developing up to this point.
In the lecture on Góngora, Lorca had explained the poet's process of
searching for "la metáfora limpia de realidades que mueren, metáfora
construída con espíritu escultórico y situada en un ambiente extraat-
mosférico" [the metaphor free of realities that die, the metaphor

constructed with a sculptural spirit and situated in an environment beyond its atmosphere] (*O.C.* 3:229) by means of limiting the imagination: "pone a los mitos de perfil, y a veces sólo da un rasgo oculto entre otras imágenes distintas" [he profiles the myth, and at times gives only one trait hidden among other different images] (241). The emotion rejected by Dalí and the form that he and other Cubists pursued in art combine in Lorca's choice of details that objectify his subject even as they appeal to feeling. Again, writing to Gasch in August 1927, Lorca states:

> En estas abstracciones mías veo yo realidad creada que se une con la realidad que nos rodea como el reloj concreto se une al concepto de una manera como lapa a la roca. Tienes razón, queridísimo Gasch, hay que unir la abstracción. Es más, yo titularía estos dibujos que recibirás (te los mando certificados) *Dibujos humanísimos*. Porque casi todos *van a dar con su flechita en el corazón*.

> [In these abstractions of mine, I see created reality that unites with the reality that surround us as the concrete "clock" attaches itself to the concept as a limpet to a rock. You're right, dear Gasch, one must unite abstraction. What's more, I'd call these drawings that you will receive (I'm sending them registered) Very Human Drawings. Because almost all of them pierce the heart with their little arrow.] (*O.C.* 3:970)

In this letter, Lorca is responding in words to Gasch's article "Del cubismo al superrealismo," which had appeared earlier in *Nova Revista*,[46] continuing a dialogue he had already begun with his practice of drawing. Observing that the drawings "van a dar con su flechita en el corazón" [pierce the heart with their little arrow], he admits the feeling they express and call forth, and Lorca seems to credit this emotive quality to the union of his abstractions—non-representational, "created reality" in the Cubist tradition—with reality, the human experience.[47] It also explains Lorca's use of the phrase "metáforas lineales" [linear metaphors]. By referring in this way to the drawings, Lorca unites his plastic and poetic work. Soria Olmedo observes that:

> the metaphor is the vehicle toward the aesthetic object's autonomy, just as abstraction and construction are for the pictorial.[48]

In Lorca's articulation, this process of abstraction and construction is the poet's process of seeking metaphors, and he does not distinguish between the two. The process of abstraction de-emotes the images involves. It would appear then, that Lorca relies on his reader/viewer to effect the emotive result he desires. The reader/viewer provides the heart that is the target of Lorca's arrows.

"Santa Lucía y San Lázaro"

Lorca's observation about metaphor and abstraction may also be applied to his poem "Santa Lucía y San Lázaro" (*O.C.* 3:143–50). In this text, as in the drawings, Lorca employs the same criteria and demonstrates the same influences of Cubism, Surrealism, Ramón Gómez de la Serna, and others noted by Hernández in the drawings.[49]

The text was written during the summer of 1927, making it the only documented writing of a literary nature during this time. Terence McMullan observes that, prior to its writing, "from January 1927 onwards, Lorca's vexation lay dormant, awaiting the therapeutic outlet of a literary safety-valve."[50] The notion that Lorca produced nothing from January 1927 must be countered with the realization that for Lorca, as already noted in this chapter, correspondence and drawing were major creative output. As the only literary text written in this period, "Santa Lucía y San Lázaro" is of particular interest. Its dedication to Sebastià Gasch links it to the aesthetic speculation contained in Lorca's important correspondence with the art critic. Ian Gibson relates the piece to Lorca's correspondence and collaboration with Dalí and goes so far as to assert that the piece "seems to have been a direct product of his [Lorca's] deep admiration for Dalí's "San Sebastián."[51] Morris observes that "Lorca's description of Dalí's prose poem as a 'prose full of unforeseen relationships and very subtle points of view' shows that he was sympathetic to the surprising juxtapositions and new angles of vision found in Dalí's writings and painting."[52] Christopher Maurer reads "Santa Lucía y San Lázaro" as a tribute to Ramón Gómez de la Serna.[53] Edwin Honig introduced it effectively in this fashion in 1944:

> "Santa Lucía y San Lázaro" (it is but one of Lorca's many prose pieces which have still to be published) for want of a better name, is called a story. Actually, we might call it any number of things: a group of movie stills, an exhibition of word paintings, a dream monolog with several silences, a montage of city memories; and there are those who, I am sure, will still insist that it is only "prose poetry."[54]

Reading "Santa Lucía y San Lázaro" as Honig describes it, in terms of visual art, as stills, montage, paintings, exhibition, and so forth highlights the commonality between the text and the drawings that are its contemporaries. In this reading, the protagonist of the text epitomizes the "artista caminante" of whom Lorca speaks in "Imaginación, inspiración, evasión" (*O.C.* 3:262) and the poet who takes a voyage in the lecture on Góngora (*O.C.* 3:237). It is this traveler who guides the reader and maintains the unity among the poem's components. This poem is, as Honig indicates, a *series* of visual texts. Both the protagonist and the reader of the text who follows him from image to image attempt to read and interpret their experience of the conjuncture of images. One place where this interpretation occurs is the composition and reading of the multitude of similes that fill the text. In this way, the poetic voice, the narrator who wanders through the city, in and out of the spaces belonging to the two saints (the inn and the cathedral for Santa Lucía and the station for San Lázaro) reads and interprets what he sees, redefining his experience in terms that imply a facilitating of comprehension. This is the function of a simile as Riffaterre explains it, to compare one object with another in order to extend meaning or chains of association.[55] There are over fifteen similes in a relatively brief text. Some are easily grasped, expressing an experience in terms of another, for example "estar pendiente de una voz es como estar sentado en la guillotina de la Revolución francesa" [to be hanging on a voice is like being seated on the guillotine of the French Revolution] (149), or "los ojos de un mulo me amenazaron como dos puños de azabache" [the eyes of a mule threatened me like two jet fists]. Others are more obscure, "el día de primavera era como una mano desmayada sobre un cojín" [the spring day was like a languid hand on a cushion] (143). Again, Lorca's manner of expression demands corresponding activity on the part of his reader. The seeming incongruence of images does not suggest that the reader is really expected to render incomparable terms comparable. Riffaterre explains, "It is simply an expansion that fleshes out a simile structure with words not comparable—and this destroys the mimesis and triggers genuine literary behavior in the reader . . . even if it is wrong behavior."[56] Some of the similes here are examples of the "imágenes cazadas" [hunted images] of which Lorca spoke in the lecture on Góngora, that is imaginative ones—"un hecho del alma" [a feat of the soul]—and that other more difficult images are in the realm of inspiration, requiring not analysis but faith, "un estado del alma" [a state of being] (*O.C.* 3:261).

As consistently noted, Lorca had experimented in his drawing with the process of reduction, and had succeeded in expression with a minimum of plastic means. This may explain what Gibson describes as a "stark, dream atmosphere, and the use of short paragraphs and phrases without verbs" in "Santa Lucía y San Lázaro."[57] Gibson attri-

butes this to the influence of Dalí, but to my view, this is not the
only feasible explanation. Lorca's drawing, especially during the time
preceding the writing of this text, also serves to explain the use of
"short paragraphs and phrases without verbs." Surely the achievement of "Santa Lucía y San Lázaro" is at least in part a result of this
process, the fruit of Lorca's continued artistic exercise.

Several aspects of Lorca's technique already delineated in the
drawings are immediately obvious as one reads "Santa Lucía y San
Lázaro." The focus on isolated images, their division and repetition
and an insistence on balance are in evidence. In the first part of the
text, dedicated to Santa Lucía, repetition is seen in mathematical
references to persons and things, first in terms of twos and then of
halves. The wholeness implied in images of "two": the mule's eyes,
the landlord singing a duet with his wife, for example, is followed
by the contrast of presence with absence, achieved by presenting one
of two things normally joined. The protagonist enters the inn at *mid-
night.* The frost dances on one (of its two) foot. A man is cut in
halves by his belt. The protagonist has half a comb in his pocket.
Later, Santa Lucía is described in terms that echo the description of
the man in the first paragraph. Her waistband is also mentioned, not
only as something that divides her body by means of its location, but
also as something that weighs her down, for Lorca tells us that Christ
is sitting on it bearing scepter and crown.[58] In this image, then, there
are present both the divided "half" concept as well as a doubling.

Another technique is the presentation of a series of enclosed,
framed, or isolated images of a single object or characteristic. These
images form metonyms, representing a whole, much in the same
way Lorca had emphasized singular "essential characteristics" of the
various subjects of his drawings. The poet's words "mi <<me
gusta>>" [my "I like it"], representing him, are reflected in the
mirror. He seeks the sight of one star framed in the window and
insists that it be only one: "las demás hay que olvidarlas" [one must
forget the rest]. This framing device is also seen in the image of a
hand against a pillow, the mule dozing on the threshold and the door
labeled "Posada de Santa Lucía" [Inn of St. Lucy]. The narrator
stands encircled by a balcony overlooking the city, and even as he
scans the vista, he is looking for that same city on the map he holds
in his hands. His searching implies that this is not a map of the city
per se, but that the image of the city is contained within the map of
a larger area. Reality is being read, therefore, in light of its representation. Comparing the actual city before him with its reduction on a
piece of paper signals to the reader that the text which follows is also
a map, a depiction, a narration of the voyage.

Lorca's statements explain that in his drawings he offers the viewer the end product of his own reading of a subject in the form of reduced sign, having chosen those characteristics that best express the significance of the subject. The analysis of the drawings finds that statement to be true. The reading process involved in viewing these drawings entails reversing Lorca's process—starting with the metonym, and reconstructing the subject from the elements portrayed in the drawing. So, too, in "Santa Lucía y San Lázaro," viewing Lorca's final choice of elements enables the reader to move backward through the text, reconstructing significance. Just as the form of the drawings is crucial to the process, so too the structure of the text of this prose poem creates what Riffaterre terms "sequence induced phenomena inseparable from the physical substance of the text . . . the end regulating the reader's grasp of the beginning."[59] Thus, in addition to the concept of considering "Santa Lucía y San Lázaro" as a series of visual images, it is helpful to read the last paragraph of the poem as another means of establishing coherence among what appear to be disparate, unlikely combinations of images. The text reads:

> Solo unas gafas y un blanquísimo guardapolvo. Dos temas de viaje. Puros y aislados. Las gafas sobre la mesa, llevaban al máximo su dibujo concreto y su fijeza extraplana. El guardapolvo se desmayaba en la silla en su siempre última actitud, con una lejanía poco humana ya, lejanía bajo cero de pez ahogado. Las gafas iban hacia un teorema geométrico de demostración exacta, y el guardapolvo se arrojaba a un mar lleno de naufragios y verdes resplandores súbitos. Gafas y guardapolvo. En la mesa y en la silla. Santa Lucía y San Lázaro.

> [Just some eyeglasses and a very white duster. Two themes of a voyage. Pure and isolated. The eyeglasses on the table, carried to the maximum their concrete drawing and their extra-flat firmness. The duster was fainting in the chair in its always last attitude, with an already barely human remoteness, a remoteness under the zero of a drowned fish. The eyeglasses were going toward a geometric theorem of exact demonstration and the duster was throwing itself into a sea filled with shipwrecks and sudden green brillances. Eyeglasses and duster. On the table and in the chair. Saint Lucy and Saint Lazarus.] (*O.C.*: 150)

The phrase *dos temas de viaje* [two themes of the voyage] raises a flag in the mind of this reader of Lorca. Coming at the end of the poem, it echoes Lorca's contention that the artistic object provides direction—a way of articulating creative experience, a map of the poetic plane, the text as the narration of the voyage. Here Lorca offers a summary that may serve as a guide to the text's (re)reading.

In this part of his poem, Lorca summarizes the imagery he has employed in two semantic fields. This repetition of related images reveals a line of order—the "poetic logic" that governs and binds them together.[60] In his "Sketch de la nueva pintura" [Sketch of the new painting], Lorca explained how elements of a work may both serve to express (on the part of the artist) and to influence perception (on the part of the viewer):

> Un gris da motivo a un fondo donde varias formas y volúmenes en armonia (en belleza) *sentida por el pintor* juegan y entrelazan sus naturalezas dando origen a un mundo que *conmueve o hace pensar al que lo mira* [my italics].

> [Gray gives reason for a background where various forms and volumes in harmony (in beauty) felt by the painter play and entwine their natures giving birth to a world that moves the one who looks at it and makes him/her think.] (*O.C.* 3:275)

This organization into fields is one way Lorca searches for and expresses "*los rasgos esenciales*" [the essential traits] of his subjects. It is for the reader to bring these images together, and, following Lorca's lead, to arrive at meaning. Examining these fields will result in an understanding of what Lorca saw as the essence of these two saints, their meaning.

These divisions might be restated thus. First, Santa Lucía and her representation are named:

> Las gafas sobre la mesa, llevaban al máximo su dibujo concreto y su fijeza extraplana . . . Las gafas iban hacia un teorema geométrico de demostración exacta, . . . En la mesa . . . Santa Lucía.

> [the eyeglasses on the table were carrying to the maximum their concrete drawing and their extra-flat firmness. . . . the eyeglasses were going toward a geometric theorem of exact demonstration . . . on the table . . . Saint Lucy.]

This field, then, would include references to eyeglasses, frames, a table—exactness, distinctness, hardness of texture, clarity, and delineated boundaries usually in the form of a circle—that same field of images with which Lorca delineates poetic imagination: "La imaginación fija y da vida clara a fragmentos de la realidad invisible donde se mueve el hombre" [The imagination fixes and gives clear life to the fragments of invisible reality where man moves] (*O.C.* 3:259). San Lázaro is aligned in Lorca's text with these images:

> El guardapolvo se desmayaba en la silla en su siempre última actitud, con una lejanía poco humana ya, lejanía bajo cero de pez ahogado . . . y el

guardapolvo se arrojaba a un mar lleno de naufragios y verdes resplandores
súbitos . . . en la silla . . . San Lázaro.

[The duster was fainting in the chair in its always last attitude, with an
already barely human remoteness, a remoteness under the zero of a
drowned fish . . . and the duster was throwing itself into a sea filled with
shipwrecks and sudden green brillances . . . in the chair . . . Saint
Lazarus.]

These are the opposite pole—suggestions of a lack of form or imme-
diacy, nuances of disorder, of softness, of cloth and of unclear connections, a drowned fish, for example. These may be aligned with
Lorca's description of poetic inspiration: "la inspiración lo [el tema]
recibe de pronto y lo envuelve en luz súbita y palpitante" [inspiration
receives it (the theme) all at once and wraps it in unexpected and
palpitating light] (O.C. 3:263). Santa Lucía is, of course, the martyr
who plucked out her own eyes to dissuade a suitor and is therefore
the patroness of the blind and of all matters of vision and eye health.[61]
It is only natural, then, that in writing about her, Lorca should draw
on multiple references to eyes and vision. More likely, the process
was the reverse—he chose Santa Lucía because of his intention to
focus on the sense of sight, a logical choice for Lorca, who claimed,
"Todas las imágenes se abren en el campo visual" [All images are
opened in the visual field] (O.C. 3:230).[62]

The landlord's enigmatic statement, which opens the piece, "Una
muchacha puede ser morena, puede ser rubia, pero no debe ser
ciega" [A girl can be dark or fair, but she should not be blind] can
be read as a reference to the virgin martyr. This is followed by images
of seeing, such as the "ojos del mulo que dormitaba" [eyes of the
mule that was dozing], "Vi mi <<me gusta>> en el espejo verde"
[I saw my "I like it" in the green mirror], "no hay nada más hermoso
que ver una estrella" [There is nothing so beautiful as seeing a star],
and "se miraron" [They looked at one another]. Multiple instances
of eyes or of function of eyes, reading, crying, looking, and so forth
occur in the text. These would include every mention of opticians'
shops. The reader is seeing through the eyes of the wandering narrator. References to the lack of vision include the already noted statement about blind girls, the description of the landords' duet as two
moles who are stumbling, searching for an exit, as well as the curious
simile "se miraron . . . equivócandose. Como el niño que se lleva a
los ojos la cuchara llena de sopita" [They looked at one another . . .
making a mistake like the child who raises a spoon filled with soup
to his eyes]. (144)[63] The pouring of hot liquid into the eyes as a
means of blinding is accompanied by the image of the spoon, to be

used for a similar purpose later in *Poeta en Nueva York:* "Con una cuchara, arrancaba los ojos a los crocodilos" ("El Rey de Harlem" [With a spoon, he was pulling out the crocodiles' eyes] *O.C.* 1: 459).[64] Another instance of the blindness image occurs when Lorca speaks of "la cabeza de una mula con anteojeras de cuera" [the head of a mule wearing leather blinders]. The shift of gender from the first mention of the eyes of a mule—"mulo" to "mula" appeals again to the eyeless, immovable Santa Lucía. It may also mark the process of the poet's identification with her.

The moment in which the poet-pilgrim confronts the eyes of Santa Lucía during cathedral devotions is key to the image Lorca has been repeating. In an important paragraph, he links her eyes to the ordered exactness that we have seen her represent in the text. Interestingly, Lorca begins his comments with terms appropriate to graphic expression. Recall the use of line in the 1927 drawings discussed above.

Espacio y distancia. Vertical y horizontal. Relación entre tú y yo. ¡Ojos de Santa Lucía! Las venas de las plantas de los pies duermen tendidas en sus lechos rosados, tranquilizadas por las dos pequeñas estrellas que arriba las alumbran. Dejamos nuestros ojos en la superficie como las flores acuáticas, y nos agazapamos detrás de ellos mientras flota en un mundo oscuro nuestra palpitante fisiología.

[Space and distance. Vertical and horizontal. Relationship between you and me. St. Lucy's eyes! The veins of the soles of her feet sleep stretched out on their rosy beds, tranquilized by the two little stars that illuminate them from above. We leave our eyes on the surface like aquatic plants, and we hide while our palpitating physiology floats in a dark world.] (146)

Much significance can be mined from this quote. First, it names distance, space, relationship, creating points on the vertical/horizontal axis. The body of the saint at rest establishes a horizontal line, repeated in the relationship between the soles of her feet and her eyes. The repetition of her eyes in the ceiling—"dos pequeñas estrellas que arriba las alumbran" [two little stars that illuminate them from above]—is related to the eyes, of course, but also to the soles of her feet, which are tranquilized by the lights overhead. This creates a vertical tension. One might well ask how an eyeless saint, whose eyes are kept in a reliquary might lie under a projection of those very same eyes. Lorca here could be referring to traditional depictions of Santa Lucía in which she appears to both retain her eyes—she is never disfigured—even as she holds another pair on a tray. Of course, this is an example of traditional art's rejection of thoroughly mimetic function. Lorca makes use of the same artistic distance from literal reality. The two references to "teoremas" [theorems] in the text as well as the addition and multiplication signs may refer to this doubling of the image. Santa Lucía's eyes function in the text as both absent and present, and this phenomena recalls many of Lorca's drawings in which two faces are superimposed, one whose eyes are empty, the other filled. These include, for example, *Sueño del marinero* [Sailor's dream], and *Payaso de rostro desdoblado* [Clown of the double face].

Secondly, the powerful image evoked when Lorca speaks of the reader placing his or her eyes on a surface like floating plants implies living under that surface, in the realm of poetic inspiration. Since our eyes meet a text or drawing at its surface, we can name these meeting points, as Gasch described, between the soul and external reality. We have already noted the presence of this theme in Lorca's more theoretical writings and its implications for his art and our reading of it. Thus, as Mary Ann Caws has noted in the work of other poets, the text becomes an interface between the author and the reader.[65] Several drawings recall these images, featuring the recurrent motif of an eye placed by itself on the page. Images of dangling nerve cells, which often accompany this eye, may also be viewed as the roots of an aquatic plant that descends, suspended into the dark water.

The eye image leads to two secondary series of representations: first, of eye glasses repeated throughout the text and secondly, the shape of the circle, or oval. Eyeglasses are mentioned directly by means of Lorca's repeated allusion to opticians' offices, to his own binoculars, the windows of the inn, the atmosphere itself, the glass cover of the reliquary in which the saint's eyes rest. The frames of eyeglasses are echoed in the framing references already noted, and also in the device of the tray, in its rigid surface and in its shape.

Limits and profiles, the product of imaginative activity according to Lorca, abound. Circles are expressed in words such as "caracola," "tomates," "monedas," "esferas del reloj," "órbita," "bóvedas," "cúpula," "el aire ovalado," and "manzana" [snail, tomatoes, coins, spheres of the clock, orbit, dome, cupola, the ovaled air, apple] among others.

Another meaning of the phrase "ojos de Santa Lucia" further relates them to circular imagery. McMullan insists that the Dalí connection explains Lorca's repeated references to the "ojos de Santa Lucía," that

> they are pebbles found on the beach at Cadaqués where Lorca visited Dalí and his family, pebbles known locally as "ojos de Santa Lucía."

Lorca's prose piece distinguished carefully between "los ojos humanos de Santa Lucía," presumably evoking the saint's traditional attributes, and "los ojos de Santa Lucia" presented in the context of "la playa" [the beach] and "el mar" [the sea] which almost certainly denote the pebbles just mentioned.[66]

Another reading of Lorca's distinction is that Lorca is certainly contrasting the human eyes of St. Lucy with the artifices included in her portrayal. As we have noted, she is almost always depicted with two pairs of eyes. Lorca summarizes the significance of Santa Lucía through a description of her eyes that identifies them with external, visible realities—with things that can be fixed, lined, drawn. It is no accident, in my view, that he refers to them as protagonists in his art. The phrases will be reproduced here as they are on the page, since their position as single phrases suggests a series of the still lifes proposed by Lorca:

Ojos de Santa Lucía sobre los nubes, en primer término, con un aire del que se acaban de marchar los pájaros.

Ojos de Santa Lucía en el mar, en la esfera del reloj, a los lados del yunque, en el gran tronco recién cortado.

Se pueden relacionar con el desierto, con las grandes superficies intactas, con un pie de mármol, con un termómetro, con un buey.

No se pueden unir con las montañas, ni con la rueca, ni con el sapo, ni con las materias algodonosas. Ojos de Santa Lucía.

Lejos de todo latido y lejos de toda pesadumbre. Permanentes. Inactivos. Sin oscilación ninguna. Viendo cómo huyen todas las cosas envueltas en su difícil temperatura eterna.

[St. Lucy's eyes over the clouds, in the foreground, with the air of birds having ended their leaving.

St. Lucy's eyes in the sea, in the sphere of the clock, on the sides of the anvil, on the great trunk recently cut.

They can be related to the desert, with the great intact surfaces, with a marble foot, with a thermometer, with an ox.

They cannot be united with the mountains, nor with the distaff, nor with the toad, with cottony materials. St. Lucy's eyes.

Far from all throbbing, and far from all discomfort. Permanent. Inactive. Without any oscillation. Seeing how all things flee wrapped in their difficult, eternal temperature.] (147)

Not all the connections between the images here are apparent, but Lorca, in addition to repeating images of fixing, of balance and limits, offers a transition into the other conjunction of imagery rejected for St. Lucy, but present in the San Lázaro paradigm. The image of cloth and of the toad suggest softer, less defined surfaces and objects, preparing the reader for the next field of imagery portraying San Lázaro, the one raised by Christ from the dead.

First, the figure of Lazarus lying in death in the tomb is repeated in several figures of death and repose, in the protagonist who wearily stretches out on the bed in his room, under a star, later re-presented by the figure in the cathedral—"las venas de las plantas de los pies duermen tendidas en sus lechos rosados, tranquilizadas por las dos pequeñas estrellas que arriba las alumbran" [The veins of the soles of her feet sleep stretched out on their rosy beds, tranquilized by the two little stars that illuminate them from above—of Santa Lucía having died on "un lecho de llamas" [a bed of flames], and of the traveler who "se complacía en hundir sus pies en el lecho de cenizas y arena ardiente" [is pleased to plunge his feet in the bed of ashes and burning sand].

The nature of those characteristics that Lorca presents as intrinsic to his Lazarus is not in opposition with the thesis of this chapter: that the same reductive, focused approach present in the 1927 drawings is also to be found in "Santa Lucía y San Lázaro." The fact that Lazarus is characterized by Lorca to reside in the pole opposite of Santa Lucía does not cancel the thesis. It is not the nature of the characteristic but rather how Lorca portrayed them in reduced, defined, and repeated form that aligns these two figures with Lorca's drawings.

Just as some of the imagery that invokes the associations with Santa Lucía are found throughout the entire text, so words that convey the ambiguity, formlessness and shadowy nature of the San Lázaro figure appear in the text before the actual section dedicated to him. Early on, Lorca speaks of "una mano desmayada" [a languid hand], the protagonist loses his guidebook (map) and his binoculars (glasses), and he describes a change in the feel of the city, from celebration to a subtle sadness:

la tristeza que afloja los cables de la electricidad y levanta las losas de los pórticos que había invadido las calles con su rumor imperceptible de fondo de espejo.

[the sadness that slackens the electric wires and raises the flagstones of the porticos that had invaded the streets with the imperceptible murmuring of the mirror's bottom.] (145)

"Las losas" may also be translated as "gravestones," a reference to the tombstone of Lazarus rolled away at Christ's command before he called Lazarus forth from the grave.

As the protagonist approaches the train station, the space of San Lázaro, a darkening occurs that results in silence that Lorca describes as "el silencio que descubría la sutil relación de pez, astro, y gafas" [the silence that was uncovering the subtle relationship of fish, star, and eyeglasses] (147). It is in the silence of reading that such relationships are discovered. The ability to make the connections between such images comes from the gift of inspiration described earlier by Lorca. This concept is repeated shortly after the above lines: "en la oscuridad, dibujado con bombillas eléctricas, se podía leer sin esfuerzo ninguno: *Estación de San Lázaro*" [in the darkness, drawn with electric lightbulbs, one could read without any effort, St. Lazarus Station]. When San Lázaro is introduced in the text, Lorca does so in terms that identify him with the poet of the lecture, "Imaginación, inspiración, evasión." He tells the reader that San Lázaro "percibía los menores ruidos . . . podía contar en la madrugada, por sus latidos, todos los corazones que había en el pueblo" [would perceive the slightest noises . . . could count in the early morning, by means of their throbbing, all the hearts there were in the village] (148). The poet described in Lorca's lecture "quiere sentir el diálogo de los insectos bajo las ramas increíbles. Quiere penetrar la música de la corriente de la savia en el silencio oscuro de los grandes troncos. Quiere comprender el alfabeto Morse que habla al corazón de la muchacha dormida" [wants to hear the insects' dialogue beneath the incredible branches. He wants to penetrate the music of the flowing of the sap in the dark silence of the great trunks. He wants to understand the Morse alphabet that speaks to the heart of the sleeping girl] (*O.C.* 3:260). Throughout the text, San Lázaro is listening, as does the poet, for things that, in Lorca's words, do not require analysis but faith (*O.C.* 3:261).

This attitude has its equivalent in the the reader. The reading generated includes the search for technique, structures, influences, but must transcend these formal elements to an appreciation beyond what Gasch had called the aesthetics of the dissection laboratory.

This point is suggested by a comparison of the identification of Lazarus with Christ in "Santa Lucía y San Lázaro" and the portrayal of Christ in a drawing by Lorca, one of the series of the "crucecita" entitled *¡Ecce homo!* In the prose text, Lorca creates an image of Christ's Passion through brief allusions to familiar objects, suggestive of that story. McMullan lists "un gallo," "me puse a llorar," "monedas con agujeros," una paliza," "le daban azotes," "me coronaba," "estación [de ferrocarril]," and "clavos de hierro" [a cock, I began to cry, coins with holes, a beating, they were whipping him, I was being crowned, station (railroad) and iron nails]. He concludes:

Christ's raising of Lazarus (his prototype) renders them both interchangeable here. Phrases like "lleno de unción" [filled with unction], "ocultando en sus pequeños ataúdes" [hiding in its small coffins] and "levanta las losas de los pórticos" [raises the stones of the portico] might equally apply to Lazarus or to the anointing, entombment and Resurrection of Our Lord.[67]

San Lázaro, as he prefigures Christ, is removed from his model all the while that he represents it, just as the depiction of Christ's suffering in the drawing ¡Ecce homo! removes the viewer's gaze from Christ to the elements of his suffering. The words that McMullan cites above as applying to the Christ image also are in accord with the other semantic field already established, the realm of darkness, of the underworld, the world of poetic inspiration.

In ¡Ecce homo! Lorca presents the elements of Christ's Passion through minimal suggestion. Readers familiar with the story and its depiction can follow Lorca's suggestions. We see a face, again represented by one eye, which is shedding tears over a stippled surface that appears to delineate the area of a cheek. Christ is usually not portrayed as weeping in the Passion; these tears may be interpreted as Lorca's reading of the event, attributing such humanity to Christ. It may indicate the presence of another's eye that views the suffering of Christ; this could be Lorca himself. To the right of the eye is a long vertical line crossed by a diagonal, which suggests a cross, both by the meeting of the two lines as well as the presence of two nails in its lower half. Symbols of the Passion surround the eye. A half moon filled in by numbered horizontal lines represents a rib cage, and recalls the words of Psalm 22, associated with Christ's death, "I can count all my bones." The number three is not written; in its place Lorca has placed a triangle out of which come three lines. An arrow, or more accurately, a lance pierces a hole representing the wound in Christ's side. The blots of ink observed in the other drawings are larger here, suggesting blood. These stains fall along curved lines and a triangle ending in three smaller lines, all of which suggest the cords of a scourge.

One is reminded in this drawing of the image of Christ's face on the veil of Veronica portrayed in so many religious paintings. Lorca's drawing is no less poignant. The subtle treatment of his theme provides a space in which the reader can identify elements, interpret their meaning, and respond accordingly.[68] In his lecture "Imaginación, inspiración, evasión," Lorca said: "No pretendo definir, sino subrayar, no quiero dibujar, sino sugerir" [I do not claim to define, but to underline, I do not want to draw, but to suggest] (O.C. 3:258).

"¡Ecce homo!" © 1994 Artists Rights Society (ARS), New York/VEGAP, Madrid

This is a change in Lorca's aesthetics since that articulated in the Góngora lecture and personified in the person of Santa Lucía.

Essentially, then, Lorca has reduced the experience of Santa Lucía and San Lázaro to their "rasgos esenciales" [essential traits] and by means of repetition has reinforced in his reader's consciousness what the essence of each is. In addition to the presence of the wandering narrator, this highlighting is another means of guiding the reader's voyage through the semantic fields. Having examined these images, we can identify these essential characteristics: the deliberate, steadfast control of St. Lucy facing martyrdom and the lack of control experienced by Lazarus, bound and entombed, waiting and hanging upon the call of Christ. Secondly and more important, Lorca has managed to demonstrate not just his experience of the realms of imagination and inspiration as he defines them, but also to employ techniques of both. In this text he both defines and underlines, he draws and he suggests.

It seems clear that Lorca has attempted in this prose poem to do what he was doing with his drawing, namely to create an artistic object that would correspond to the demands of "totalismo" [totalism], a text that would be a union of the principles of Cubism and Surrealism. By assigning to each saint the essence of one of the two aesthetics, and by combining tightly drawn comparisons and balanced polarities with subtle, suggestive imagery, Lorca shows that they are not mutually exclusive. His protagonist, wandering, trying to find his way through and between the two spaces finally arrives "home" in a third space, where both aesthetics are present. Read in light of the drawings that are its contemporaries, "Santa Lucía y San Lázaro" is understood as a written expression of the dynamics examined in *totalismo*.

Honig, describing Lorca's prose poem, speaks in terms applicable to the series of drawings under consideration as well:

> It is the silences, the white spaces between Lorca's engraved images and the sky which tremble so, and which suggest the kind of drama he spun so fabulously in his greatest plays.[69]

It is the silences, the spaces between the images that permit the viewer to consider and interpret the images individually and in relation to each other. Thus, it is important to view the text not as one would a single drawing, but, as Honig indicates, as a series of such work, an exhibition of word paintings, reminiscent of the experience of viewing the suite of drawings "marked by a cross." Indeed, Lorca's deliberate use of this pointer in the drawings, almost as part of their titles, and his subsequent references to the "little cross" in his remarks to Gasch support the view that he saw those specific drawings as an ensemble. Descriptions of persons, what we might call portraits, as well as the still lifes proposed by Lorca in "Santa Lucía y San Lázaro" also point to this thesis. McMullan's description of the text as "an implicit yet coherent aesthetic statement" links the poetics of "Santa Lucía y San Lázaro" with that of the "drawings with the little cross," for, as we have seen, both are the result of focused observation and expression.

McMullan has observed:

> Two distinct aesthetic approaches to existence are embodied in the duality of the Spanish title [of the poem]. One (Santa Lucía), shallow but in its way perfect and reassuring, encapsulates an aseptic beauty where bright, pure surfaces, schematic outlines, and transparency combine with the transcendental image of an essential reality, timeless and static, defined with geometrical precision. The other (San Lázaro), turbid and anguished, probes the unfathomable depths of human insecurity and vulnerability, a deceptive region of gut responses and raw nerve ends, its visceral immediacy shot through with alarming intimations of mortality."[70]

This is not only an affirmation of the division made in this analysis, but a demonstration of the transitional nature of this literary text. The dynamic assigned by McMullan to the St. Lucy "aesthetic approach" is very much that observed in the drawings analyzed in this chapter. Those assigned to St. Lazarus, especially its visceral quality and the distinction of "gut-response and raw nerve ends" can be easily applied to the drawings that would follow in the New York period. Once again, Lorca's visual experience is transformed to provide himself and the reader with access to the realm of the soul, in Gasch's now familiar words, "El alma del poeta y el alma de las cosas = Poesía"[71] [The soul of the poet and the soul of things = Poetry]. It also confirms the ongoing experimentation on Lorca's part with the two aesthetic approaches delineated in this text and in "Imaginación, inspiración, evasión." The wandering narrator and his rambling discourse prefigure the uninterrupted lines that enters Lorca's drawing at this juncture and shows itself in *Nadadora sumergida* [Submerged swimmer] and *Suicidio en Alejandria* [Suicide in Alexandria]. The space and silence of which Honig speaks, present in the drawings of the summer of 1927 as well as in "Santa Lucía y San Lázaro" will continue to be key elements in this second series of drawings/prose poems as well as in Lorca's "Oda al santísimo sacramento del altar" [Ode to the most holy sacrament of the altar].

Two Drawings and Their Corresponding Poems

Nadadora sumergida [Submerged swimmer] and *Suicidio en Alejandría* [Suicide in Alexandria], published in 1928, are important texts to this chapter, since they are the only examples by Lorca directly connecting specific poetry and drawings. He wrote to Gasch in 1928: "Si te gustan los dibujos dime cuál or cuáles piensas publicar y te mandaré sus poemas correspondientes" [If you like the drawings, tell me which one or ones you intend to publish, and I'll send you their corresponding poems] (*O.C.* 3:963). These drawings were *Nadadora sumergida* and *Suicidio en Alejandría*. It comes as no surprise that Lorca should show the drawings first; following his lead, then, I shall first examine the two drawings and then the prose poems.

Both are line drawings obviously related to those that Lorca composed in the summer of 1927. The most eye-catching difference is the line, more tremulous than the definite strong lines of the earlier drawings, and yet precisely because of its rhythm, charged with more movement. Indeed both would appear to depict actions in process. In both drawings Lorca makes use of this wandering line, yet the drawings very definitely convey readable subjects.[72] These two drawings have received some attention by critics, most notably Loughran, who analyzes the graphic texts independently of their literary counterparts.[73]

In *Suicidio en Alejandría*, Lorca follows the pattern of a double portrait used by himself and Dalí during their collaborations. He depicts two intertwined figures pulling apart, linear except for their faces and genitals, which are drawn by what Fourneret calls "manchas de sangre, siempre sangriento" [blood stains, always bleeding] (71). The figures portrayed in the drawing are so entangled it is virtually impossible to distinguish one's members from the other's.

Two spaces are established, land and water, and each of the figures has one foot in each space. The placement of the figures at the water's edge is a sexual reference but may also hint at Lorca's imminent embarkment for the new world. The depiction of the two realms of water and land suggest reading this drawing as a representation of the two fields of literature and the plastic arts and the impossibility of separating them from one another.

In addition to these characteristics, Loughran notes the repetition

"Suicidio en Alejandría" © 1994 Artists Rights Society (ARS), New York/
VEGAP, Madrid

of figure 8's: "Lorca's enumeration from one to eight at the bottom of the drawing precisely beside the one appendage with more than five digits" (200). This appendage has eight digits. In addition to the foot with its eight digits and the enumeration already cited by Loughran, the central configuration of the figure—where we see the stains of which Fourneret speaks, which seem to represent the essence of these figures: their blood, their genitals, perhaps their hearts—is that of an eight.

In the drawing *Nadadora sumergida*, a rectangle from which one line proceeds appears to be the source of the entire drawing.[74] The form resembles an X, the four lines formed by the four appendages, feet and legs and/or hands and arms. The drawing is designed in such a way that it can be viewed from either direction (rightside up or upside down) and remain balanced. A central oval-shaped body is balanced by a dot and V-shaped lines at one end and short lines suggesting hair at the other. Retracing Lorca's lines in the drawing reveals a quantity of figure 8's, or at least a high frequency of the type configuration that forms half of an 8, as well as many actual 8's in hands and feet. The 8, of course offers the same picture no matter the direction from which it is viewed.

A first reading of the drawing sees a growth of what appears to be hair in the upper section of the central oval, below the upper set of appendages.[75] This suggests that the figure's arms are raised above its head in a posture assumed by a "submerged swimmer" struggling to reach the water's surface. At the top of the second set of appendages appears a dot that could be a navel and a V-shaped line that suggests female genitalia. To the left of the figure's center is a group of prolonged marks resembling a shower of sorts. This is the first such appearance of this motif in Lorca's drawings, but it will appear in later drawings as well, serving various functions. In two drawings that follow *Nadadora sumergida* chronologically, *Gitano malísimo* [The evil Gypsy] and *Marinero del <<Moreno>>* [Sailor from "Moreno"], this figure also occurs. The lines appear to be tears or in the case of *Marinero del <<Moreno>>*, the sea, forming a border; the sailor is depicted between this water image and the land represented by the tavern. So it seems appropriate to interpret these lines as representing the sea. Such lines represent blood in drawings such as *Manos cortados* [Severed hands] or tears in *Firma con Luna reflejada* [Signature with reflected moon], and *Payaso de rostro desdoblado* [Clown with a double face]. Again, given the title of the drawing, the interpretation of these lines as blood or as tears would be appropriate. Most critics see the lower appendages as hands, in which case the "drops" would become hair on the swimmer's head and the other group of lines

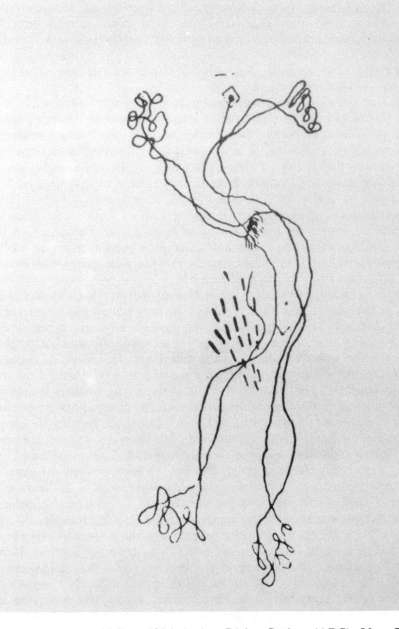

"Nadadora sumergida" © 1994 Artists Rights Society (ARS), New York/
VEGAP, Madrid

might become pubic hair.[76] Later we shall see how the written text suggests a reading of the swimmer's position.

In the letter in which he sent the prose poems to Gasch, Lorca situated the texts in his aesthetics:

Ahí te mando los dos poemas. Yo quisiera que fueran de tu agrado. Responden a mi nueva manera espiritulista, emoción pura descarnada, desligada del control lógico, pero ¡ojo!, ¡ojo!, con una tremenda lógica poética. No es surrealismo, ¡ojo! la conciencia más clara los ilumina. Son los primeros que he hecho. Naturalmente, están en prosa porque el verso es una ligadura que no resisten. Pero en ellos sí notarás desde luego, la ternura de mi actual corazón.

[Enclosed are the two poems. I hope you like them. They answer to my new spiritualist manner, pure disembodied emotion, detached from logical control, but careful! careful! with a tremendous poetic logic. It is not Surrealism, careful! the clearest self-awareness illuminates them. They're the first I've done. Naturally, they're in prose because verse is a confinement they can't withstand. But in them you will find right away my true heart's tenderness.] (*O.C.* 3:965)

In his "Sketch de la nueva pintura" Lorca defined this "new spiritualistic manner" as "un modo espiritualista en el cual las imágenes ya no son dadas por la inteligencia, sino por el inconsciente, por la pura inspiración" [a spiritualistic mode in which images are not given by intelligence, but by the unconscious, by pure inspiration] (*O.C.* 3:273). In spite of Lorca's insistence that this is a new way for him to draw and write, there has not been a complete abandoning of the technique he employed earlier.[77] The control evidenced in his organization of the text permits his images to surface. Furthermore, in spite of its resonances with the Surrealist aesthetic, one must read this definition bearing in mind not only Lorca's insistence that his were not Surrealist texts, but also that in the lecture on painting as well as in "Imaginación, inspiración, evasión," Lorca acknowledged the richness of the Surrealist use of dreams and the unconscious, but insisted on the need for more concrete expression. The reader familiar with Gasch well asks if Lorca is not, in fact, referring once again to *totalismo*.

Looking to the text of "Suicidio en Alejandría," one is immediately struck by evidence of artistic control—its arrangement on the page— short paragraphs or sentences divided mostly by equations and, at the bottom, by a column of descending numbers. It literally appears to be a puzzle of sorts to be unraveled, decoded by the viewer. The number sequence begins with the highest ($13 + 22 = 35$) and ends with the lowest (the number 1). This suggests that the poem ends at the beginning and provokes a reverse reading of its verses. Loughran's observations about the drawing, "The essential circularity of the figure eight denies escape from its confines and must always return to the earth from which it emerges,"[78] support such an approach. Furthermore, adding the numbers reveals that the pairs represent the joining of an even number with an odd, adding up to an odd sum. The pairing of odd with even may suggest a heterosexual relationship in the joining of opposites. In contrast, the presence of odd or unresolved sums interspersed through the verses creates a sense of incompleteness, which compels a repeated reading of the poem. This suspension of meaning may imitate the ambivalence of those contemplating suicide; or the relationship itself is seen to be a suicide. In Lorça's case, the prospects of remaining locked in a heterosexual relationship, or in a homosexual relationship that did not offer the possibility of openness, could be such a reality.

The focus on numbers leads to the awareness that the number 9 is also prominent in the poem.[79] The difference between each of the pairs of numbers equals nine, and it is in the sentences between 8 and the "9 y 18" configuration that the suicide is reported. Attention to this pair of numbers reveals a doubling theme, since "9 y 18" is the same as "9 y 9 + 9." The fact that Lorca claims to portray a double suicide gives further motive for a double reading of the poem.

The last line of the poem, "Nunca olvidaremos los veraneantes de la playa de Alejandría aquella emocionante escena que arrancó lágrimas de todos los ojos" [We the summer vacationers of the beach at Alexandria will never forget that moving scene which drew tears from everyone's eyes], sounds like the beginning of a recollection, and describes the scene Lorca has depicted in his drawing. Beginning then, from this phrase, the eye of the viewer is lead to the 0, a starting point, and up a column ending in 9 to the next section, which continues the description of the maritime scene beyond what is shown in the drawing, "Un golpe de mar . . ." [A surge of the sea]. Next, one sees three sets of equations, beginning at the bottom with 1 (y 10) and ascending to 3 (y 12). Again, Lorca repeats what he has shown in the drawing, "Al llegar este momento vimos a los amantes abrazarse sobre las olas" [When that moment arrived, we saw the lovers embracing over the waves].

In the phrases between 6/15 and 7/16, Lorca states: "reconozcamos que la mejilla derecha es un mundo sin normas y la astronomía un pedacito de jabón" [Let us recognize that the right cheek is a world without norms and astronomy is a little piece of soap]. In addition to echoing his contention, stated in the lecture on Góngora that "le da lo mismo una manzana que un mar, porque sabe que la manzana en su mundo es tan infinita como el mar en el suyo" [An apple is the same to him as a sea, because he knows that the apple in its world is as infinite as the sea in its world] (*O.C.* 3:233), the movement from small to large (cheek > world) and the reversing of that movement from large to small (astronomy > piece of soap) suggests a forward/backward reading, and implies a validation of such a reading. It also invites the search for other relationships. Here again, Lorca's metaphor is provocative, demanding increased activity on the part of his reader.

The next two phrases are read as homosexual references when seen in light of Lorca's imagery in some other drawings. The words "yo, un niño, y tú lo que quiera el mar" [I, a child, and you, whom the sea would love] suggest Lorca's depictions of sailors and youths. In *Sueño del marinero* [Sailor's dream], from 1927, the sailor set against a geometric, lightly shaded background is centered between a youth and a young girl. The youth can certainly represent the sailor himself, but in Lorca's scheme of things, this is unlikely. He seems to be implying a choice. *Hombre y joven marinero* [Man and young sailor], from 1929, is clearly homosexual in theme. Its composition closely resembles that of *Aleluya del marinero y su novia* [Alleluia of the sailor and his bride], from 1926. Against the background of a house and tavern there rests the figure of a large, burly man. In this drawing, however, the man is holding a young, effeminate sailor on his lap while a woman in the background waves her arms out a balcony to no avail. The presence of pairs in the drawing: two men, doors, windows, trees, houses, contrasted with the single woman, underlines the drawing's message. In the poem, the phrases containing the references to the youth and the sailor are followed by the repetition of "Bésame, bésame" [Kiss me, kiss me].

The next division of the text contains the verb "morimos" [we die], which is read in the present tense, since further along the verbs "se suicidaban, nos suicidábamos" [they were killing themselves, we were killing ourselves] are definitely past. The present "morimos" is read first, followed three sections later by "se suicidaban." One notes that the next phrase "nos suicidábamos" is impossible unless the narrator is somehow removed from the already past act of suicide. An objective position, such as that of viewing the drawing, would make the sequence, indeed the statement possible. When the reader arrives at #12, a reference to a "terrible ceremonia" [terrible ceremony], presumably the suicide, ends with the first paragraph on the page. The last sentence in this paragraph can be read as an ending for the poem, "Había necesidad de romper para siempre" [There was a need to break forever].

There is no way to ascertain, of course, if Lorca intended the poem to be read in this order. But the visual clues in the drawing and the poem offer that possibility and an attempt at such a reading allows a valid derivation of meaning. Perhaps this is what Lorca meant when he told Gasch that this new way of writing (or, in our case, of reading!) was: "desligada del control lógico, pero ¡ojo!, ¡ojo!, con una tremenda lógica poética. No es surrealismo, ¡ojo! la conciencia más clara los ilumina" [detached from logical control, but careful!! careful! with a tremendous poetic logic. It is not Surrealism! careful! the clearest self-awareness illuminates them] (O.C. 3:965). The resource of the visual text illumimates the poetic logic of the poem. In fact, my reading of both texts leads me to conclude that the written texts may be considered as Lorca's reading of his drawings.

The poem "Nadadora sumergida" [Submerged swimmer] follows this same premise. It reads as a detective report, and its dedication, "pequeño homenaje a un cronista de salones" [little homage to a chronologer of salons] implies the presence of a narrator, "cronista," while it suggests an ironic perspective. The text's arrangement on the page is not so unusual as that of "Suicidio en Alejandría;" only the last paragraph is set off by spacing. However, this poem is as enigmatic as "Suicidio en Alejandría."

It is the last paragraph that connects the poem directly with the drawing, since it speaks of the body of "la condesa X, . . . muy aficionada a la natación" [Countess X, a great fan of swimming]. In addition to the precise form of an X, and the reference to swimming, the body contains "un tenedor clavado en la nuca," [a fork stuck in her nape] that enforces the interpretation of the drops in the drawing as blood, as well as affirming the second reading, that the swimmer's head is in the lower half of the drawing.

The possibility of the swimmer being either upside down or rightside up is reinforced in the text by the presence of two women. Perhaps the drawing is also depicting two at once. Unlike "Suicidio en Alejandría," "Nadadora sumergida" would appear to be meant to be read from beginning to end, although there is one discrepancy to this reading. In the end of the text, Lorca states that "se ignora el nombre de su maravilloso asesino" [the name of her marvellous assassin is unknown], yet in the beginning, there are many references to endings and good-byes, and in the course of the poem, he provides details of an argument, of physical harm, and addresses someone (the reader? the police?): "Ya sabe usted lo demás" [you know the rest].

"Nadadora sumergida" offers an example of how the presence of irony can exert control over poetic subject matter. The tone with which Lorca writes the text is detached; although he speaks of rejection, death, murder, he does so in a tone that mimics the gossip of a salon. This same attitude can be read into the drawing. The swimmer is drawn with no indicators of the kind of violence we will see in later drawings of cut-off hands, decapitations, and so forth. In "Imaginación, inspiración, evasión" Lorca discussed his "nueva manera espiritual" [new spiritualist manner]:

> El poema evadido de la realidad imaginativa se sustrae a los dictados de feo y bello como se entiende y entra en una asombrosa realidad poética, a veces llena de ternura, y a veces de la crueldad más penetrante.

> [The poem escaped from imaginative reality avoids the dictates of ugliness and beauty as it is understood and enters into a frightening poetic reality, sometimes filled with tenderness, and sometimes with the most penetrating cruelty.] (*O.C.* 3:262)

The poetic reality that Lorca describes here resonates with his description, in other texts already cited, of the poetic realm. In that same lecture, Lorca spoke as well of the role of irony in effecting poetic evasion (*O.C.* 3:264). Irony, it seems, permits the same kind of distance from reality that drawing does, allowing an emotional space in which the poet can regroup and produce a text free of the complications of emotional response to such beauty and ugliness, tenderness and terror.

In conclusion, if we return to the comments with which Lorca offered these drawings/poems to Gasch, we recall that, for their author, they contained "la emoción pura descarnada" [pure, bare emotion] but that they were governed by a "lógica poética" [poetic logic] that suspends order and sustains the text, enabling one to derive significance from it. Each of the texts analyzed expresses and evokes powerful emotion, yet visually and verbally, that emotion is controlled, guided, and directed.

In this series, it is the drawings that more intensely express the emotion associated with love, rejection, separation, struggle, and death. The drawings have a sense of spontaneity, and of their connectedness with the hand that drew them. The poems are once removed from this experience of emotion. This, coupled with Lorca's use of irony and playfulness as he writes, give me the impression that he is writing about the drawings, creating a story about them, but not revealing what really inspired them. This explains his objectivity in the texts: "La conciencia más clara los ilumina" [The most clear consciousness illuminates them]. In both instances, knowledge of the drawings facilitates a new reading of what the two poems. The emotion is in the line.

"Oda al Santísimo Sacramento del Altar"

The poem "Oda al santísimo sacramento del altar" [Ode to the most holy sacrament of the altar] is a contemporary to *Nadadora sumergida* and *Suicidio en Alejandría* and shows the culmination of the evolution traced thus far in Lorca's drawing and writing. The first three parts of the poem were written during the summer and fall of 1928; the fourth and final section was finished early during the poet's stay in New York in 1929. Hernández connects the phenomena present in the drawings of this period with the poem quoting from "Mundo" [World], part two of the Ode:

> El Lorca de la madurez—una madurez fatalmente juvenil—alcanza un timbre de voz y de línea en el que se mezclan lo escueto y lo delicado y, junto al dibujo neto, también, cuando es necesario, la solemnidad meditativa:

> > Noche de rostro blanco. Nula noche sin rostro. Bajo el sol y la luna. Triste noche del mundo.
> > Dos mitades opuestas y un hombre que no sabe cuándo su mariposa dejará los relojes.

> [The mature Lorca—fatally, youthfully mature—realizes a timbre of voice and of line in which the unadorned and the delicate are mixed, and, along with the clean drawing, also, when necessary, a meditative solemnity:

> > Night of the white face. Void night without a face. Beneath the sun and the moon. Sad night of the world.
> > Two opposite halves and a man who does not know when his butterfly will abandon the clocks.][80]

This "meditative solemnity" is the same observed in drawings such as *¡Ecce homo!* or *San Sebastián*. Such solemnity is discussed by Lorca in a letter he wrote on 14 July, 1929, to his family from New York, an interesting statement concerning the Eucharist, that also recalls his insistence on the "human elements" of art:

> Lo que el catolicismo de los EEUU no tiene es solemnidad, es decir, calor humano. La solemnidad en lo religioso es cordialidad, porque es una prueba viva, prueba para los sentidos, de la inmediata presencia de

Dios. Es como decir: Dios está con nosotros, démosle culto y adoración
. . . Son las formas exquisitas, la hidalguía con Dios.

[What Catholicism in the United States doesn't have is solemnity, that
is, human warmth. Solemnity in religious matters is cordiality, because
it is a living proof for the senses, of the immediate presence of God. It
is like saying: God is with us, let us give him worship and adoration. . . .
They are exquisite forms, nobility with God.] (*O.C.* 3:833)

In these comments, written even after the first two sections of the
ode to the Eucharist, Lorca returns to the theme of the senses, of
giving images form, "prueba viva" [living proof]. One notes as well
that in this poem Lorca is retrieving the religious imagery already
discussed in the drawings *San Sebastián, ¡Ecce homo! Pavo real,* and
Poema del anzuelo, and in the poem "Santa Lucía y San Lázaro."
Lorca discussed the ode in a series of letters written to Jorge Zalamea in the summer and fall of 1928. It would seem that he wrote it
in an attempt to avoid expressing and revealing his feelings, since
he both advises Zalamea against such writing and says that writing
the poem is a precaution:

Y luego . . . Procurando constantemente que tu estado no se filtre en tu
poesía, porque ella te jugaría la trastada de abrir lo más puro tuyo ante
las miradas de los que no deben nunca verlo. Por eso, por *disciplina,* hago
estas academias precisas de ahora y abro mi alma ante el símbolo del
Sacramento, y mi erotismo en la <<Oda a Sesostris>> que llevo
mediada.

[And so . . . striving constantly that your state does not filter into your
poetry, because it would play the dirty trick on you of opening that
which is most pure in you to the stares of those who should never see it.
Therefore, by means of discipline, I do these academic exercises for the
moment, and I open my soul before the symbol of the Sacrament, and my
eroticism in the Ode to Sesostris, which I have half-finished.] (*O.C.* 3:981)

In an earlier letter to Zalamea, Lorca had also spoken of the ode and
of beginning another new kind of poetry:

Después de construir mis Odas, en las que tengo tanta ilusión, cierro este
ciclo de poesía para hacer otra cosa. Ahora tengo una poesía de ABRIRSE
LAS VENAS, una poesía EVADIDA.

[After constructing my Odes, for which I have such enthusiasm, I'm
closing this cycle of poetry in order to do something else. Now, I have a
poetry in which veins are opened, an escaped poetry.] (*O.C.* 3:978)

If, as Lorca claims, this poem is an "academic exercise," if he is opening his soul in it instead of his veins, as he would in later work, if he is in fact *constructing* the ode, then he would be returning to the aesthetics of Cubism, of the "Oda a Dalí," and the lecture on Góngora. Reading the poem reveals that much of the aesthetic in the 1927 drawings, Lorca's "obras de fusión" [works of fusion], is seen in this text. The exercise of control through formal rigidity evident in his choice of form, an alexandrine, a verse of fourteen syllables, is accompanied by the focus on a theme, as well as by many of the techniques already observed in Lorca's other work at this time. Indeed, as the poet himself stated to Zalamea, the "Ode to the Most Holy Sacrament of the Altar" is part of an aesthetic cycle, and a fitting representative of its poetics.

Part one, "Exposición," refers first to the rite in Catholic worship during which the Host is placed in a monstrance for the purpose of adoration by the faithful. In addition, of course, the title refers to its place as the introductory section of the four-part poem. Furthermore, the text serves as another "exposition" of Lorca's aesthetics. Lorca presents a series of elements pertaining to his subject, in this case the Eucharist in the monstrance, and, indirectly, to the arrest and vigil of Christ preceding his death that is celebrated on Holy Thursday and on every occasion during which there is exposition of the Eucharist. These include the monstrance, its column, oils and Christ's shroud (symbolized in altar linens), mantillas, angels, and the words by which the priest, "el hombre sudoroso" [the sweaty man], reenacts Christ's Passion and death in the Eucharist.

In surprising juxtapositions of these elements with other images, Lorca repeats a technique previously examined in the drawings and prose poems. First, he isolates images, then arranges those images in relation to others, highlighting those characteristics of his topic that he wishes to explore in the poem. For instance, the use of a visual device already noted specifically in *Pavo real* [Peacock] or in *Arlequín ahogado* [Drowned harlequin] as well as in "Santa Lucia y San Lázaro" is found in "Exposición" in the repetition of circular forms, often found as elements of the unusual juxtapositions already cited. These include "frasco," "ruedas," "el blanco," "panderito" "cúpula," "boca," "circundada," and "témpanos" [flask, wheels, the bull's eye, tambourine, cupola, mouth, encompassed, and timbrels]. Another cluster of images develops a semantic field along the concept of containment. Expressions like "clavado," "vivo en el Sacramento," "dentro del ostensorio," "en el frasco de vidrio" [nailed, alive in the Sacrament, inside the monstrance, in the glass flask] occur most often in the first two stanzas of the poem; they appear consistently but less frequently in those that follow: "anclado," "expresión exacta," "forma limitada" and "nieve circundada" [anchored, exact expression, limited form, encompassed snow]. Both the image of the circle and the concept of limit or containment have their origin in the Catholic visual experience of the Eucharist. The round Host is, in fact, encased in a circular glass container called a "luna" and then placed in the monstrance for exposition and adoration by the congregation.

On another level, one can see that Lorca is celebrating in this poem the ideal for which he has striven in earlier expression. Specifically, Lorca reads the Eucharist to be the finite, disciplined expression of that which exceeds and therefore can only have a limited expression in human life. The Sacrament has its parallel in the lived experience Lorca mentions so frequently as the inspiration and the object of his poetic activity, that in fact he strove to articulate in the drawings we have already studied: "En estas abstracciones más veo yo realidad creada que se une con la realidad que nos rodea" [In these abstractions of mine, I see more created reality which unites with the reality which surround us] (*O.C.* 3:970). The physical characteristics of the Eucharist—specifically its appearance as bread and wine serves as a meeting place, a point of union between the divine and the human. In a sense, the Eucharist as Lorca understands it is, like his texts, also a surface that joins two realms even as it is part of each.

Not only in the analysis of "Exposición" but in the other three divisions of "Oda al Santísimo Sacramento del Altar" as well, analogies can be drawn between the nature of the Eucharist as Lorca delineates it, and Lorca's activity in drawing and writing. The Sacrament is seen as a sign; in "Exposición," Lorca refers to it as "forma," "vértice," "ángulos" [form, vertex, angles], something that has the power to "expresar concreta" [concretely express]. It is measured; we read words in the second part, "Mundo" [World], that echo the stylized, geometric appearance of the line drawings, words like "luz in equilibrio," "manómetro," "tres voces iguales" [light in equilibrium, manometer, three equal voices].[81] It is as well a place where differences meet "naipe y herida," "punto de unión y cita del siglo y el minuto," "brisa y gusano," "meta de desamparo," "amor y disciplina" [card and wound, point of union and engagement of the century and the minute, breeze and worm, goal of abandonment, love and discipline]. Not only differences, but also specific time references are united here, temporal superimpositions seen in prediction (*naipe*/card) and actual event (*herida*/wound) as well as in a specific instance (*minuto*/minute) and its larger context (*siglo*/century). In part

three, "Demonio," Lorca refers to the Eucharist as "sacramento definido" [defined sacrament] as well as to its "unidad sencilla" [simple
unity] and its power to "hacerte visible" [make you visible].[82] This
artistic goal is shared by Lorca's graphic work.

In "Exposición," Lorca presents God in the Eucharist as one pursued, just as the reality behind his drawings has been pursued and
captured by the artist. Christ in the Host is throbbing, "latiendo,"
beating like the heart of a captured frog. We can recall here how
Lorca would later describe himself as artist in "Poema doble del
lago Eden":

Porque yo no soy un hombre, ni un poeta, ni una hoja, pero sí un pulso
herido que sonda las cosas del otro lado.

[Because I am not a man, nor a poet, nor a leaf, but I am a wounded
pulse which probes things from the other side.] (O.C. 1:490)

The image of the surface, of the interface appears again. Both the
poet and the Host represent a deeper reality than their surface, the
white surface of the page/poem/drawing or the thin white surface of
the Host. To these surfaces, Lorca links the notion of fragility and
suffering. These images and their union will be repeated in the poetry and the self-portraits executed by Lorca in New York in
1929–1930.

In seeming contrast to fragility's depiction, one reads in the text
a certain impassivity present in the Eucharist. It is "una piedra,"
"una piedra de soledad donde la hierba gime" [a stone, a stone of
solitude where the grass groans]. This does not appear to be an expression of remoteness in the face of human circumstance, especially
the suffering already noted, but, rather, according to the terms of
this discussion, a statement of the immutability realized when one
has arrived at the essence of an experience—the essence searched
for by Lorca in his treatment of the subjects of his drawings, in his
own emotional struggles, and now in his consideration of the
Eucharist.[83]

The image of solitude is further associated with the concept of
simplicity and economy of image and enhanced by the fact that diversity is dispensed with: "pierde sus tres acentos" [loses its three ac-
cents]. And, echoing the theme of immutability, Lorca states that
the Eucharist, "una forma flotando" [a floating form] on its "columna
de nardo bajo nieve" [column of nard under snow] is raised above
the "mundo de ruedas y falos que circula" [the world of wheels and
phalli that circulates]. The purity and whiteness of the Eucharist,

described as white on white, standing on a vertical column, is contrasted with sexual imagery, "ruedas y falos" [wheels and phalli]. The contrast between stoney solitude and sighing grass, between vertical, linear and circular images is highlighted by their juxtaposition. These sorts of joinings will be very apparent in the New York drawings.

The style seen in the drawings that Lorca drew prior to his writing of this poem is expressed in "Exposición" in images of focus, like that of "el dulce tiro al blanco" [the sweet shot to the target] (which literally repeats the bull's-eye image from *San Sebastián*), in images of purity: "harina para el recién nacido" [wheat for the newborn]; in geometric exactness: "expresión exacta" [exact expression], "vértice de las flores, donde todos los ángulos toman sus luces fijas" [vertex of flowers where all the angles take their fixed lights] and of reduction: "forma breve," [brief form] "forma limitada para expresar concreta muchedumbre de luces y clamor escuchado" [limited form to express a concrete mob of lights and heard clamor].

In part two, "Mundo," Lorca establishes the context in which the Eucharist is seen as sign and form. Stanzas 1–7 contain a multiplicity of images, most of them violent and destructive, almost all of them characterized by the juxtaposed imagery already noted in "Exposición," but here to a more frantic degree, with the seeming lack of logic evidenced in work like "Nadadora sumergida" and "Suicidio en Alejandría." In stanzas 8–11, Lorca returns to the theme of Eucharist as a source of order, "luz en equilibrio" [light in equilibrium], "un manómetro" [a manometer]; of understanding, "clave de llanura celeste" [key of celestial plain] and of union. The language of these verses is more restrained, although no less dense in imagery, a balance of contrasts incredible in their junctures: "donde naipe y herida se entrelanzan cantando" [where card and wound are joined together singing], "tu signo expresa la brisa y el gusano" [your sign expresses the breeze and the worm], "orbe claro de muertos y hormiguero de vivos" [clear world of the dead, and anthill of the living]. As noted in the analysis of the similes in "Santa Lucía y San Lázaro," the apparent nonsensical relationships between the words open the text to the reader's activity. A final contrast summarizes the theme of this section and suggests a source of such significance: "Mundo, ya tienes meta para tu desamparo" [World, here you have the goal of your abandonment]. The ordering of "meta" and the disorder and turmoil of "desamparo" are united in what Lorca calls "¡Sacramento inmutable de amor y disciplina!" [Immutable Sacrament of love and discipline].

Lorca's personal struggles at this time, as he expressed them to

Jorge Zalamea, can shed light both on his citing of "love and discipline" as the hope offered the world by the Eucharist in the last verse of "Mundo" as well as the theme of the third part of the poem, "Demonio" [Demon]. Lorca wrote to Zalamea in the fall of 1928:

> Yo también lo he pasado muy mal. Muy mal. Se necesita tener la cantidad de alegría que Dios me ha dado para no sucumbir ante la cantidad de conflictos que me han asaltado últimamente. Pero Dios no me abandona nunca. He trabajado mucho, y estoy trabajando.

> [I, too have had a bad time of it this summer. Very bad. It's necessary to have the quantity of happiness that God has given me in order not to succumb to the quantity of conflicts that have assaulted me recently. But God never abandons me. I've worked a lot, and I'm working.] (*O.C.* 3:979)

The same contrast between opposites—happiness and conflicts reflected in the poem is noted here in mathematical language, by which Lorca opposes happiness and conflict and balances his equation: "se necesita tener la cantidad . . . ante la cantidad" [It's necessary to have the quantity . . . when facing the quantity]. In addition, the union of love and discipline again joins the concepts so often held together by Lorca—form and feeling, technique and affectivity. Both are essential to his art. In the same letter, Lorca discussed the third part of the poem, "Demonio:"

> La <<Oda al Sacramento>> está ya casi terminada. Y me parece de una gran intensidad. Quizá el poema más grande que yo haya hecho. La parte que hago ahora (tendrá más de trescientos versos en total) es <<Demonio, segundo enemigo del alma>>, y eso es fuerte. Me parece que este Demonio es bien Demonio. Cada vez esta parte se va haciendo más oscura, más metafísica, hasta que al final surge la belleza cruelísima del enemigo, belleza hiriente, enemiga del amor.

> [The "Ode to the Sacrament" is already almost finished. And it seems to me of great intensity. Perhaps the greatest poem that I have done. The part I'm doing now (it will have more that three hundred verses in all) is "Demon, second enemy of the soul," and that one is strong. It seems to me that this Devil is really a Devil. More and more, this part is becoming more obscure, more metaphysical, until finally beauty emerges, the very cruel beauty of the enemy, wounding beauty, the enemy of love.] (*O.C.* 1:982)

Lorca is not merely seeking an order or an aesthetics that resides solely on the plane of appearances. It is precisely such superficiality that he decries in "Demonio."[84] Again, the initial half of the text is devoted to a reality other than the Eucharist, in this case, an incomplete, rootless love personified in the "enemy of the soul." Lorca begins "Demonio" by describing the Demon in terms of beauty, attractiveness, light, and temporality.[85] Then, in verses 9–13, Lorca returns once more to the Sacrament, and through a series of oppositions shows its nature in relation to the Demon just presented. The Eucharist is "unidad sencilla" [simple unity] to the Devil's "mil calidades" [thousand qualities]. In the face of the Demon's "mágico prodigioso de fuegos y colores" [prodigious magic of fires and colors], Lorca contrasts "este Sacramento definido que canto" [this defined Sacrament that I sing]. The constancy of the Eucharist, "aleluya reciente de todas las mañanas," [just-out comics of every morning] provides a "norma y punto sobre los cuatro cientos sin afán deportivo" [a norm and point over the four hundred without sporting effort]. A contrast is found in the last stanza of "Demonio," when Lorca compares the "semillas" [seeds] of the Sacrament to the "perdigones" [buckshot] of the Demon. In appearance, seed and shot are deceivingly similar; in fact such an ambiguous image will often occur in later Lorca drawings. The nouns that qualify these two associations "semillas de alegría" [seeds of happiness] and "perdigones de dolor" [shot of sadness] summarize the theme of Lorca's text. The Sacrament by serving as a sign offers seeds, with potential for growth, transformation, finding new significance, whereas the Devil, the "father of lies," offers lead shot, dead, lifeless, heavy with no possibility for meaning beyond its appearance in the present.

Finally, in "Carne," Lorca allows the stabilizing presence of the Eucharist to be all but usurped by the "flesh" of human experience—a usurping portrayed first in the uneven distribution of verses to the two themes. His return to the Sacrament occurs only in the last of "Carne"'s eleven stanzas. In the first ten stanzas, Lorca portrays "flesh" as sin, beginning with a reference to Eve, later by a reference to Adam and to the taking of fruit seen to be the introduction of sin into the world. Included in these stanzas are references to diverse sexual expression, including references to Sodom.[86] Much of the imagery in this section of the ode resembles the apocalyptic, sometimes frenzied language we will see in Lorca's later poetry. Indeed, it is important to remember that this concluding section was composed during his stay in the States. We are approaching *Poeta en Nueva York*, and the images and style of this last section, while seen as the result of the evolution studied thus far, is close to what would later appear in the New York drawings and poetry. Vegetal images of destruction and decay: "musgo baboso" [slobbery moss], "flores calientes" [hot flowers], as well as "hilos y nervios" [threads and nerves], "venas" [veins], animals like "caballo" [horse] and "el caimán enlunado" [the enmooned caiman] are familiar images in the drawings executed by Lorca after 1929.[87] More importantly for the focus of this study, however, Lorca's technique in this division can be read as the result of the sort of meandering imagery found in *Suicidio en Alejandría* and *Nadadora sumergida* over which is exerted the control found in drawings such as *San Sebastián* and *¡Ecce Homo!* The surprising metaphors and juxtaposition of diverse elements in the production of rich imagery to be later noted in "Martirio de Santa Olalla" [Martyrdom of St. Olalla] continue in less mimetic expression serving Lorca's purposes as he concludes his text. The heartbeat of Christ in the first section, "Exposición" is echoed here in "ritmos de sístole y diástole" [sistolic and diastolic rhythms], thus bringing the poem full circle.

Lorca's concluding verse reiterates the theme of immutability: he sings to the Sacrament's "absolute silence," to the constancy of its "unsleeping form" and he equates its role in the world with that of poetry. Taking recourse once more to the image of the heart beat, to the pulse discussed above, he expresses the relationship of the "flesh" to poetry: "ángeles y ladridos contra el rumor de venas" [angels and barks against the noise of veins].

Marie Laffranque considers the "Oda al Santísimo Sacramento del Altar" a synthesis of Lorca's development up to this point.[88] In effect, the poem continues Lorca's efforts. He defines the Sacrament as *"poesía"* in the terms defined by Gasch and adopted by himself in drawing and art. By "opening his soul to the Sacrament," Lorca produces a meeting place for the soul of the poet and of the subject in which the reader may confront meaning.

In this poem, especially in the last section, Lorca's expression, formed by the artistic and poetic experiences of the years immediately preceding the composition of this poem, has already begun its departure from the aesthetics articulated during the summer of 1927. They will never be lost; Lorca's poetic creed would always revert back to his search for the image, and the consistency with which he had integrated experiences and aesthetics up to this point would continue, remaining a hallmark of his creative process.

3

Reading Space and Subject

A reading of Lorca's writing and of his drawings reveals consistent portrayal of a scene or setting and a human subject, as well as attention not only to what is seen but to the act of seeing itself. Nigel Dennis, among others, notes "the primacy of the visual in Lorca's work in general, and that, in particular works, such as *Impresiones y paisajes* [Impressions and landscapes], a markedly pictorial sensibility is in evidence."[1] The role of seeing in the creative process and the depiction and transformation of the visual image varies according to the development of Lorca's aesthetics. Although studies of this visual primacy, of the act of seeing and being seen in Lorca's poetry, do not often include consideration of his drawings, observations made therein consistently describe the dynamics present in the drawings as well.[2]

In Lorca's texts, the act of seeing takes in both setting and subject, and the relationship between the two; this seeing becomes the means of transformation of the setting, the subject, the poetic voice, even of all three. Sometimes, the seer is a character within the text (as we have seen in "Santa Lucía y San Lázaro"); in other instances it is the poetic voice who observes. Both setting and subject can serve to convey double significance, the setting through its being established by Lorca as uni- or multidimensional and the subject as projection of the poet/artist at work. This reading of the text involves looking for these relationships and their depiction. This study of setting and subject, especially their multiplication, reflection, and projection in Lorca's poems and drawings leads to new insights into the transformations of both setting and subject that occur in Lorca's work.

I have shown that for Lorca, both writing and drawing are a means of articulating the voyage through the poetic realm, the "far-off dark wood," the sea over which the poet casts his net. Blanchot describes this in other terms, analogous both to Lorca's articulation of his experience and also to his means of capturing it.

105

The poem or literary work seems to depend on a discourse that can never break off because it does not speak, but is. The poem is not this discourse, it is a genesis; the discourse never begins only repeats itself over and and over. But the poet is someone who has heard the discourse, has become its interpreter and mediator and has reduced it to a silence as he speaks it. . . . And he who writes is equally he who has "heard" what is endless and ceaseless, who has heard it as discourse, penetrated its significance, submitted to its demands—he who has lost himself in its depth and yet, because he has endured it as it should be endured, has brought it to a halt, made it accessible in its discontinuity and, containing it forcefully within such limits, has uttered it and measuring it, has mastered it.[3]

Both Lorca's drawings and poetry show how he establishes the poet/artist's role as interpreter and how he subsequently "hears the discourse, penetrates, submits." His declarations suggest that after "hearing the discourse" his first act is to record this inner sensation through drawing then "make it accessible" in other drawings and in written texts. Lorca makes use of a poetic figure through which to portray this entry into the poetic realm. By emphasizing the act of seeing, of perceiving, Lorca provides a means by which his reader/viewer may also engage the process of "bringing the discourse to a halt, making it accessible" to the perceiver. It follows, of course, that the reader must perform the same functions on the text as the poet has performed on the discourse. The reader will see, read, interpret. This occurs in liminal space; Blanchot observes that "a poem is only a poem when it becomes the shared privacy of someone who writes and someone who reads, the passionately unfurled space of a mutual conflict between speaker and hearer" (110). It follows for the purpose of this study that this interaction also takes place between artist/poet and viewer/reader. Furthermore, we may extend the process to accentuate the role of the reader who has already "heard the discourse" recorded in Lorca's drawings, and with this discourse in his or her memory, approaches the verbal texts. It is in articulation, in "containing, uttering, measuring" that the poetic material is mastered, and the one through whom or in whom it is articulated—poet, subject, reader—is transformed.[4]

The central problem of the portrayal of space and time in poetry and drawing contrasts the traditional view that sees this question as a barrier between the two with the position of other aestheticians who provide a means of overcoming such a barrier by establishing analogies or parallels between space and time in the arts. Beyond the representation effected in the arts, one must consider the reading of these elements. Modern aesthetics and studies of the process of perception argue that space and time are necessary components for the reading process of either medium. Rudolf Arnheim explains:

> We are led to the startling conclusion that any organized entity, in order to be grasped as a whole by the mind, must be translated into the synoptic condition of space. This means presumably a translation into visual imagery since the sense of sight is the only one that offers spatial simultaneity of reasonably complex patterns.[5]

Such techniques as repetition force the reader to remain in a limited space in a way that highlights literature's spatiality. The viewing process highlights painting's temporality, that is the repeated scanning necessary to draw meaning from a work.[6] Particularly in the twentieth century we see an effort in the arts to bring these two elements together. Lorca was not unaffected by such a development.[7]

In his exploration of the visual experience as a springboard toward deeper levels of meaning in the drawings and poems, Lorca frequently makes use of multiple or simultaneously present spaces, for example, physical settings, mental or imaginative space, both physical and figurative reflections, and panchronic perspective. In *Teoría de la expresión poética,* Carlos Bousoño provides an instrument with which to analyze this phenomena, what he calls superimpositions. More than the joining of two objects, which is the traditional understanding of the image, Bousoño extracts examples of a broader union from traditional and contemporary poetry.[8] He defines superimpositions as

> el resultado de superponer dos esferas (una real y la otra imaginaria o ilusoria) que la realidad mantiene separadas: y se distinguen por la naturaleza de tales esfuerzas.

> [the result of superimposing two spheres (one real and one imaginary or illusory) which reality maintains as separate: and which are distinguished from one another by the nature of such spheres.] (393)

According to Bousoño's theory, such superimpositions consist of the joining in the temporal, spatial, significative and situational realm (389). Likewise, Cohen asserts that in painting:

> Painters have available a number of strategies for showing duration, sequence, cause and effect, progressive and retrogressive movements through time. One of the simplest of these is to show, within the same frame, two or more actions or scenes succeeding each other in time.[9]

An analysis of Lorca's work shows how he employs the techniques described by both of these theorists.

Early Drawing and Writing

In *Impresiones y paisajes* [Impressions and landscapes] (1918), largely conceived during outings with his art professor, the young Lorca recorded a vision of the Spain of his day. Although not a collection of poetry, *Impresiones y paisajes* is important as an early example of Lorca's perceptive and descriptive talent. Although we know that Lorca drew as a child (there remain some of his schoolbooks with drawings on their pages), a careful look at both the 1986 and 1991 catalogs reveals that there is no drawing in either volume dated before 1923, and then a series of fifty-three caricatures. This is not to say that Lorca did not draw, but the lack of any evidence to the contrary suggests that it was at least not a predominant pastime.

In *Impresiones y paisajes*, Lorca uses the scenes depicted as a background to his thoughts, questions, and impressions, as a springboard for themes or observations he wishes to make.[10] His accurate depictions of monastery interior and exterior, for instance, serve as a support to his perception of the fruitless retreat of the monks and nuns who lived therein. Lorca's descriptions of fields, of villages, of festivals and the people who gave soul to them underline his deep love for his native soil, and form the basis for his aesthetics in participation in life (131). Finally, his musings about what he sees reveal what he is feeling. Lorca betrays a Romantic tendency in his portrayal of nature as reflective of human sentiment (12). We shall see this tendency not only in *Impresiones y paisajes* but also in a poem contemporary to that work.

A reading of *Impresiones y paisajes* reveals many passages that resonate with Lorca's later drawings of buildings and scenes of life in Spain, as well as other passages without a direct counterpart in his plastic expression. A study of Lorca's style in this excerpt from "La montaña" [The mountain] reveals that his visual talent has indeed informed his perception and consequently his writing. The passage reads:

> Apenas estamos en plena sierra. Luchan las cumbres unas con otras para levantarse más, las primeras se acusan salvajes, llenas de tomillos y encinas, otras más lejanas alzanse grises, pálidas y moradas, y en los confines asoman algunas su violeta fundido con el cielo. Avanza el coche lentamente por la carretera que es como un enorme anillo que abarcara los

vientres de los montes. Brilla el paisaje su tono opaco y sobrio. . . . Vive en el ambiente una soledad augusta y salvaje. Hay derrumbaderos inmensos de piedras rojizas. Hay garras sobrehumanas con terciopelos de musgos polvorientos. Hay contorsiones de bárbaras danzas en los árboles sobre los abismos.

[We are hardly in the jagged mountain range. The summits battle with each other to rise higher, the first confess themselves to be wild, full of thyme and evergreen oak bushes, others farther away rise gray, pale, and mulberry, and in the confines some show their purple tones blended with the sky. The car advances slowly on the highway, which is like a huge ring that embraces the belly of the mountains. The landscape shines its opaque and sober tone. An august and savage solitude lives in the atmosphere. There are immense precipices of reddish stones. There are superhuman claws covered by velvets of dusty mosses. There are contorsions of savage dances in the trees over the abysses.] (*O.C.* 3:76)

In this painterly passage, Lorca proves his visual capabilities, constructing his text in much the same way as a painter designs a landscape. Lorca establishes the elements crucial to pictorial representation almost immediately. The viewer begins to ascend the mountain range, and, by following the order of the description, moves from foreground to sky thus taking in the fullness of the space in which Lorca is operating. The shape of the mountains and their rising against one another determine the form or line of the piece, an ascent accentuated by the presence of the highway climbing the peak, drawing the viewer's eye with it. The use of words like precipice, ring, claw, and chasm forces the reception of the mountain range beyond a one-dimensional level. Through the "line" of the highway against the mountain, Lorca guides the eye of the reader's imagination. Rings encircle, claws grasp, chasms reflect mountain height in their depth, and the use of the dance image completes the poet's efforts to establish volume. Since dance involves the whole of the body, it suggests here a full, rounded twisting of road on the surface of the mountain and of mountain range against the sky. Lorca's use of texture foreshadows his admiration of the Cubists and their attention to surface. He foregrounds his passage in the savage underbrush, a rough ensemble of oak and thyme, moving gradually to the blur of distant forest, to velvet and moss over the harshness of rock, and eventually to the smooth grandeur of mountain peak blended with sky. This is a painter's technique; if the initial vision had been less than rough, the viewer's eye might linger over the foreground, never moving on to the beauty lying in wait. Furthermore, Lorca imposes color in a progression from the dark green of tree and underbrush to the gray mist and purples of distant heights, moving away from a literal reproduction toward the vision created by the marriage of mountain, mist, and muted light. The text is a visual masterpiece. Ironically, there is no evidence of such skill in evoking visual imagery in Lorca's graphic work at this time.

In the poetry contemporary to *Impresiones y paisajes*, Lorca executes equally successful representations. Examples of masterful evocation of a visual scene include "Campo" [Field] and "Se ha puesto el sol" [The sun has set] both written in 1920, and a more symbolic treatment of landscape and its relationship to human and divine realites evoked in its context in "Luz" [Light].

The poem "Luz," written around 1918 is a contemporary of *Impresiones y paisajes*. In this poem, Lorca again demonstrates his visual acuity and his ability to reproduce a visual experience in words. In addition, in "Luz" Lorca establishes a relationship between the poetic self depicted in the poem and the environment in which that self is wandering.

First, Lorca describes the temporal and physical setting of the poem. The sunset he describes is not only felt—"sentida"—it is reflected in the person of the poet. The moment of sunset, or of decline—"ocaso"—is repeated in the "aire" of the poet and reiterated by means of rhyme "aire de fracaso" [air of failure]. The verb *desangra* [bleeds] implies such a weakening as well as suggests the color of sunset, a blood red seen also in the poet, "rojo el corazón" [his heart red]. As daylight dissipates, the poet too is fading: "apagada la frente" [his forehead dim]. Next, in the second stanza, the poet leaves the path, a line on the mountainside on which he had walked. In words that recall the sinuous twisting and turning road described in *Impresiones y paisajes*, Lorca describes the poet as: "la sombra luminosa que marcha pretentiendo enlazar a los hombres con Dios" [The luminous shadow that marches, claiming to unite men with God]. Just as the line of the path seen against the mountainside, the poet is described in terms of contrast, of movement and of joining—all functions of line. As the light is fading around him, the poet does not see completely; he walks without noticing, "sin notar." By identifying the poet with the land in this "magic hour," this moment of decline, of transformation, Lorca provides an entry into the mystery that poetry attempts to articulate.

The reader's eye next moves from the man-mountain relationship to another mutual reflection. Stanza 2 shows the sky-earth configuration through opposition. Both are "sueños" [dreams]: the sky is a living dream, the earth a dream long dead. That same sky is a vessel for an almost infinite sadness: "tiene la gran tristeza de no presentir nunca donde su fin está" [He bears the great sadness of never having a presentiment of where his end lies]. We read further that the sky is a reflection of a greater, truly infinite sadness: "Dios es la tristeza suprema e imposible" [God is the supreme and impossible sadness]. This implies another plane. From earth (sueño) to sky (sueño/tristeza) to God (tristeza) one descends semantically by referring to God as "su porqué profundo" [his deep why], thus not only returning to a lower plane, but, in the light of divine omnipresence, also exquisitely enveloping all three spaces.

In the last stanza, Lorca repeats this multiplication of planes by means of the divinity/sky/earth configuration. The verse "Las estrellas son almas que al misterio quisieron escalar" [The stars are souls that tried to climb to mystery] contains all three planes and renames them. God is no longer sadness, but mystery; the blue sky is now a field of stars and the earth is represented by people/souls. Furthermore, his description of the stars as "luz de piedras" [light of stones] unites earth with the divine that transforms all: "La esencia del misterio las hizo luz de piedras" [The essence of mystery made light of the stones]. The stars, and by implication, the souls that they reflect and in which they are reflected cannot participate fully in the mystery that surrounds them. In visual terms, Lorca has shown the coexistence of three distinct planes and united them through shared characteristics. Yet he has delineated the limits of any relationships between these spaces. It is the poet who stands between earth and sky, walking the path up or down the mountain, who serves precisely as the line drawn between them. The viewer's eye follows the path of the wandering poetic self. The poem's last verse echoes the despondence expressed in the opening lines. Even on the page, the top of the text, its opening verse, is reflected by the final one on the bottom and the poetic self is depicted in the middle ground.

This poem is an explicit articulation of the experience of hearing the "discourse" of which Blanchot speaks. Walking through the space of dream, attempting to bridge earth with heaven, "los hombres con Dios" [men with God], the poet's observations in stanzas three and four are his artistic rendition of his experience. By his presence on the mountain that (visually) bridges heaven and earth and also pierces the clouds and sky, the poet "penetrates" the surface of mystery. By identifying himself with his environment, he limits his experience of mystery and masters its articulation. He is not only the reflection of the mountain but also of the stars, because he, too, wishes to "escalar el misterio" [climb the mystery]. Finally, in his acknowledged inability to completely express the poetic experience, he is the reflection of God whose "porqué profundo tampoco puede hablar" [whose profound why cannot speak either].

In contrast to the open space described in the text from *Impresiones y paisajes* and in the poem "Luz," Lorca depicts architectural space in "Patio húmedo" [Humid patio] through the use of repetition. Literature depends on various kinds of verbal repetition—for example, in Casey's words, "repetitive patterns [that] delimit and guide the movements of the reader's imagination."[11] Beginning and ending the poem with the same verse suggests the enclosure of a patio. By populating the patio with nonhuman inhabitants—"la casualidad," "los años dormidos," "La Quietud" [chance, the sleeping years, quietude] Lorca brilliantly conveys the decrepitude of the enclosed place. Describing the relationship between "La Quietud" who "se ríe de la Muerte que canta melancólica en un grupo de lejanos cipreses" [Quietude (who) laughs at melancholic Death, who sings in a group of far-off cypresses], Lorca establishes two opposing poles, juxtaposing laughter with melancholy and the patio in the foreground with far-off trees. The reference to the trees delicately implies another outside space. This parallel establishing of spaces, inner and outer, enclosed and open can be seen in the drawings Lorca began in the early 1920s.

As indicated, the earliest drawings catalogued were executed in 1923. Among them is *El hombre malo* [The bad man], typical of the caricature series with one striking difference—the presence of a tavern door off to the right, and two lines indicating ground and part of the horizon behind the central figure. Subsequent drawings show progressive attention to setting, and to a multiplaned representation. In *Salón de casa noble* [Drawing room in a noble house], Lorca presents a setting with no human subjects; a well-established foreground in which we see various pieces of furniture each at a different distance from the back wall. Furniture against the wall, a small shrine on a shelf and pictures suggest perspective, but for the most part the drawing maintains a sense of flatness. Similarly, Lorca has drawn in arches, ceiling beams and wall decorations, but he seems to lack the skill or, in light of contemporary aesthetics, the desire to effectively distinguish one plane from the other. He is successful in his execution of the door and the vista onto which it opens. In the background through the open door, one sees a sun, and the cupola of a church as well as lines suggesting other buildings. Another drawing done the same year, *Sala con balcón que da a un huerto* [Drawing room with a balcony opening onto a garden], offers both the interior and exterior space visible from the salon, the foreground very well defined by floor tiles, the outside referred to by a glass door and a tree drawn (supposedly) beyond it.

The rendering of space and perspective is more and more successful in subsequent drawings, although with the encroachment of Cubism, the emphasis on classical perspective will diminish significantly in later drawings. Drawings such as *Casa con torre* [House with tower] and *Plaza con iglesia y fuente* [Plaza with church and fountain] are typical of the descriptions found in *Impresiones y paisajes*, featuring bright vivid colors, obviously affected by the Andalusian sun. Blue, green, and yellow predominate. In both drawings, Lorca seems to be interested in the front of the building, yet he manages to suggest in the first a depth in space by drawing trees behind the house. In the second drawing, the plaza contributes to a sense of depth, coming out from the church toward the viewer, and being broken midpoint by a fountain. Lorca also draws the left side of the church away from the viewer in a further attempt to establish volume in his drawing. By contrasting the brightness of walls and roof with the blueness of the Spanish sky, in *Casa con torre*, and by paying attention to the details of windows and doorways so critical to Andalusian architecture, Lorca portrays a visual experience of his homeland.

Another drawing contemporary to these is *Jardín con el árbol del sol y el árbol de la luna* [Garden with the tree of the sun and the tree of the moon], drawn in 1923. Although the background, foreground, and some details of this drawing are fairly conventional and very similar to the drawings already mentioned, the viewer is struck by the presence of the two trees on either side of a central fountain. Here one sees clearly Lorca's use of conventional landscape or background to support an innovative symbol. The trees in this drawing are not realistic. The "árbol del sol" resembles a distorted sunflower, and the "árbol de la luna" might be a green, inverted crescent. Each tree has its own fountain as well.

Concluding that this drawing is more about human experience than mimetic representation, the reader makes use of its symbols in order to interpret it. Ascribing traditional qualities of femininity and masculinity to moon and sun respectively explains a codice of the drawing. The moon tree is located closer to the house, and the sun tree seems to be giving off smaller versions of itself into its fountain, clear allusions to the interiority of the feminine and the sowing, seeding activity of the masculine. The third fountain is located between them, perhaps symbolizing their union. The presence of a window reminds the viewer that this garden is also a somewhat enclosed intimate space, resembling so many Andalusian homes. It is also a reference to another outside space, contrasted with the containment of the water.[12] This joining of sun and moon is not Lorca's invention; Mario Hernández cites his familiarity with the miniature illustrations of a fifteenth-century text, one of which is precisely a painting of the "árboles del sol y de la luna."[13] This image occurs consistently in his writing: in poems such as "Balada de un día de julio" [Ballad of a July day] as well as in "Canción" [Song], later reworked and published as the "Casida de las palomas oscuras" [Casida of the dark doves] in *Diván del Tamarit*.

Drawings and Poems of Andalusia

Lorca uses color most in the drawings dating from 1924 to 1927 that feature scenes from Andalusia, although in later drawings and most certainly in writing, he does not abandon it entirely. Prieto notes that Lorca uses color in these early drawings even when it is not needed and makes it explicit when that intensity is not necessary visually: "He naturally revels in color when he thinks it is poetically useful."[14] This poetic use of color is obvious throughout the corpus of the Andalusian texts, where Lorca employs colors in both drawing and poetry with a consistency that enables us to identify his palette: reds, yellows, and greens; black and white that set off the others' vibrance and suggest tenderness, happiness, innocence, and the deep sadness of crime and pain (10). The contrast of color with blackness, as in "Romance de la guardia civil" [Ballad of the Civil Guard] underlines the characteristically simple division of Lorca's Andalusian world: there are two opposing forces at work. The honest vitality of the common folk, especially the Gypsies, finds its vibrant colors covered over by the blackness of their oppressors.[15] Colors, then, become kernel words generating chains of synonyms and associations.

One drawing from this period, entitled *Muchacha granadina en un jardín* [Girl from Granada in a garden], is divided into two spaces, the foreground, an interior space where the girl stands, and an outer garden. Her garb is characteristically Romantic, familiar to Lorca since similar costumes were worn during public festivals in his home town.[16] This, along with her pose may also be a manifestation of Lorca's sensitivity to the aesthetics of the neoromanticism of his time.[17]

The expression of this girl is very sad; she shares the big oval eyes, long face and downturned lips of many of Lorca's portraits. She is dressed in yellow, a yellow reflected outside in the sunlight. Red flowers, perhaps symbolic of love or passion, are in her hair, clasped to her bosom, and in a basket in the outside space as well. The function of the color red in both spaces is twofold: on a visual level, it draws the viewer's eye across the drawing, down from the girl's waist and out the door. Symbolically, of course, we see a connection between what she treasures and what is beyond her reach. This repetition of red as well as the shades of yellow in both inner and outer spaces suggest that the woman is simultaneously present in two, even three spaces; her physical situation, inside opposed to outside, as well as the inner, mental space of her longing. Even this longing is projected outward to its object. The inclusion of a fountain inside the wall is typical in Lorca's work but is also typical of Granada, and it is difficult to determine just how much significance it has beyond a portrayal of the poet's native city. Obviously, as a sexual-life force symbol the fountain's position inside the house indicates the enclosure of the vitality of this young woman. It suggests that she stands not in the house per se but rather in an inner courtyard, neither inside nor outside as it were; in liminal, confined space. Indeed, there is even also a parallel between the contained, confined fountain and landlocked Granada.[18] The girl and the fountain in the interior are repeated in the colors, trees, and flowers outside the house. The presence of these external elements transforms the portrait of the *muchacha granadina* and indicates the artist's awareness of the many levels of meaning and relationship present in and between his subject and her surroundings. Lorca's constant references to windows, doors, balconies, and arches, especially as he describes Andalusia in his writing at this time, feature as well the conflict between interior and exterior space, and reveal his awareness of the bispatiality of his world.

Through the juxtaposition of two physical spaces with references to the spaces in the girl's mind, Lorca effects a temporal superimposition, as Bousoño defines it in poetry, the joining of present and past closer in memory than they are in actual time relationships.[19] The mental spaces suggested in the drawing may well include the future for this young woman.

A similar transformation occurs in a poem from Lorca's play *Mariana Pineda*.[20] Lorca was working on the play as early as 1923; he read it to the Dalí family in 1924. In Act I, scene 4 (*O.C.* 2:176–77), the protagonist's friends have returned from a bullfight, and, quite naturally, attempt to relate the spectacle to Mariana. This purpose determines the structure of the piece, that is, in its composition it follows a rhetoric of description as well as a secondary rhetoric of narration, both of which direct the reception of the text by the reader.

Through the speaker, Amparo, Lorca relates the arrival of the crowd at the bullring, their gathering in the plaza, and the subsequent performance of the bullfighter. It is Amparo's experience through which the poetic discourse is heard; her reflection on her experience as she recounts it as well as Lorca's use of foreshadowing in the play allows the reader to penetrate the surface of the bull-fight's meaning.

His choice of narrator allows Lorca a particular perspective. Her eyes are the mirror, the screen that offers to Mariana Pineda and to Lorca's reader/audience a secondhand experience of the spectacle. Amparo's perspective forms her experience of the bullfight and her articulation of that experience. As a young woman, Amparo's interests, and therefore her perspective, limit the breadth of her focus. She pays attention to the appearance of the spectators, to the prowess of the bullfighter, and to the atmosphere generated in the bull ring.

Appropriately, Amparo posits her description in a certain setting: "En la corrida más grande que se vió en Ronda la vieja" [In the greatest bullfight seen in ancient Ronda]. This exaggeration shows how the setting can be determined by the one who describes it. In what sense is this the greatest bullfight ever seen in Ronda? Her judgment lends importance not only to the event but to herself as narrator of the event. Thus, Amparo performs a reading of the bull-fight. She is lost in the experience—caught up in the spectacle and in retelling it. She shows the arrival of the spectators in procession-like fashion, concentrating on visual elements that would characterize each group, their clothes and their mode of transportation. The inclusion of the girls' fans and the young men's wide, gray hats as well as their horses and carriages add a costumbristic touch to the description. Her listeners: Mariana, the reader of the poem, or the audience at the play, follow Amparo into the arena, that she describes, naturally, as circular, "un zodíaco" [a zodiac]. This choice of terms establishes a multilevel of reading, based on the perceptions of space. Amparo is offering a physical description of the arena as well as a celestial reflection or projection as it were of the arena's shape. Its color, "pajiza," [straw-colored] parallels the surface of the Gypsy nun's embroidering that will be discussed shortly. It is Amparo's blank canvas as well as the blank space upon which Mariana's death will be foreshadowed.

The use of that specific term *zodíaco* implies destiny, fate, the future, juxtaposed with the present bullfight, already past as it is now portrayed in Amparo's discourse. This is a temporal superimposition. The observations of Harriet Turner in her analysis of the "Romance del emplazado" [Ballad of the summoned one] are equally applicable to this text:

Foreshortening between fact and premonition, as each is brought to bear reflexively upon protagonist and reader, determines the rhetorical impact of the ballad. From the outset, Lorca intends to equate fact and premonition, reversing their identity so as to capture the summoned man between thumb and forefinger of a time framed by past and future."[21]

In this text, the coming together of the past bullfight in which only five bulls are slain and the present narration of events to Mariana evokes the future—Mariana's death. In this coming together, both Mariana's presence and absence are crucial elements, as we shall discuss shortly.

Next, Lorca draws a line against the background of the arena. Across this circle, almost cutting across it, walks the bullfighter. Cayetano steps into the middle of the ring; Amparo singles him out among the crowd and the other participants in the bullfight: "destacándose gallardo entre la gente de brega" [standing out gallantly among the common crowd]. His counterposition against the black bulls raised in Spain, *by* Spain, "frente a los toros zainos que España cría en su tierra," suggests that the center of attention is not merely the center of the bullring, but of the second, larger space of the entire nation. Once again, Lorca has established a doubling of space and/or images. The use of the imperfect subjunctive is echoed in a refrain that occurs in the poem's middle and reiterates the absence of Mariana from the spectacle: "¡Si hubieras visto con qué gracia movía las piernas!" [If only you had seen with what grace he moved his legs!] Amparo is lost in her experience, out of herself as it were, thoughts turned to Mariana. This refrain also serves to bring together two distinct times: the moment of the bullfight from which Mariana was absent, and the time of Amparo's narration, in which she is present. The two moments overlap, meeting in the person of Amparo, who witnesses and gives witness. In this way, Mariana and the reader see the fight through Amparo's eyes, creating another sort of superimposition of narrator, listener, reader.

The kind of superimpositions described by Bousoño in poetry are effected in drawing by doubling, a motif predominant in Lorca's drawings at this time, beginning around 1926. The imposition of one face upon another suggests at times the falling away of a mask, at others the presence of an unseen reality, the soul, or some aspect of personality. Santos Torraella warns the viewer to take careful note of the eyes when any doubling occurs, as their appearance signals the contrast between dreams and alertness, absence and presence, death and life, not-being and being.[22] His reading would restrict Bousoño's idea of superimpositions to the coming together of opposites for the purpose of negating. Other less polarized interpretations of double figures, as already seen in the Dalí texts, may be possible.

Probably the best known example of doubling is the drawing *Leyenda de Jerez* [Legend of Jerez] or *Joven y su alma* [Youth and his soul]. In both, a clearly outlined young man is embraced from behind by a shadow of himself, perhaps a representation of the soul or death itself. In *Leyenda,* the youth stands in the foreground in clown costume against a background of a tree and distant house, and on the right, in closer proximity, a tavern. Three crosses appear on the wall of the tavern and are reflected on the street below. By varying the surfaces in this drawing (through the use of blue crayon, straight lines drawn in black, stipple, and other patterns), Lorca identifies at least six different planes or grounds. This does not include the two buildings. The tavern door is open, covered by a curtain suggesting an intimate interior, perhaps one from which the youth has fled. It is evident that the youth is suffering, from what is not so clear. Hernández underlines the narrative nature of *Leyenda* and indicates that there are letters written on the surface that may spell *alma*.[23] This drawing was titled by Lorca, so the reader must also take into account the poet's suggestion as to the narrative nature of the piece. Although he titled the drawing "Leyenda," Lorca subtitled this piece "Poema surrealista" [Surrealist poem] and in his lecture on painting named 1926 as the year of Surrealism. Although Soría Olmedo claims that Lorca was referring to totalism when he mentioned 1926, either aesthetic might be represented in the empty eyes of one figure and the cloud/dream of the other.[24]

The portrayal of death in its embrace is consistent with the intimate, personified entity we meet in all of Lorca's work. Two other double studies are *Sueño del marinero* [Sailor's dream] and *El beso* [The kiss], in which Lorca makes use of a rare triple representation. In *El beso,* already discussed in chapter 2, one notes the influence of the Dalí portraits and observes Lorca's use of a red background in the form of a solid red head, under a detailed face over which lies the mere outline or shadow of the man portrayed. As already seen in *Muchacha granadina,* color is used as a mediator between spaces. The red of the background is picked up in the central figure's tie and pupil, and in the shadow's lips. In these drawings and in others like them, the presence of more than one face represents the distinction between an inner and outer self, through what Caws refers to in other texts as "a simple alteration in the viewing line, directed outward or inward."[25] Many such drawings are of clowns, playing on the mask theme, representing the dual nature of those who wear such a mask, highlighting the simultaneous existence of the theatrical persona and the person himself.

Returning to the poem, we note that Amparo's tone is admiring, making Cayetano a hero; she dispenses quickly, in four lines, with his success over the bulls, with a rapidity that imitates his prowess, and concludes her account of the afternoon's activities with a brief description of the plaza, of the atmosphere, and of the afternoon itself.

In its descriptive aspect, the poem exemplifies Lorca's genius for creating visual images. The geometrical patterns have already been noted: the circle of the bullring, the path of the bullfighter that crosses it, as well as the progression of the afternoon shadow over the arena. In spite of an abundance of colors and words associated with them, one notes Lorca's rather limited palette; the majority of his color images refer to shades of black or red. These link a host of synonyms or associated words: Lorca, through Amparo, delights his reader/viewer with the variety of their expression: "negra," "azabache," "grises," "zainos" and "manzana," "bermejas," "sangre," "hocicos" [black, jet, gray, black, apple, vermilion, blood, snouts]. With the exception of two references to green, "verde" and "sierra," the other colors are neutral: "pajiza," "blancas" [straw-colored, white]. Lorca insists throughout the poem on the presence of color: the wagons are painted; surely the costumes of the spectators are anything but drab. By only naming certain colors, Lorca succeeds in establishing the focal point, guiding the reader's attention to the black death of the bulls, the red of the bullfighter's suit, of the beasts' snouts and of the wounds he opens in their bodies. Set against the pale sand, a vivid visual scene is created.

In this poem, we find several references to light. Those familiar with the bullfight make an immediate association with "sol" [sun] and "sombra" [shadow]. In addition, the presence of gold and silver, of the glittering sequins of the girls' fans as well as the bullfighter's "traje de luces" [suit of lights] allow for the play of light across the surface being described. This glistening light recalls the movement of colors in the prism. The steel of the sword that glistens as it is raised and the reference to stars' light in the word *zodiaco* are other indications of light as a crucial element in Lorca's portrayal of the bullfight scene.

A third element of any visual experience is that of movement. This element is omnipresent throughout the poem. Whether Amparo is describing the filling-up of the arena with people, the turning wheels of carts and wagons, or the constant fluttering of fans in the sunlight, one receives the impression of activity. Cayetano's movement is more concentrated and focused. In fact, the stillness of the crowd as they watch the bullfighter creates a contrast, a tension that may be perceived as concentrated movement, the movement of eyes, a central component. Eventually, even the plaza moves; having absorbed the tension, the arena and the afternoon vibrate in the aftermath of death.

Another reading of the poem reveals opposition between the expressed and the unexpressed, what is referred to in visual terms as positive and negative space. The articulated description of a familiar experience makes the poetic discourse accessible, orders it according to the ritual of the bullfight, and contains it in the space of the arena. The reader, aware that beneath the beauty and splendor of the festivities lies the grim reality of death, is not deceived by Amparo's circumventing this aspect of the bullfight. She uses the word *matar*, to kill, and the word *sangre*, blood, only once each. The alert reader finds in the poetic language a recounting of the brutality of the bullfight: in the predominance of the color red, and in her describing how Cayetano has caused five flowers to open: "en la punta de su estoque cinco flores dejó abiertas" [he left five opened flowers on the point of his sword] instead of explicitly describing the wounds suffered by the bulls in the course of the fight. The image of flowers is continued by comparing the bullfighter's triumph to the action of cutting and gathering, as one would flowers. However, a bouquet of blossoms is not harvested here, but rather the snouts of his victims, red like red-winged butterflies:

> y en cada instante rozaba
> los hocicos de las fieras,
> como una gran mariposa
> de oro con alas bermejas.

> [And at each instant brushed against
> the beasts' snouts
> like a great golden butterfly
> with vermilion wings.]

(*O.C.* 2:177)

Once again, the result of this merging of times and spaces is transformation—here, of bloody bulls' noses into golden, flying butterflies. Both the symbol of the butterfly representing poetry and the image of killing the bull as creative or artistic activity come together in this verse. Previously, in his lecture, "Imaginación, inspiración, evasión." Lorca had linked the bullfight with the creative process:

Dijo el arquitecto Corbusier en una reunión íntima de la Residencia de Estudiantes que lo que más le había gustado de España era la frase de <<dar una estocada>>, porque expresaba la intención profunda de ir al tema y el ansia de dominarlo rápidamente, sin detenerse en lo accesorio y decorativo. Yo también—agrega—soy partido de esta posición de la estocada, aunque, naturalmente, no sea un espada de limpia agilidad. El toro (el tema) está delante y hay que matarlo. Valga siquiera mi buena intención.

[In an intimate gathering at the Students' Residence, the architect Corbusier said that what he liked most about Spain was the expression "to strike a sword thrust" because it expressed the deep intention of approaching the theme and rapidly dominating it without detaining oneself in the accessory or decorative. I, too—he adds—take this position of the sword thrust, although, naturally, it may not be a sword of clean agility. The bull (the theme) is in front of me and must be killed. At least this would be my good intention.] (*O.C.* 3:262)

Lorca's final insistence that the plaza and the afternoon vibrate almost with a life of their own reiterates his vision of an extended, vital space and time. The place of Cayetano in the center of the bullring and of the Zodiac as well as of Spain herself in such a cosmic ambiance prepares the reader for a final, metaphorical reading of the poem.

The reader/audience of the play is aware that the historical Mariana Pineda met a tragic end. So, the bullfight is a metaphor for her death. The reader must make this tranference of meaning, since Mariana's death occurs at the end of the play. However, in the context of the entire play, this poem serves as an echo of the play's first lines. These consist of a romance sung by children lamenting the death many years ago of the heroine in an ill-fated attempt at revolution. Before the first character appears on the stage, the listener knows by means of a *romance* that Mariana Pineda is doomed:

¡Oh, qué día tan triste en Granada,
que a las piedras hacía llorar
al ver que Mariana se muere
en cadalso por no considerar!

[Oh, what a sad day in Granada.
that made even the stones cry,
upon seeing that Mariana dies
on the scaffold for not giving in!]

(*O.C.* 2:166)

Thus, the poem brings the initial warning together with the play's tragic end. In addition to the reference to death inferred by this *romance*, several other clues in the poem insist on Mariana's inevitable doom. Most direct are the repetitions already noted. The first is that of the five bulls killed in the arena; a clear reference to the sixth, missing victim. Amparo's lament over Mariana's absence brings home her role as this missing character, and further implies her fate with the words "si estuviera conmigo" [if you had been with me].

In fact, on its most profound level, the poem is a description and, in the context of the play, a prediction of Mariana's public execution. That execution is never portrayed on stage. When the reader arrives at the end of the dramatic text, this is the only execution scene he/she has read. Wearing the colors of the slaughtered bulls, "verde y negra" [green and black], Mariana will meet a similar fate. Just as the violence of the bullfight fades as the spectacle is mythified, so the tragic, brutal execution of Mariana Pineda has been effaced, and her fate mythified in the street songs of the children of Granada. The poet has mastered his theme.

"La Monja gitana," [The Gypsy nun] a poem written in August 1925 and found in the *Romancero gitano* may be similarly analyzed. Although the subject matter is popular, the influence of Cubism and of the poetic-plastic dynamic that Lorca demonstrated in the "Oda a Salvador Dalí" that same year are seen here. In this poem, as in the "Romance de la corrida de Ronda" and the "Oda a Dalí," Lorca identifies an artist at work, and, by means of spatial play and the delineation of reflection and perspective, he portrays the identification of subject with setting and their mutual transformation.

The nun embroidering may be seen as an embodiment of the poet writing, the artist drawing. For her, the "tela pajiza" [straw-colored cloth] is the canvas, the blank page, and even as she embroiders the cloth, she is "embroidering" other flowers, the "flowers of her fantasy" that religious convention would not allow on altar linens. This creative act of embroidering, of sewing, is taken up in other imagery present in the poem. Among its semantic functions, the word *araña* recalls the image of the spider—one who weaves, Arachne of classical mythology, weaving her cloth—and infers the weaving of narration. The reference to "malvas" [mallows] recalls a plant related to cotton, from which cloth is woven, and the use of the phrase "mantel de la misa" [altar cloth] and "llagas de Cristo" [wounds of Christ] refer to sacred uses of cloth—the altar linens symbolizing the burial cloth of Christ. This cloth image is reinforced by the words "lunas en el mantel de la misa" [moons on the altar cloth] that refer to placing the Eucharist, the Body of Christ, in a "luna" or round glass container

in a monstrance. Finally, the image of the "celosía," the latticework
and of chessboard pattern—"el ajedrez"—also suggest this weaving
activity. Indeed, the "light playing chess," that is, creating patterns
through the lattice is another artist, drawing lines across the surface
of wall and/or floor.

Secondly, Lorca establishes the setting for his poem with visual
images. He too begins with blank space—the white of plaster, the
walls against which the scene unfolds. Through displacement, he
erases the expected "cal y canto" [robust]; "cal y mirto" [lime and
myrtle] offers a pattern of dark lines against this whiteness reminiscent of drawing or writing. The primacy of sight in Lorca's poetics
explains subsequent images; not content to name those things that
form the background, the poet provides images of what they might
look like. Indeed, one way to decipher many of Lorca's images is to
draw what he is describing while thinking of the object/person being
described. Thus, the church with its towers easily suggests the bulk
of a bear with its legs in the air. The image of the bear in earlier
poetry evokes sound; Lorca writes in "Veleta" [Weathervane]: "Aire
del Norte / ¡oso blanco del viento!" [Air from the North / polar bear
of the wind!] and here too it may refer to the sound of wind around
the church. The two are not mutually exclusive. The "araña gris"
[gray spider] against which fly "siete pájaros del prisma" [seven birds
of the prism or from the prism] may be seen as the colors of a stained
glass window, encased in or colliding with gray lead, resembling the
legs of a spider and perhaps her web. Many critics read this image
as that of a chandelier, but the unlikely placement of such in a convent garden suggest searching for other interpretations. An earlier
poem of Lorca's, "Balada triste" [Sad ballad], contains these lines:

> ¡Mi corazón es una mariposa
> niños buenos del prado!,
> que presa por la araña gris del tiempo
> tiene el polen fatal del desengaño"

> [My heart is a butterfly,
> good children of the meadow,
> which imprisoned by the gray spider of time
> has the fatal pollen of disenchantment.]

(O.C. 1:27)

In these lines, too, gray holds back color, as the lead might be seen
to hold back colored glass. The idea of being prisoner is echoed in
Lorca's treatment of space and the nun, and the image of the butter-

fly, a symbol for Lorca of poetry itself, held captive by time all reinforce that this poem is a treatment of poetic/artistic activity.

Space is consistently evoked in images that suggest a sense of simultaneity, and of overlapping—Bousoño's superimpositions. The poem's title, an apparent oxymoron, is also an example of a significational superimposition in which the speaker "innocently" brings together two terms, leaving the reader to realize the contradiction and their significance together.[26] "Monja gitana" opposes a free, nomadic culture with the confines of cloister and Catholic culture. The opening lines of the poem suggest enclosure, both physical and mental. The words "cal y mirto" recall "cal y canto," a reference to the walls of a house, here a reference to the enclosed convent garden in which the nun appears to be sitting. This is further enforced by the reference to the church building in the distance, providing a physical backdrop as well as representing the institutional church that governs not only her physical enclosure, the cloister, but also the artistic restraints under which she works. While she sits in one garden, the nun is creating two others—the flowers she is actually sewing into the cloth, "alhelíes" [gillyflowers], and those she would sew given the freedom, "girasol . . . magnolia . . . azafranes" [sunflowers, magnolia, crocus]. In the original manuscript of this poem, Lorca included the phrase "Girasoles y magnolias flotando en cielos de oliva" [Sunflowers and magnolias floating in olive skies].[27] Although he eventually deleted it from the text, this phrase offers yet another example of two spaces reflecting one another—she holds a sky in her lap.

The references to other convent spaces—the kitchen and the chapel, where, we may assume, daily routine is ongoing—provide a background for the figure of the nun, a counterpoint to her imagining, and an enrichment of this concept of multispatial representation, in the concurrent evocation of more than one space. Like any writer or artist, she raises her eyes from her work, looks off into the distance, observes, imagines, then returns to her cloth, her gaze becoming a guide for the reader: looking, and indicating the superimpositions. It also places her in liminal space, where she can mediate the activity of all the other spaces of which she is aware.

We may also presume that in a reversal of the perception portrayed, the nun may be viewed from these other spaces. Thus Lorca's depiction of her from these multiple points of view suggests that he is utilizing these perspectives to draw a 360 degree portrait of his subject. Lorca, discussing the poetry of Góngora, analyzed the same technique in which that author:

dobla y triplica la imagen para llevarnos a planos diferentes que necesita
para redondear la sensación y comunicarla con todos sus aspectos

[duplicates and triplicates the image in order to bring us to the different
planes needed to round out the sensation and to communicate it in all its
aspects]. (*O.C.* 3:234)

and:

explica las cosas para redondearlas.

[he explains things in order to round them out.] (243)[28]

John Crosbie, citing these observations of Lorca, suggests that these
same principles be looked for in the reading of the *Romancero gitano.*[29]
   The multifaceted image we have in "La Monja gitana" is the same
kind of portrait we see in some of Lorca's more Cubist drawings, as
well as in other work of the period.
   In addition to simultaneous evocations of space, time is telescoped
in the image of the grapefruit, "cortadas en Almería" [cut in Almeria],
suggesting the presence of memory, as Turner describes it in the
"Romance del emplazado":

   . . . the metaphor projects a remembered identity, still another reflection,
   in the double sense of something visualized and something recalled; thus
   it also points back toward the past.[30]

The dynamic of superimpositions provides another interpretation
to the phrase "malvas en las hierbas finas" [mallows among fine
grasses], another unlikely juxtaposition of elements. This phrase is
certainly a reference to the nun, either by virtue of her birth or
disposition ("como una malva" means meek and mild, like a lamb).
The image of wildflowers among cultivated plants may also be read
as an allusion to the presence of random thoughts—her imaginings—
in the midst of determined, disciplined thoughts and activity, basing
themselves in some firsthand experience and transcending that experience toward past or future. References to the two horsemen as
well as to clouds and mountains, arid distances, plains and suns are
other spatial and temporal clues. Again, they suggest real places,
remembered or seen over the convent wall, imagined spaces, depictions of the nun and her actual environment, or all three. "Yertas
lejanías" [far-off drylands] evoke distant spaces, but because it suggests aridity and dryness, the phrase is simultaneously a certain reference to her celibacy. "Veinte soles" [twenty suns] recapture the image

of the chandelier's prisms in the beginning of the poem. Havard's reading of these suns as male images, initiated in the body of Christ, continued in the two horsemen, and later in the rising rivers brings together literal and symbolic significance.[31] The rigidity of the convent walls is repeated in the steep plain in the distance; the height of the walls with their latticework extends to the rising heights in the distance.

We can observe that this nun/artist is also listening to a discourse, as Blanchot defined it, indeed to multiple discourses. Her awareness of her surroundings and all they dictate for her life is accompanied by her presence to things outside the convent, as well as to the murmurings of her heart, memory, and imagination. Just as she concentrates on her embroidery, so the poet here focuses his writing, brings the discourse heard to a halt, limits it, confines it, makes it accessible. The progression from white and dark "cal y mirto" to colors—prisms, grapefruit, suns, and so forth—and then back to the black and white of shadows reflect Lorca's control over his subject matter, bringing the poem back to its starting point (as he had in "Luz") in the person of the woman who returns to her sewing. In fact, we have been observing three sewings at once: the altar linen that is the final product of discipline, her imaginings, and the poem itself—a reflection of discipline and technique triumphing over feeling and imagination.

Lorca introduces the element of light into the "Monja gitana" and maintains that image throughout the text. The words that form along the seeing/light continuum begin with the reference to the spider and to prisms: "Vuelan en la araña gris/siete pájaros del prisma" [the seven birds of the prism fly in the gray spider]. This repeats the contrast between bright color and dull background seen first in "alhelíes" and "tela pajiza." She wishes to sew sequins, "lentejuelas," thus extending this reflected light into the space of her imagination. The sequins with which the Gypsy nun wishes to embellish her work recall the "traje de luces" described by Amparo, thus connecting the creative activity of the two women for the reader. An examination of the original text reveals the inclusion of the words, "Agata, espejo, y madera / La iglesia retumba y gira sobre una luz picoteada por los pájaros del prisma" [Agate, mirror, and wood / the church and turns and rumbles over a light pecked by the birds of the prism]. Thus, the church building appears not only to be a mirror, but also to be mirrored. Later, the nun's eyes serve as a surface in which images are reflected, "Por los ojos de la monja galopan dos caballistas" [Two horsemen gallop through the eyes of the nun]. This reference to the horsemen indicates that she is either seeing them in the distant heights or imagining them in her mind's eye. In either case, she is caught up in the experience, out of herself in an experience of transcendence. This is an example of situational superimposition. The reader knows that the nun cannot see, presumably two other areas mentioned, the kitchen and the chapel, but again, her mind's eye takes note of them. So, her visualizing includes not only fantastic flowers, sequins, horsemen, landscapes, but also real, experienced spaces, people, and activity. Her eyes become mirrors in the sense Dennis intends when he observes:

> The mirror, or indeed any reflecting surfaces, can be understood to be the point at which the self confronts its image or separates into its representation. Consequently, it is both a meeting place and a place of departure. This is emblematic, in a sense, of an essential principle of perception which Lorca's poetry proposes: the eyes are the surface at which the inner world branches out into the outer world, functioning as crossroads at which sense, understanding, direction, and navigation all become critical.[32]

The distance that the nun observes above the walls of the garden and the distance she envisions through the eye of her imagination are reunited in her person. Havard interprets the poet's exclamation, "¡Qué bien borda! ¡Con qué gracia!" [How well she sews! With such grace!] as the presence of the poet/observer.[33] It might also refer to an act of self observation. Similarly, the reality represented in the flowers she embroiders on the cloth she holds are duplicated in the flowers she "would embroider," the flowers of her fantasy. Both mental and physical space, then, meet in the person, in the "eyes" of the nun. The images of enclosure and captivity are balanced by the images of flights of fancy, the activity of imagination that permits escape, and her eventual return to her work, to the enclosure, to the space in which she resides.

Transformation or metamorphosis occurs in the poem in its imagery, in the objects described, in the nun herself, and in her setting. The colors of the prism, repeated in the variety of flowers mentioned by Lorca in the poem, become birds. The church with its towers becomes "un oso panza arriba" [A bear on its back]. The grapefruits are transformed into sweets in the convent kitchen, a reference to a common activity associated with nuns. The positioning of the grapefruits (being sweetened) next to the wounds of Christ in the text indicates another transformation. In his reading of the poem, Havard sees this as a reference to nasturtiums, "a flower known in Spanish as the 'wounds of Christ' because of the stains on its five petals" (17). Such an interpretation is one more example of the multiple functions of words in Lorca's imagery. Havard has noted that at this point in the poem, transformation occurs on two levels: the sweetening effect of wounds turning to flowers, and the next transformation from the image of the (male) Body of Christ to the image of the two horsemen (17). Sweetening may also imply ripening, in which case the fruit would be read as a symbol of this woman. This association would identify her with Christ, whose passion was sweetened by his Resurrection, or, given Lorca's feelings about the conventual life, such ripening may be a transitional stage in eventual decay—a waste of her life.

The evocation of the kitchen activity, in any reading, joins the reference to the nun's activity, sewing an altar cloth to the chapel and the Eucharist. Thus, her perspective permits daily life to be transformed, the suffering of Christ to be sweetened, even as her imaginings transform her solitude and enclosure. She is one with her creation; her "corazón de azucár y yerbaluisa" [heart of sugar and lemon verbena] identifies her as a sweet or fragrant plant. The interplay between fantasy and concrete experience as it occurs in the person of the Gypsy nun witnesses to such transformation. As Flint observes, in the *Romancero gitano*, "the principal aim of the themes of metamorphosis . . . may be designated as the fragility of the limit between matter and mind."[34] Even as the nun's attention returns to the present, the light through the lattice is transforming her surroundings. Lorca has expanded his subject through multiple impressions, then organized them in a style that is expressed in the poem's closing lines, as the nun returns to her sewing, and the geometric patterns of the light fall to the ground before her.

A third poem from this period, "El Martirio de Santa Olalla," [The Martyrdom of St. Olalla] also from *Romancero gitano*, serves as another example of Lorca's poetics during this period, especially as an interesting case of the poet's recourse to the visual element in his poetry. Karl Selig ascribes this importance to the text:

The "Martirio" poem is within the framework of the collection [*Romancero gitano*] something of a culmination, as it restates, transmutes, and re-articulates elements, aspects, images, and literary/verbal icons of previous poems.[35]

In addition, the poem suggests analysis along the lines already established in this study, those of the relations between subject and setting and how such relations are established and if, when, and how they are effective. The narrator of the poem is the one through whom the discourse is mediated; whose perceptions establish the planes represented in the poem. In each of the poem's three divisions, Lorca highlights the setting and/or subject: in part one he establishes the setting, in part two the representation of the protagonist, and in part three the union of the two.

In the first part of the poem, "Panorama de Mérida," Lorca creates a "word painting" by establishing a plastic context for the piece, by identifying it through title and content as a visual entity, a panorama, and by the creation of a multiplaned representation of his subject. As an inspiration for this poem, we can cite the precedent of paintings of Christ's Passion: in this first of three parts, Lorca mentions the lounging soldiers, the instruments of torture, and most specifically the red crest of a cock, all associated with scenes depicting the arrest and trial of Christ, in addition to Selig's mention of the hagiography tradition (45). Havard sees in the references to Minerva, the Roman goddess of war, references to another artistic tradition of sculpture, albeit broken sculpture in the images of arms without leaves, or perhaps hands, to recumbent busts and to broken noses (157). In his choice of title, "Panorama" as well as in the elements of a panorama included here (a street, mountain, water suspended in the air, rocks), Lorca establishes a background that he then fills with people (the soldiers) and animals (a horse, the cock, and the bull). Some are present in the scene at hand; others may be revealed only through the narrator's perception. Sounds in the distance, for example, much as those behind the scenes in the "Monja gitana" are noted in the mind's eye of that perceiver. The initial function of all these elements is to serve as a setting. Lorca's descriptive abilites again provide a background as if it were a visual text; in this instance at least, that setting as a visual text—painting or drawing—would not be a setting in the classical mode. The penetration of the surface takes place as the poem unfolds. The fractured images of nature: for example, of suspended water, broken stars places the space of Mérida with in a larger one: Ramsden observes that "Nature, both telluric and cosmic, participates in the scene."[36]

The establishing of a multiplaned representation is achieved by Lorca through the use of verb tense, through simultaneous activity, through the presence of repetition and especially through the creation of suspense. All but two of the verbs in this first part are in the present tense, bringing them to a temporal foreground; the two verbs that are expressed in the imperfect suggest a background: the frozen water gilds the rock's edge, and blasphemies arise occasionally from the group of soldiers depicted as part of the panorama.[37] In addition, some activity, the soldiers' playing or sleeping, is secondary in nature compared to the foregrounded images of waiting or imminent collapse. Another example of background or preparatory activity is the sharpening of knives and hooks accompanied by the arresting, high-pitched cry of the victim: "al gemir, la santa niña quiebra el cristal de las copas" [upon wailing, the holy child breaks the crystal of the glasses]. This image is the first reference to the saint found in the poem. She is already fractured—her brokenness represented by her sighs—as well as the cause of fracturing. Repeated imagery also suggests more than one plane in the text. Spatially, the texture of a splintered dawn is seen again in the broken glass, and temporally, the premonition expressed in cock's crow, the girl's cries during her present suffering, and the bull's bellow create an echo, uniting two different times in one sound.

Holding this first section together is the element of suspense, created by the relationships between opposing elements in the text's composition. The primary opposition represented is that of Olalla, the virgin martyr, innocent and powerless, and the Romans, presented in both sexual and violent imagery.[38] These oppositions are largely conveyed by Lorca's choice of verbs. The poem begins with the contrast between the horse leaping and running in the streets and the idle soldiers sleeping and gaming. The girl moans and the bull bellows while a wheel spins, sharpening instruments of torture. In addition we note the tension of incompleteness: waiting, "aguardar," and almost awake, "casi despiertos." The anticipated collapse, "para derrumbarse todo" strengthens the heaviness of the dread expressed. This recalls the emotion generated by the imagery associated with San Lázaro.

In addition to the use of verbs, Lorca uses opposites in color: the whiteness for Olalla, the crystal and the daylight both of which are splintered and shattered; the red and black for her foes in the blasphemies of the cock's crest, in the bull and in the anvil. Other words express gender opposition, with an emphasis on male images: the horse, the cock, the bull, the soldiers. The image of the wheels, "ruedas," and the knives they sharpen, "cuchillos," is found in Lorca's "Oda al santísimo sacramento de altar" as "ruedas y falos" [wheels and phalli], which suggests the simultaneous presence of male and female imagery. The moans of the girl are accompanied by the bellow of the bull, "brama," which also refers to the state or season of rut. The juncture of these images implies, as well as oppositions, the portrayal of a world in which all are contained.[39]

The most outstanding components of the second section, "El Martirio" are Lorca's use of color, the choice of elements in the text and the establishing of movement through vertical, horizontal, and static images. Lorca's use of color in this section is rich. Whereas, as we have seen, in "Panorama" his palette was limited to red, black, and green, here we encounter specific mention of green, red, white, yellow, gray, and silver, references to things associated with specific colors, blackberry bushes, skies, blood, flames, manes, and swords, as well as a nonspecific reference to colorful flowers.

In addition to an increment of color, "El Martirio" is more heavily populated than the preceding section by a diversity of components both human and nonhuman. Many of these images provide the color already mentioned. Only a few are characters in Lorca's history: the consul, Olalla, the centurions (although these appear to be ghosts or metaphorical, in either case not primary characters), and other participants and witnesses, represented by "crines y espadas" [manes and swords]. In fact, it is Olalla herself, or more accurately, her muti- lated body that, by means of its fragmentation, in torture and in the poet's description, usurps the bulk of this text. Her suffering be- comes the vessel for all that has previously been felt, described, or articulated: cruelty, corruption, violence. The fragmentation of Olalla's body—in Lorca's description of it and literally in her torture and martyrdom—continues a persistent motif in the text. As Selig notes, "Panorama de Mérida" included many references to the disor- der and breakdown:

> Decline, decadence, disintegration, fragmentation . . . And this stress on fragmentation can be considered the thematic/topical equivalent to what formally might be indicated by disjuncture, and both seem to be indica- tive of an expressionist technique and mode.[40]

The highlighting of individual body parts in the poem and the scat- tered mannequins in part three point as well to the influence of Dalí and Surrealist landscape.

Olalla's wounds and the evil they represent are further transformed (much as the grapefruits in the Gypsy nun's kitchen were transformed into the wounds of Christ and both sweetened, and as the bull's wounds became flowers), described metaphorically in a host of vary- ing images: "flora desnuda," "escalerillas de agua," "pájaro en las zarzas," "cielos diminutos," "arbolillos" [nude flower, ladders of water, bird in the brambles, tiny skies, little trees.] Flames are "un bisturí" [a lancet], and the crime "pasión de crines y espadas" [pas- sion of manes and swords]. In visual terms, this section of the poem is a very "busy" piece, much more complex than the scene of the panorama of the first section and the starkness we will consider in "Infierno y Gloria" [Hell and Paradise]. This is appropriate to the central piece of a triptych.

The establishing of movement through vertical, horizontal, and static images serves the same function as line in the visual arts, and the suspense noted in "Panorama de Mérida." As in "Panorama" verbs are the preeminent source of this effect. They express upward, downward, and arresting action. The verb *to rise*, "sube," which introduces the text, is accompanied by the verbs "brota," "brinca," "llegan al cielo" [shoots forth, leaps, reach the sky] as well as by other words that suggest upward movement: "llamas" [flames] and "cielo" [sky]. Similarly, the verbs "tiembla" [trembles] and "vibra" [vibrates] and the image of a bird struggling in a bush establish another position, this time more static, at eye level. The expanse of Olalla's back, its length and breadth as it were, contributes to this arresting function. The repeated image of the tray, on which rest her breasts, combines a horizontal line with upward movement. This image of amputated breasts is not a singular occurrence in Lorca's work. In "Rosa de los Camborios" we read "con sus dos pechos cortados puestos en una bandeja" [with her two severed breasts placed on a tray]. The "Romance de la pena negra" contains the line "yunques ahumados sus pechos" [her breasts smoky/smoked anvils]. In "Santa Olalla," "El Cónsul porta en bandeja senos ahumados de Olalla" [the Consul carries the smoky/smoked breasts of Olalla on a tray]. Also in "Santa Lucía y San Lázaro," we find references both to breasts on a tray, referring to the martyrdom of Saint Agatha, and also to Lucy's eyes "en una bandeja." Finally, Olalla's amputated hands falling onto the floor, the streams of white milk flowing from where her breasts once were and the dousing of the rising flames by the blood shed from her back all create a downward movement that completes the balance. This description of Olalla includes her whole body but in terms that reflect some vanguard tendencies, what Selig refers to as anatomization (47). The violence endured by Olalla is not represented in the overpowering imagery seen in *Poeta en Nueva York*, but is more evocative of feeling than in the earlier texts of *Nadadora sumergida* and *Suicidio en Alejandría*. The balance is achieved in controlled fashion through reduction and transformation. As in the series of line drawings done by Lorca in the summer of 1927, we see body parts singled out in a sort of metonymy, a reduction that not only suggests the whole but also, by means of its limitedness, arrests the attention of the reader/viewer and controls or forces a reaction.

Finally, Lorca unites the setting of his poem with Santa Olalla. The human subject becomes one with her surroundings. Through such a relationship the poet achieves a balance and recuperation of the suffering and sacrifice depicted thus far. Flint's observations apply in this case:

> Through telluric imagery, Lorca specifically emphasizes the representational capacity of the body: aspects of the natural world are described in terms of the human body; the human body, conversely, is often depicted in terms of the natural world, and on several occasions, both interact in ways that indicate the permeability of the boundaries between them.[41]

Such permeability is seen in the third section of the poem as well, where once again Olalla is the liminal space where opposites can meet. The third section's title, "Infierno y gloria," in itself suggests two opposing spaces, and a drawing found on Lorca's original manuscript over this title suggests one plane proceeding from another. The starkness of "Infierno y gloria," [Hell and paradise] which serves as the poem's epilogue, much as "Panorama de Mérida" had served as its introduction, is in contrast to earlier more colorful imagery. In this final section, Lorca creates a starkness—a silence that anticipates and then echoes the very silence it calls forth in the one who reads the text. This silence is in part caused by the contrast between the expectancy of heat and red imagery created by the word *infierno* [hell] and the resultant shock when the reader meets white and snow instead. "Infierno y gloria" begins and ends with the color white, progressing from the white of snow to the white light of glory. As seen in other work, Lorca emphasizes the white page, the canvas before he begins his work. Throughout this section, Lorca employs only black and white, but combines them, offering images of whiteness, of blackness, and of black on white.

Lorca concentrates three times on the image of Olalla, and through the use of repetition, depicts the final stages of her martyrdom— Olalla hangs from the tree, she is dead on the tree, and finally, she is white on the tree—as well as on three configurations of the black and white scheme. In the first, her blackened body smudges the snow. Next, inkwells spill black ink and black mannequins dot the snow-covered landscape. Finally, blackbirds converge on the now snow-covered, charred body of the martyr—black on white on black. The verbs in this section are almost all verbs of covering, of black on white: "tizna," "vuelcan tinta," "cubren la nieve," "escuadras de níquel juntan los picos en su costado" [blackening, they dump ink, they cover the snow, squads of nickel join their beaks in her side]. It is striking to realize that when Olalla's body is black, it darkens the snow; once it is snow covered, it is itself covered by the blackbirds.

For Havard, the image of ink on a page represents official sanction of the saint's death.[42] In the context of this study, these images of black on white, specifically of the inkwells and ink might serve as Lorca's autograph, as his emphasis of his accomplishment. As poet and as artist who knew well the blank page, Lorca would regard his setting down of the story of Olalla as a fitting record of her suffering.

The whiteness of the earth and the white light of heaven concentrated in the gold or silver monstrance are separated by the horizontal line of a burning sky. Specific upward images, "ruiseñores en ramos" [nightingales in branches], and downward images, "gargantas de arroyo" [gorges] establish a connection between earth and heaven whose effect is the depiction of a *locus amoenus*. Some color is added by the reference to stained glass windows, but this section ends in the register in which it began: "Olalla, blanca en lo blanco" [Olalla, white on white]. The word "blanco" recalls for the reader the imagery present in Lorca's drawing of another martyr, San Sebastián and the circle that served as mouth and target for the arrows in his portrait.

"Infierno y gloria" serves, as noted, as an epilogue in this poem, but in visual terms, it functions as the third panel of a triptych, with the controlled panorama in part one to frame and balance the middle, more active section that carries the central theme of the poem. Recapturing images, such as that of the "torsos yacéntes" [recumbent torsos] in part one, the "manos cortadas" [severed hands] of Olalla in part two, and the armless mannequins in the third section unifies the entire poem. The contrast of the frozen water of the "Panorama" and the snow of "Infierno" with the flowing of milk, streams, and blood in "Martirio" and the stream in "Gloria" affirm the transformation in a cause-effect relationship.[43] Thus, in this final section, the reader is led back over the whole of the text in order to effect a unified reading of its entirety.

Drawings and Poems in New York

The avant-garde tendencies noted in "El Martirio de Santa Olalla" continued and developed in the work that followed it. The poems and drawings that Lorca executed during his stay in New York evince his exposure to and experimentation in vanguard art and literature prior to his arrival in the United States. His poetry shows these influences, and many aspects of the drawings done at this time reflect the abstraction of Cubism, the freedom and even nightmarish quality of Surrealism, as well as Lorca's own refinement of technique during the late 1920s. This evidence of contact with outside forces and its eventual integration into the poet's creative activity is consistent throughout Lorca's career. He consistently makes use of such sources, adapting them to his own uses. Hernández asserts:

> One of the notes that define Lorca's graphic work and make it unique as a totality is the strange blend of influences that appear there. These influences are not superimposed, they are naturally integrated into a homogeneous and intensely personal whole.[44]

Such a synthesis, coupled with attention to inner and external reality bore fruit in the series of line drawings executed in 1927 as well as the powerful drawings done during Lorca's stay in New York in 1929–1930. The New York experience, therefore, must be analyzed in light of its personal, aesthetic, and historical context. This combination of forces resulted in work that represents what Andrew Anderson refers to as a parentheses in Lorca's work—work that surely influenced what followed it, but was never repeated in its intensity or mode of expression.[45]

In Lucía García de Carpi's judgment, *Poeta en Nueva York* and *Viaje a la luna*, Lorca's filmscript, are two written works especially related to Lorca's drawings.[46] Whereas in earlier work, Lorca had referred to poems in musical terms, such as "Canción" [Song] and "Concierto interrumpido" [Interrupted concert], he seems more inclined at this time to affirm the interrelation of poetry and the visual arts so espoused by the avant-garde at the beginning of the century. *Poeta en Nueva York* contains three poems entitled "Paisajes" [Landscapes] and one entitled "Panorama." In addition, the titles of other poems imply a centering on specific physical space. As many have noted, in the New York work, the city becomes a protagonist not merely a background. It is the human subject that appears to be diminished.

In both drawing and poetry, Lorca applies to his New York work the techniques he had mastered in the 1927 line drawings. He continues to choose certain characteristics of his theme or subject, isolate them, and then explore that subject's significance. However, many New York drawings and poems contain disquieting imagery indicating ferocity, fear, weakness, menace—vital human experiences. This is explained in part by multiple influences: the Surrealist proclivity to death and violence noted in these works by García de Carpi, the notion of the Surrealist, whether painter or poet as "slave to the pure faculty of seeing" cited by J. H. Matthews, and the Neoromantic tendency toward vital forces observed by Castro Lee.[47] The elements of background, setting, and human subject on which Lorca places his emphasis are interrelated in light of his experience of urban America in 1929.

Whereas some of Lorca's drawings of clowns, youths, or even sailors before his arrival in New York in June of 1929 may be read as unexplicit self-portraits, Lorca's plastic work now took a decidedly deliberate turn toward self-identification. In *Poeta en Nueva York*, in a series of drawings considered to be self-portraits, and in other drawings linked to them by theme and style, Lorca explored his sense of self and his experience in the metropolis. As he had earlier recorded his impressions of the Spanish landscape, Lorca now focused on New York. At a reading of his poems from *Poeta en Nueva York* in 1932, he described this new environment:

> Los dos elementos que el viajero capta en la gran ciudad son: arquitectura extrahumana y ritmo furioso. Geometría y angustia . . . las aristas suben al cielo sin voluntad de nube, ni voluntad de gloria . . . éstas ascienden frías con una belleza sin raíces, ni ansia final, torpemente seguras sin lograr vencer ni superar, como en la arquitectura espiritual sucede, la intención siempre inferior del arquitecto. Nada más poético y terrible que la lucha de los rascacielos con el cielo que los cubre.

> [The two elements that the traveler grasps in the big city are: extrahuman architecture and furious rhythm Geometry and anguish . . . the edges rise to the sky without the will of a cloud, or the will of heaven. . . . these ascend coldly with a rootless beauty without final desire, clumsily certain without managing to conquer or overcome, as spiritual architecture does, the always inferior intention of the architect. Nothing more poetic and terrible than the fight of the skyscrapers with the sky that covers them.] (*O.C.* 3:349)

Both this extra-human architecture and furious rhythm are portrayed in *Poeta en Nueva York* and in the drawings that are its contemporaries.

It is important to read the self-portraits not only individually but also as a suite, noting changes and evolution in their various motifs. The first drawing to be discussed, *Autorretrato en Nueva York* [Self-portrait in New York], portrays the city as a jungle of concrete buildings whose windows are formed by apparently meaningless letters and numbers. The poet's figure in the center of the drawing consists largely of a full, circular face, with bushy eyebrows and moons on its cheeks—a reference to the moles or "lunares" on Lorca's own face. He uses small, delicate hands to defend himself against several animals. Against the lower left of the piece is a park filled with dying flowers and with figures similar to those that appear in the drawing *Bosque sexual* [Sexual forest], which Helen Oppenheimer finds suggestive of the images in the poem "Paisaje del multitud que orina" [Landscape of the urinating multitude].[48] Lorca may be referring to

"**Autorretrato en Nueva York**" © 1994 Artists Rights Society (ARS), New York/VEGAP, Madrid

an inability to flourish under the tyranny of human disregard for beauty and properness. A second portrait of the poet appears in the form of a seed spreading wings over the city, and lowering its roots in the form of tentacles. The fragility of these tentacles resembles Lorca's hands in the lower form and in subsequent drawings and seem to represent a searching, a reaching out. Here, they are clearly looking for a place to land, to put down roots. In addition to providing a contrast between natural forces and urban sterility, this image's frightened face and its dangling tentacles recalls other images of nerve endings in Lorca's drawings and his depiction of the frightened child listening to lullabies: "planicie con los centros nerviosos al aire de horror y belleza aguda" [a plain with nerve centers exposed to the air, of horror and of sharp beauty] (O.C. 3:291).

At first glance, the drawing seems to represent a sketch of any city, but presumably of New York and so titled because it was drawn during Lorca's stay in that city. There is just enough realistic detail present in this drawing for the reader to identify the city; fantastic elements are added in order to challenge the viewer's appropriation of the drawing. The familiar city image is enhanced by a perspective in the drawing that represents the outline of a skyline. Even the seed blowing in the wind has a familiar air to it; although not pertinent to an urban setting, it is at least recognizable. Furthermore, what would be quickly identified as windows are in fact a series of alphabets, and the thin lines of the circle in the center of the drawing reveal eyebrows, eyes, moles, hands. The presence of the larger of the two self-portraits destroys the viewer's ability to consider the skyline, in isolation, at least, any further, and the juxtaposition of the larger and smaller faces challenge the identifying of either as a point of origin, that is, as *the* self-portrait.

The relationship between the setting, the human representation(s) and even the animals is dependent, as we have observed consistently, on the reader's viewing. It is the reader who must bring together the elements of the drawing to derive meaning from their relationship. The figure of the poet appears to be frightened; he is once again caught in a liminal space between the buildings that soar over him and the animals below him. Neither is acccessible to him, both appear to be a threat. Flint's observation about Lorca's poetry at this time is appropriately applied to this drawing: "Not having an identifiable, integrated body, and hence lacking a stable self, leads to the experience of death."[49] The image of the larger face has been superimposed on the background of the urban landscape, explicitly establishing the importance of this setting to Lorca's sense of identity. Not only does the drawing depict how Lorca is experiencing himself at this time, but also how New York as a presence contributes to those feelings.

If we read the animals in this drawing as reflections of the poet's inner reality, then their presence here is a reflection of his fear and terror, even of his protest, and represents a new way to double an image and to allow more than one portrait of the same subject in the same text. In this reading, the self-portrait would truly include the New York portrayed in the drawing, the large face, its seeming multiplication in the face imposed on the floating seed, the beasts, the repeated alphabet with its missing letters, and the fancy columns in a desolate urban setting—all facets of the poet's self-image. This would make the entire drawing a self-portrait.

Reading the series of self-portraits as one portrait brings to light important characteristics and traces a sort of progression as well. None of the rest of the series of five drawings referred as Lorca's self-portraits show identification with the city of New York. Each of these sketches features the same central figure, whose eyes are empty in all of the drawings of the series. This figure, sometimes a bust, sometimes drawn as full standing, is executed by means of one continuous line, depriving the representation of any sense of volume, of presence in space.[50] It is important to note, however, that this does not infer weakness in Lorca's technique. To the contrary, in this series, he demonstrates a real control of his pen, the lines of his drawings betraying strength of hand, and real connection with the emotions, tension, and inner sensations inspiring the drawings. Examination of these drawings reveal that Lorca most certainly executed his figures in one line, never lifting the pen from the paper. Perhaps the first time he drew the figure was a time of experimentation, but once he identified its expressive potential, he made use of this figure, changing its appearance, but always swiftly, apparently spontaneously, executing masterful lines, not always evident in the drawings' reproductions. The figure in the self portraits also appears in other drawings, among them a drawing of St. Christopher, and two of St. Rodegunda.

With the exception of *Autorretrato en Nueva York*, no self-portrait has a background. Present in each drawing are strange animals, a composite of horse and lion, almost mythical in their makeup and ambiguous in their function. Hernández suggests that these animals spring from Lorca's acquaintance with medieval art, in which such fabulous figures appear in heraldry as well as in apocalyptic works.[51] The position of these animals in relation to the human figure shows an important development in the drawings.

Composition and other elements (the posture of the Lorca figure and animal, for example) are purposefully varied throughout the series. I read in this progression a process of domination of the inner/outer forces that threatened to overwhelm him personally and artistically. Lorca, the subject of these drawings, would appear to be representing visually what Dennis observes in his poetry at this time:

> The subject attempts to engage in dialogue with itself, questioning insistently the nature of the relationship between itself and its visual representation. Instead of a single, fixed, unchanging identity, the speaker perceives only multiple, shifting, surrogate forms.[52]

In *Autorretrato con bandera y animal fabuloso* [Self-portrait with fabulous beast] the poet is portrayed side by side with an animal, drawn to more natural scale. He appears here to be protecting himself not only with his hands (he has three), but also with a banner on which letters appear. The third hand, which holds the banner, can be seen as the one with which he draws and writes. This recalls the imagery of *Arlequín* [Harlequin]. Hernández suggests that the animal against which Lorca continues to defend himself portrays the "beast" asleep in Lorca, his insecurity, his sexual identity.[53] Whatever threat the animal poses in other drawings, it seems to have been resolved in Lorca by the time he drew *Autorretrato con animal fabuloso abrazado* [Self-portrait with embraced fabulous beast].

Here the human figure dominates, and the poet clasps an animal to his breast. Not only has the animal been embraced, it seems to have been named. Floating letters include "R," "A," "F," "E." It would appear then, that Lorca expressed vulnerability in the face of, or because of this animal. Apparently, he sought to dominate whatever forces its represented, through letters, writing, drawing.

This search for stability and identity is also expressed in the poem "Vuelta de paseo" [Back from a walk], which Lorca begins and ends with the verse "Asesinado por el cielo" [Assassinated by the sky], a line that establishes both the two-planed relationship of sky/earth (man) as well as the hostile relationship between them. Speaking of this poem at a reading of *Poeta en Nueva York*, Lorca described his position relative to the city and established his poetic persona as a wanderer, much like the poet in "Luz" and in "Santa Lucía y San Lázaro":

> Yo, solo y errante, agotado por el ritmo de los inmensos letreros luminosos de Times Square, huía en este pequeño poema del inmenso ejército de ventanas donde ni una sola persona tiene tiempo de mirar una nube o dialogar con una de esas delicadas brisas que cercamente envía el mar sin tener jamás una respuesta.

"Autorretrato con bandera y animal fabuloso" © 1994 Artists Rights Society (ARS), New York/VEGAP, Madrid

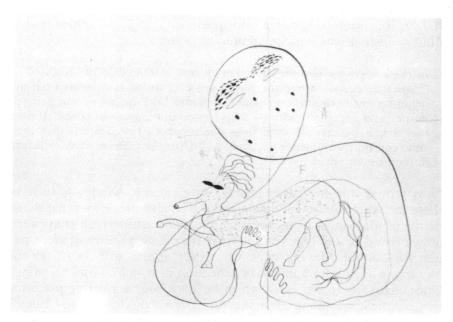

"Autorretrato con animal fabuloso abrazado" © 1994 Artists Rights Society (ARS), New York/VEGAP, Madrid

[I, alone and wandering, worn out by the rhythm of the immense lit up signs of Time Square, was fleeing in this small poem from the great army of windows where not even one person has time to look at a cloud or dialogue with one of those delicate breezes which the nearby sea sends without ever receiving a reply.] (*O.C.* 3:349)

The line "asesinado por el cielo" is also important because it provides the poet with an empty space in which to begin his task. His point of reference, himself, has already been emptied, eradicated, blanked out, and he employs vocabulary suggesting negation and annihilation throughout the poem. Into this empty space he begins to place a new identity, to draw lines much like the lines already depicted in *Impresiones y paisajes*, "Luz," "La monja gitana," and other texts. "Dejaré crecer mis cabellos" [I shall let my hair grow] suggests freedom, a new look, a new identity. The reference to long hair suggests dark lines, even the lines that depict the hair drawn on the animals in the drawings.

The next verse provides "las formas que van hacia la sierpe" [the forms that go toward the serpent]. While Lorca may well be referring to any number of things: bread lines or subway tunnels, for example, the visual, plastic reference of curved, sinewy lines resonates with the lines in the drawings read as self-portraits. Since this poem's focus is on the poet-persona, such a association would be validated. In fact, it is interesting to read this poem in light of the self-portraits. Flint's observations may be applied to both:

> In *Poeta en Nueva York* the theme of change is immediately expressed in "Vuelta de paseo" where the poet's sense of dislocation stems from his being caught between formlessness—"entre las formas que van hacia la sierpe" and a fragile rigidity—"y las formas que buscan el cristal" [forms that search for crystal]—and from doubts about his identity—"Tropezando con mi rostro distinto de cada dia" [Running into my face which is different every day].[54]

"Las formas que buscan el cristal" may refer to windows, such as those in "Autorretrato en Nueva York," but also to the fact that these particular drawings, by virtue that the lines with which they were drawn could be easily reversed, were they drawn on transparent paper, for example. In the same vein, they appear to be a search for identity, a search for a mirror or reflection in which to find meaning. Once again, the paper is shown to be a surface, a meeting place for two realities, a looking glass that in "Poema doble del lago Eden" [Double Poem of Lake Eden] will become the surface of the lake. Stanzas 2 and 3 contain images equally intriguing in their resonance with other aspects of these self-portraits. The most striking is "el niño con el blanco rostro de huevo" [the boy with the white egg face], a perfect description of the face in this series. References to little animals are also consistent with the New York iconography.

Apart from the images of the self-portraits conjured up by a reading of this poem, one notes that here, as in the other texts analyzed thus far, Lorca is expressing his stance in relation to the discourse to which he has access as poet/artist. The anguish and ambiguity of serpentine forms, of figures searching for transparency, of tattered water all speak of an experience that defies literal, mimetic representation. In fact, Lorca's use of expressions such as "que no canta" [which does not sing] and "Con todo lo que tiene cansancio sordomudo" [all that has a deaf and dumb fatigue] and most important, the image of the butterfly that I read as poetry, "mariposa ahogada en el tintero" [butterfly drowned in the inkwell] validate his purpose.

Just as in verse 1 "las formas buscan el cristal," so the poet pursuing identity seeks his reflection. The impact of "tropezando" in the last verse is echoed in "asesinado" and suggests that the poet is searching for his reflection in the sky. This reflection is denied to him. He is limited to his own space; there appears to be no transcendence. The images of brokenness already discussed enforce the state of the poet, and in light of this denied reflection, one can read "tattered water" as the only mirror available to him.

Another example of Lorca's treatment of setting and subject is to be found in *Animal fabuloso dirigiéndose a una casa* [Fabulous animal heading for a house]. This drawing recalls earlier work; it is much richer visually than the self-portraits, its figures are solid, and planes are present and easily identified. Two other drawings done in New York with which it shares characteristics are *El hombre y el joven marinero* [Man and young sailor] and *Escena del domador* [Scene of the tamer]. The use of color links these three to some of the drawings seen in earlier work. In *Animal fabuloso dirigiéndose a una casa*, a tentacled eye watches against a blue background, as a wild animal approaches a house surrounded by cut-off hands (Lorca's most frequent symbol of sexual and creative frustration) laid out in the form of footprints. The house, in black and white, clearly represents the poet by its curtained window, to all extents and purposes a signature, and by the letters ABCDEFG repeated twice, terminating in the poet's initials. The animal comes in from the right, and the footprints/hands lead off to the left. The handprints form a trail of transformation, both in the number of fingers/toes, beginning and ending with five, and in the design of each hand. There are softer, red strokes of pencil around the animal, suggesting shadowing, or a reworking on Lorca's part of this part of the drawing. The red shadows can repeat the ears, and emphasize those black circles that also represent ears. In this drawing, Lorca has highlighted the three senses—sight, hearing, and touch—that he perceived as most crucial to the poet, "master of the five senses" (*O.C.* 3:229).

The red lines over the animal's back, when examined by magnifying glass, are seen to be letters, difficult to distinguish, but suggesting Federico. In the "sky" is an eye connected to a series of nerve-like tentacles, the form suggesting another animal of some kind created by a smoothing of the crayon strokes. Two letters, "W" written in black and in red and a red and stippled/black "A," are also in the sky, near the tail of this cloud-like form.

Clearly, this drawing treats the poetic experience. The contrast between inner and outer space, the predominance of external sensory experience and animal forces, as well as the portrayal of danger, anticipation, tension make it a visual counterpart to Lorca's earlier descriptions of the poetic voyage while at the same time, rendering visually some of the emotion portrayed in *Poeta en Nueva York*. The use of lines and figures (the hands) to guide the eye downward, then from right to left is also seen in *Florero sobre tejado* [Vase on a rooftop], in which a flower vase and animal are seated on a rooftop and smaller urns guide the viewer's eye. Are the roof and animal in this drawing the same in *Animal fabuloso dirigiéndose a una casa*?

The presence of letters in these drawings is intriguing. The loss or fracturing of the alphabetic system suggests a loss of control over language, the frustration of the poet already seen in "Vuelta de paseo." Such incompleteness also suggests an inability to name, to identify, to be identified. It demands interpretative activity on the part of the viewer. Lorca's earlier assertion that he resolved difficulties in writing by turning to drawing suggests that he is portraying a union of sorts between writing and drawing, between language and image in which each completes the other. Lorca's choice of "W" and "A" seems to be especially significant. In fact, in two drawings, he highlights the "A" by pushing a pen or pin point through the paper around it. It is intriguing to realize that "A" and "W" viewed from either side of the drawing's surface reveals the same letter. Mary Ann Caws, speaking of reversible text in painting observes:

> It is interesting, if perhaps not altogether appropriate, to remind ourselves here that the inward/outward concern . . . is a constant: the alchemical fascination of texts written on both sides, in and out, . . . the fascination with script and direction, with the direction of the script, is an enduring part of visual and verbal drama, as of the Dada circus.[55]

Her comments, linked with Lorca's identification of himself in "Poema doble del lago Eden" as a "wounded pulse which probes things from the other side" suggests that the seemingly thin, flimsy, almost ethereal surfaces of these self-portraits are in fact only surfaces, one side portrayed of reality. The motif of the roof is seen by Hernández to represent the "place of communication with outside forces" (*Dibujos*, 172). This would identify the roof in Gasch's terms as true art, as poetry. I read the roof in these drawings as serving the same function I have already noted in Lorca's poems and drawings. The poet is on the other side of the drawing. The animal, or the flowers of creative expression are above that surface. In *Florero sobre tejado*, such an interpretation would see Lorca's achievement not just in the creation of artistic meaning (vase with flowers) but also in the portrayal of his own vital forces (animal). In addition to the flowerpots drawn over the landscape instead of the hand/footprints seen in *Animal fabuloso dirigiéndose a una casa*, letters and numbers are scattered about. Lorca has expressed a union of sorts: the natural, vital force represented by the animal and the artistic containment expressed in the vase of flowers.

The eye seen in *Animal fabuloso dirigiéndose a una casa* is also present in the drawing called *La Vista y el tacto* [Sight and touch] in which an eye, its iris a light shade of blue, is again attached to a series of nerve-like lines. The presence of two squares suggests two planes, and the small dots in front of these squares form a set of crossing lines or two diamonds in the shape of an 8, suggesting the presence of two more planes, or a reflection of the larger surfaces. Indeed, these rectangles might indicate glass slides used with the microscope; the nerve drawings clearly imitate the slides of nerve cells studied by Cajal, and viewed by Lorca in the laboratory. Even the coloration reflects experimentation with cell staining.

Recalling Lorca's declaration in the lecture on Góngora that the poet has to be the master of the senses provides a reading for this drawing. The roots reaching downward and the arrow rising upward express the state of poetic tension experienced by Lorca. It can be read as a self-portrait of sorts, or at least the portrait of a poet, eye open, hands reaching, nerves exposed.

All of the texts analyzed thus far treat the experience of seeing and not-seeing. Each self-portrait can only capture one moment, one gesture, one expression, "mi rostro distinto de cada día" [my face different for every day]. That is why I read them together, as one composite, many-angled composition. In "Vuelta del paseo," perhaps a return from the poetic voyage, the poet, whom Lorca said was to master sight, sees nothing. There are no references to sight or seeing. Rather the images are of mutilation and horror. The first stanza, through images of serpents, mirrors, hair, suggest the figure of Medusa, who could not be looked at, who was vanquished only when Perseus looked at her reflection.

In "1910 Intermedio" [1910 Interlude], Lorca superimposes his gaze of 1910 with that of 1929. He negates what he sees in the present, and recalls childhood visions and memories. The metonymic figure of the eyes stands for seeing and what was seen. In stanza 3, there is a spatial doubling. Lorca's child eyes are in an attic, a place of memories—empty boxes, must, statues. Thus he empties the values of the memories expressed. It is here where memory—how the past is seen—gives way to adult, disenchanted vision: "El sueño tropezaba con su realidad" [Dream ran into reality].

The emptying process is obvious in the poem; Lorca uses such words as "vacío" [emptiness] and "dolor de huecos" [the pain of hollows]. In the self-portraits, this emptying results in the outlined portrayal of the poet; here we read the image of empty shells, and boxes that store silence. What or how the poet used to see is no more.

The images recorded in the drawings done at this time betray deeply felt emotions, violence, death. Drawings such as *La muerte de Santa Rodegunda* [The Death of St. Rodegunda] are especially disturbing. They are direct, expressive, graphic images. The drawing of St. Rodegunda with the same figure employed in the self-portraits implies that Lorca identifies himself with this saint. In each of the two drawings, the figure of the saint is portrayed as vomiting blood, bleeding from her breast (perhaps amputated breasts) and from the genitals. Her suffering is depicted more graphically than that of St. Olalla, but the details of their suffering are the same. This suggests another reading of the "Martirio de Santa Olalla" in which the reader would search for self-portrayal on the part of Lorca.

Paul Ilie has noted that in the poetry of *Poeta en Nueva York* Lorca expresses imagery typical of an oniric world, a nightmarish scenario, but "somehow" maintains rational control.[56] I believe that the practice of drawing is one explanation for Ilie's "somehow." Recording his feelings in these images and then describing the feelings portrayed in the drawings—not necessarily the drawings themselves—Lorca maintains enough of an artistic distance to preserve control of his material. The drawings are first drafts.

Lorca's play with setting, space, and transformation continued beyond his New York period. He is increasingly involved in play with the relationship between the drawn image and words and letters. These components are all explored in *Bailarina española* [Spanish dancer], drawn in 1932. Lorca's use of the two media, pen and pencil, in the drawing allows him to distinguish several planes in the drawing. The dancer's hair, face, neck, arms, waist, two of her skirts, the shadow of the man drawn on the poster, his red cane and the box in front of which the dancer stands are all executed in soft, thick lines of lead, whereas, the dancer's eyes, nose, mouth, hands, and the remainder of the poster are all delineated in the thin, firm line of pen/ink.

There are two dancers, the larger, flesh-and-blood woman, who dominates the foreground, and the smaller, less detailed male dancer present in the poster to the rear of the *bailarina*. Doubling also takes place in the presence of the shadows of these two figures. We see as well the establishing of multiplaned representation through the presence of the forward plane in which the dancer stands, and the backdrop of the poster. The words on the poster at first glance seem to merely provide a realistic touch. But closer reading reveals that these words, too, establish levels of meaning. "Celveza"—beer, might well appear on a poster; what is interesting is Lorca's rendering of the Andalusian pronunciation of *cerveza*, giving the word a more vital force, as well as lightening the tone of his piece. "Alte," arte follows this pattern, but the designation of "alte puro" [pure art] immediately deepens its significance. "Mielda" [mierda—shit] suggests an appraisal of "alte puro." A study of opposites—male and female, light and shadow, popular and artistic—is present in this drawing. Thus, the dancer is present not only in the foreground, but in the image of her male counterpart in the poster, as well as in the reference to her craft, "arte."

The two planes to the dancer's left (the viewer's right) depict first a window in which is seen a type of plant, then a window through which is seen a roof with a crescent moon. The opposition of the poster to these openings reinforces the static nature of "arte puro." But Lorca is also playing with his viewer. One cannot be sure that the two "windows" are not in fact also posters. Of course, the reader knows that he or she is already looking at a drawing, which would make this a meta-drawing. This leads to the search for more significance, questions perhaps about the distance from "reality" to art. What is Lorca saying about art, its subjects, technique, value?

The use of color in these windows as well extends the space of the woman, much as color extended that of the *Muchacha granadina en un jardín*. Comparing these two drawings reveals a greater interest on Lorca's part in the later in symbolism and in the dialogue between art/the artist and the world it represents.

Llanto por Ignacio Sánchez Mejías

The presence of the poet/artist and Lorca's efforts to articulate the discourse to which he has access is seen in "Llanto por Ignacio Sánchez Mejías" [Lament for Ignacio Sánchez Mejías], a four-part poem that he wrote in 1935. This poem represents one of Lorca's most evocatively visual works, and serves as well as a culmination of his experience in art and writing. "Llanto por Ignacio Sánchez Mejías" may be read as a rite of passage for both Lorca and the bullfighter he eulogizes. Maryanne Caws has defined such a rite of passage in other texts as consisting of separation, a liminary period, and reintegration.[57] For Lorca, the period when he wrote the "Llanto" represented the third stage. Having separated himself from Spain, and having spent a limbo-like year in New York, where he both explored the language of Surrealism and experienced his own personal depths, he now experienced the reintegration of himself into the Spanish scene, and a period of integration in his art that produced rich, mature work. Aesthetically, the period after New York marked a return to balance between form and content, the retention of the freedom of the image while identifying himself with Spanish traditional themes, in this poem, the bullfight and with Spanish poetry itself. It is interesting to note that, although he produced rich poetry and prose on the bullfight theme, Lorca did not draw bullfight scenes. The exception is *Torero sevillano* [Sevillan bullfighter], one of the 1927 line drawings.

In this poem, we shall see those aspects of Lorca's work that have been the thrust of this chapter. Lorca portrays the text as an artifice, and therefore himself, the poetic voice as artist. The original manuscript reveals Lorca's indications as to where space should intervene between stanzas, even verses. In his text, he superimposes multiple space and time references, bringing together many perspectives of Ignacio, living, dying, and dead—the three stages of passage just delineated. Emphasis is placed on seeing and on being seen, the spectacle of the bullfight, witnessing Ignacio's tragic end, the "viewing" of his body, and the act of searching on the part of both Ignacio and the poet. Finally, the poetic voice identifies himself with his subject, assuming in the last section of the poem the voice and place of Ignacio, serving as a living memorial to the bullfighter.

An analysis of the piece, not as a poem, but rather as a four-piece drawing reveals Lorca the drawer at work. Each of the four parts is a separate artistic entity, yet fits with the other three sections to form one unified work, a portrayal of the death of a bullfighter. This division is not infrequent in visual art; as we have seen in "Martirio de

Santa Olalla," the function of a triptych, for example, is to present variations of a theme, to extend an artistic idea, and precisely by means of its divisions, to insist to the viewer that what he or she sees is not reality, but a representation. The division into four on Lorca's part is not explained by the poet. He perhaps chose an even number to assure the piece's balance, or to reproduce the traditional three stages of a bullfight, as well as the triumphant march of the bullfighter around the plaza after a successful fight.

The first section is entitled "La cogida y la muerte" [Goring and death], creating the expectation that the story told here is of a bull tossing and killing a bullfighter. We shall see, however, that this poem is narrative only in its references to some details of Mejías's death.[58] Rather, instead of recounting the events of the bullring, Lorca seeks a representation of the emotional experience of the bullfighter's passing. Lorca uses a juxtaposition of color to contrast the pageantry of the bullfight (recall the *romance* from *Mariana Pineda*) with the tragic demise of his protagonist. His list of nine white elements: a sheet, lime, cotton, crystal, a dove, arsenic, stream, snow, and eggs as well as the unstated whiteness of the dead body provides a perfect background for the black of bull, leopard, and nickel as well as the red of iodine and wounds blazing like suns against the bullfighter's green suit. The light of sun as it starts to set at this hour of the afternoon creates a glowing effect picked up by all the elements and changes the stark whiteness, by reflecting the blood of the dead bullfighter: "El cuarto se·irisaba de agonía" [The room iridesced in agony]. Just as the Gypsy nun experienced the sun's movement through her space by means of prism and shadow, and the arena at Ronda was described in terms of light, so this space will hold the rainbow's hues as well as the black tone of shadow.

Form is established by the use of horizontal and vertical lines: the flowing of the sheet carried by the child, the sowing motion of the wind, the bulk of the bull and the coffin all lead the viewer's eye along horizontal lines. In contrast, the fight of the earthbound leopard with free-flying dove, perhaps representing the struggle of the soul to leave the body, along with the rising of steam away from arsenic and the position of horn thrust into thigh create vertical movement. Any depiction of a bullring would include references to both horizontal and vertical lines, so as to include not only the drama on the ground, but also the crowd in the stands who participates as well. In fact, the crowd, the "groups of silence in the corners," constitutes negative space and frames the entire piece.

The poem contains references to many spaces at once. The references to exterior space, to the bullring, and to where a coffin is waiting, are complemented by the description of an interior, the room where Sánchez Mejías suffered and then died of his wounds. The tension created between the two is representative of the preliminal moment, the moment of separation. Such tension is further expressed when this interior space is joined to the outside, not by an open door, but by the window broken by the crowd in a frenzy. The image of the child carrying the sheet is repeated in the wind's bringing the clouds.[59]

This first section as it correlates with the bullfight ritual does indeed resemble the initial procession and pageantry as bullfighters and participants enter the ring. The solemn repetition of "a las cinco de la tarde" [at five in the afternoon] adds a popular tone to Lorca's presentation and mimics the rhythm of the procession. This rhythm is expressed visually in that the consistent repetition of the refrain allows the viewer's eye to rest as it moves from image to image. In drawing, the function of this repetitive line is to return the viewer's eye to a central point. The irony is that, for the reader, this bullfight is over before it begins. This is an example of temporal superimposition. Lorca is repeating "a las cinco de la tarde" as he speaks of the bullfight, when in fact the phrase refers to the time when Mejías's body was transferred for burial.[60] Thus, Lorca is uniting two past times into one, consolidating all events, all details into the one moment of the bullfighter's death. Anderson notes that in this section, Lorca mixes present and past tense verbs, to the same effect.[61]

This explains the title of the second part, which at first glance, would seem anticlimatic. Knowing already that the hero is dead seems to override the need to consider again his spilt blood, "La sangre derramada." One might read into it an analogy between the poem and the progression of the bullfight, of the first bloodletting as the bull is thrust with lances, and the *banderillas* are placed in his shoulders, marking him for death. But Lorca is not moving through the piece with narrative logic; rather he is highlighting one detail of his first portrayal, and in so doing, painting a close-up, new portrait of his protagonist. The knowledge that this is an elegy and that Ignacio is dead serves to telescope time, as we have already observed in other poems. Once again, Lorca draws against a white background, this time created by moonlight, clouds, and jasmine. The only reference in this section to the color red is to the blood in the sand, described in one place as a "dark tongue," but both examples are to black and white in the moon's gray light. All other references to color in this section are to white, gray, silver, and black. The title of this section, then, creates a chromatic expectation that is not fulfilled. Lorca's portrayal of the hazy darkness supports his insistence that he does not want to see the blood spilt on the sand of the arena. The moon, a frequent emblem of death in Lorca's work, is reflected in the blood of the bullfighter, death on death.

Lorca's stance in the first section of the poem may well be seen as a recounting of a tale secondhand. The poet is the one on whose perception the representation depends; ironically, this second section begins, echoes, and ends with the protestation, "¡Qué no quiero verla!" [I do not wish to see it!] The poet would seem to reject this way of knowing. Yet throughout this section, in all the descriptions of Ignacio that it contains, he lends his perception and his expression. This secondhand telling is descriptive of Lorca's imagining of the scene—he was not an eyewitness.[62] Intertextually, it evokes Amparo's avoiding the details of death in her description of the bullfight. The space of the poem, then, is the mental space of the narrator.

The moon passing over the arena is described in terms of "un hocico de sangres derramadas" [a snout of spilt blood], indicating that Ignacio's death is one in a long line of such events. Lorca appears to split his text into three separate portraits of Ignacio, the first climbing through the seats of the plaza, up the steps of the arena "con toda su muerte a cuestas" [carrying all his death on his shoulders]. In addition to establishing a vertical line, this first Ignacio characterizes what remains of his form as disintegrating. Neither the outline of his profile nor of his body are well defined enough to see. This recalls the self-portraits in New York and their fragile outlines of human form. This is the moment of liminality—Ignacio is still in the arena, but he is not really in it because he is dead. The fading image may be the effect of moonlight, or an expression of how death causes a fading of presence into memory. In this way, space as well as form is undefined in ambiguity. The only clear image that remains is the poet's memory of the bullfighter's blood spurting from his wounds, here artistically exaggerated to cover the stands with its shining wetness. It is ironic that the only blood reflects the light, and the light that it reflects is that of the moon, the persona of death. This image of the moon reflected over the water is consistent in Lorca's work, both in his poems and drawings.

Between this fading, first portrait and the second, Lorca intersperses a dreamlike landscape image, of cows in far-off lands grazing and listening to the sounds of the bull's victory. In a temporal vein, they represent the line of pedigree, placing the bull too in a historic context. Spatially they represent constellations, once more joining or opposing heaven and earth. The reference to celestial cows, to Taurus, perhaps, places the bull that killed Ignacio beneath a projection of itself in the constellation. This intermission in the narration elasticizes the piece's spatial perimeters and establishes a relationship between the other-world quality of the first portrait and the vibrant second. It equally establishes the bull capable of finishing such a hero as almost supernatural.

The second portrait depicts the bullfighter at his greatest moment, the moment of confrontation with the bull that would kill him. He appears almost sculptural, described from head to spurs in glowing terms, a clear echo of the panegyric of Jorge Manrique in his *Coplas por la muerte de su padre*. The crucial elements of a bullfighter: heart, sword, and wit are delineated in the superlative, with strong, bold lines that accentuate his noble qualities. Space is doubled here as well, moving from bullring to mountains, as if to imply that Ignacio is too great to be confined in the arena.

Finally, the blood flowing is portrayed in a third portrait of a prostrate Ignacio, apparently already buried. The whiteness of the drawing is softened by the green of moss and grass infiltrating his body. This process of decomposition is the third stage of the rite of passage, of reintegration. The being of Ignacio, concentrated in his blood, is shared with all that is earthly. Lorca depicts it as flowing overland, returning to the place where the bull was raised, joining the space of the arena where it died. Instead of flowing into the river, multiplied again in its counterpart in the stars, the blood forms a puddle, repeating its appearance on the arena floor.[63] The key to this containment is the poet's refusal to acknowledge the blood and the death it symbolizes. To this end, he also negates the blood's natural color, using the stagnation of green instead of red's vibrance. Lorca also refuses to impose poetic imagery on this harsh reality; he will not beautify the spilled blood by means of light or song or crystal, all poetic ornaments. He seems to be insisting on the simplicity of his composition in keeping with the tragedy it portrays. Lorca's less frequent use of a refrain in this second section distinguishes it from the first. The space created permits longer narration, while the use of the refrain continues to unify the piece and guides the viewer through its entirety.

The second part of the poem clearly marks Lorca's practice of multiplying an image in this case, tripling the bullfighter's. Mejías's portrayal as one who stands to meet the bull, falls in death, but then rises invites the reader to consider the threefold movement of the picture's drama. The variation of line strength clearly copies Lorca's earlier experiments with superimposition. Furthermore, the final portrait resembles many of the faces of death contemporary to the double studies. The invasion of eyes and skull by green growth is a common trait in Lorca's portrayal in drawings and writing of death's consequences.

The form of the third division of the poem, entitled "Cuerpo presente" [Body laid out] is created by the tension between the static quality of a body at a viewing and the poet's desire for Ignacio to escape death, as well as his own process of coming to terms with it. The foreground is established as a flat plane, a stone slab against which rains wash; this is also a dividing image, through which seedlings and clouds may not pass. The stone thus becomes the dividing line of the piece, and as soon as this line is established, Lorca positions the dead body of the bullfighter on the stone, between sky and earth. The rain falling on the corpse drives home the reality of death, for it serves not to awaken him but rather to further the process of decomposition. Lorca insists on immobility as well; immobility of flesh, of stone, of spectators. This immobility is only temporary; Lorca is dreading the moment of the carrying-off, of burial, and he calls frantically for someone to help the bullfighter escape.

Space is stretched in Lorca's search for a place where Ignacio can be free from the effects of death, where he will not grow complacently accustomed to death. The inverse reflection of the bullring in the moon who waits to begin her waning enlarges the arena of death. There is no limit to space here, but neither is there any space free from the infiltrating mist of death. Rain and stone provide the piece's color, or lack thereof. Along with the bull's breath and the mist rising from the river, they provide a neutral, hazy color and texture that suggests the coldness associated with a corpse.

This third division of the poem resonates with the drawing *Hombre muerto* [Dead man] of 1932. In this colored, but muted drawing, the empty-eyed stare of the principal figure dominates the foreground, and is backgrounded by a landscape of grayness broken by tombs through which plants rise. The line of black figures in the farthest stretches of the background may be read as a funeral procession, performing exactly the action dreaded by Lorca, leaving the body of the departed to decompose and blend with other natural elements, spirals rising from tombs, past and future. The foregrounded figure, like the poetic voice in the poem, seems to be looking off into the distance into a space where escape is possible. "Cuerpo presente" strikes a clear parallel with the third and final movement of a bullfight, that of the death of the bull and its removal from the ring, in this case, of a similar treatment of the bullfighter.

The final event of a successful bullfight is the triumphant pass of the bullfighter around the ring, acknowledging the cheers of the crowd, and receiving gifts and tokens of affection. Any bullfighter knows that such adulation is fleeting. In this last division, Lorca makes the *paseo* [procession] in the place of the bullfighter—the "absent soul," searches for something more lasting than a moment's fleeting glory and offers his tribute to a valiant bullfighter.

This part of the poem spatially portrays a village through which the poet, or the viewer's eye passes. Details of a country town, livestock, children, houses, harvests are stretched out along the line of the poet's path. This line stretches in a temporal sense beyond the village in the foreground, however. The poet is directing himself toward the future, telling the story of Ignacio for subsequent generations as well as waiting for the moment when his equal in Andalusia will be born.

Reintegration is realized in the final verses. The white mist of the earlier imagery is dispelled by the light of a future day, and the colors of harvest and nature are imposing themselves once again on the poet's vision. The return of reds to the artist's palette and the return of life and vitality to the countryside are evoked by the image of grapes, the suggestion of mouths kissing, and in the return of the harvest. In contrast with all who do not know the bullfighter—whose memory might fade if not for the poet—Lorca's determination provides the strength that draws clear, strong lines away from the present before us, off into the distant future. As in "La monja gitana," the final verses effect a return to the present. Although a past memory, the breeze calls the poet's attention like the flash of light through the convent lattice.

Even more crucial to the analysis in this chapter is Lorca's offering of himself in this last section as the one who will be poet/artist/expresser of his experience of the life and death of Sánchez Mejías: "No te conoce nadie . . . pero yo te canto" [No one knows you . . . but I sing of you]. The poet must acknowledge his separateness from his environment—neither people nor animals, nor nature herself remember Ignacio. His determination to maintain the bullfighter's memory, in fact, less of a promise than an acknowledgment of what he has just completed, is articulated in terms that unite his task to the visual artist's: he will sing—we may read "draw"—Ignacio's "perfil" [profile], "gracia" [grace], and "elegancia" [elegance]. In this way, by means of the poet's work, others will know Ignacio, and so the poet will be united with all that surrounds him.

The readings of texts in this chapter have been based on the thesis that the apprehension of the text—both drawing and poem—occurs for the viewer in space and time. Analyzing them reveals careful attention on Lorca's part to the use and portrayal of both elements. I would conclude that this is evidence of the role of seeing and drawing in his own creative process. At those early periods when

Lorca was not drawing so actively, his poetry is not so evocative of more than one space at a time. When doubling starts in the drawings, Lorca begins to invoke more than one space simultaneously through words and images, especially through temporal, spatial, and significative superimpositions. The registering of vital, bodily sensations so natural to the drawing process results in powerful drawings and poetry from the New York period. Such vitality is integrated with personal sentiment and a cultural context in the "Llanto por Ignacio Sánchez Mejías."

4

Reading Arabesques: Lines and Words Together

We have studied the importance of drawing for Lorca, his participation in the artistic movements of his day, specifically in the 1920s in Spain, and have shown how these influences shaped his aesthetics, his drawing, and his writing in a limited time period. Next, we read his work in a chronological panorama, considering the portrayal of setting and subject and their transformation in both media. In this final chapter, we will focus on Lorca's late work, his drawings after 1930 and the poetry of the *Diván del Tamarit*. It explores the phenomenon of the arabesque in his work, specifically its dynamics associated with the metaphor, and Lorca's signatures as the union of written word and visual image.[1]

Lorca's work consistently shows Arab influence. The poet's roots in Granada, his exposure to Arab art forms, and his articulation of the value he placed on this artistic and literary heritage explain the presence of arabesque lines in his drawings.[2] The arabesque vine motif does not appear throughout Lorca's drawings chronologically. Rather, it is seen mostly in the drawings dating from 1932, and, in the drawings executed from that date until the poet's death in 1936. It is especially noteworthy in the many elaborate signatures among Lorca's drawings. The phenomenon of the arabesque appears in Lorca's drawing in two forms, the actual reproduction of arabesques, that is, lines that contain a vegetal motif and, more frequently, in his use of sinewy, serpentine lines in the construction of a drawing.

Vines, Vases, and Identity

The arabesque motif appears in the drawings of vases drawn by Lorca as containing abstract or realistic leaves, stems, or flowers. Along the same lines, we find repeated drawings of ornate fishbowls, drawn, again, with arabesque flourishes. Both the vases and fishbowls are Oriental in their design; a characterization further emphasized by Lorca when he refers to his *Pecera japonesa* [Japanese fishbowl]. In some drawings a vase serves as an aquarium.

One drawing, *Jarrón de los tres peces* [Vase of the three fish], contains fish hanging as if from poles, arranged like flowers. Lorca's comparison of the process of drawing and writing to fishing/hunting suggest that these fish might represent "captured" images. The doubling of a vase in another, with its resultant difference in lines, solid and stippled, in vase and flowers recalls the many double portraits in Lorca's drawings. In those drawings he produced to accompany editions of his work, we see Lorca's reading of his own work. One of the few vases drawn before 1930 shows the imposition of a vase over a map of Spain in a drawing Lorca designed in 1928 as a cover of the *Romancero gitano*. This suggests that the vase is holding Spain, or that it is proceeding from Spain. Either would corroborate the content of the poems in this collection. All these factors, including the positioning of a vase on a rooftop—which, as we have seen, may represent a writing or drawing surface—suggests that the vase/containers represent Lorca's art in poetry, drawings, plays, and so forth. Furthermore, the superimposition of the vase over the map of Spain recalls the face of Lorca against the New York skyline. In this reading, we see the influence of later artistic expression on Lorca's reading of a text he had produced prior to his New York experience.

When we turn our eye to Lorca's signatures, we find that the same flowers and stems remain, though the poet's name replaces the vases. This is a variation on the self-portrait theme, since in addition to the flowers, Lorca often embellishes his signatures with drawings of the moon and of lemons, common symbols in his drawing and writing. Moreover, each of these images has a basic structure in common that I shall discuss later in light of the drawings and in light of Lorca's poetry.

In time, Lorca's signature became more stylized as the representation of his public persona and gave evidence of his awareness of his development artistically but also in the evolving perception of his work by the public. In 1935 he dedicated a copy of his *Impresiones y paisajes* with a double signature "De Federico y Federico" [From Federico and Federico], imitating in one of the signatures the manner in which he had written his name in 1918, the year the book was published. His repetition of the straight/curvy line motif, the consistency of the use of accompanying images, and the control of line he demonstrates betray the presence of purpose and intent of expression in the majority of the signatures.

"Jarrón de los tres peces" © 1994 Artists Rights Society (ARS), New York/
VEGAP, Madrid

Lemons are a frequent component of Lorca's signatures. They are not attached to his name in the same way that vines are. Usually there are two lemons, their branches crossing over. Similar composition is used in signatures where the fruit has been identified (by others) as a quince. The lemons are sometimes colored, sometimes drawn in black and white. There seems to be no significance to the absence of color here. It is most probably a question of Lorca's having pencils available to him. The signatures that contain lemons include many that represent the years from 1924 to 1934.

The moon is another constant in these signatures. Sometimes the moon is a crescent, sometimes Lorca draws a temporal superimposition, drawing the crescent and then by stippling fills in the full moon, representing its entire cycle at once. The moon is often personified in the drawings, as it is in his poetry. It almost always has an eye, sometimes a face. In *Firma con luna reflejada*, it weeps over the poet's name. In a signature from 1935, the moon even wears a hat. Finally, in a signature dated 1931, Lorca combines the sun (a rare image, although it appears several times in 1931), moon, and lemons in a signature.

The most common motif employed by Lorca is the use of the *F*, *G*, or *L* of his name as a stablizing line to support swirling lines to which he adds leaves and flowers. Often, three circles form over the *G* and then terminate in a descending line over the *L*. The vine ends in a flower that is spilling its contents below the poet's name. One signature that resembles the vines contains lines that form both vine and a curling arrow. This drawing is unusual not only in the addition of the point and fletching of the arrow, but also because careful observation reveals that the point of the arrow and the fletching are leading in opposite directions. This may be accidental, but given Lorca's cleverness on other occasions, such a conclusion should not be foregone. The lines of the signature are flowing, and graceful, but the division and lack of harmony implied by the opposing movement of point and feathers, only evident after careful reading of the drawing, opens the signature to multiple interpretations.

Lorca's signatures express a common theme, the interaction between word and image.

In *Firma con luna reflejada*, for example, three common motifs—the crescent moon weeping over "Lorca," its reflection below his name, and vines ending in flowers—are united in a double image. The vines growing from the poet's first name move across his second and form a semicircle. The leaves from the descending vine connected to *García* create an eye and mouth. In many of Lorca's drawings of faces, mouths, and leaves are indistinguishable. This sort

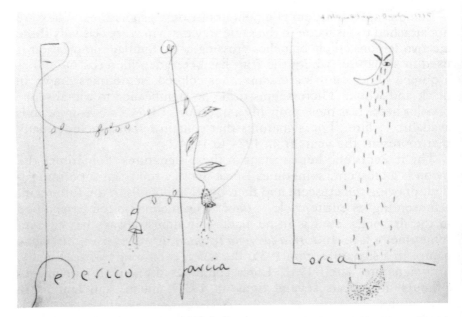

"Firma con luna reflejada" © 1994 Artists Rights Society (ARS), New York/
VEGAP, Madrid

of substitution is what Bousoño refers to in poetry as "significative superimpositions," when the two meanings of one word are simultaneously appropriate in a given phrase.[3] Here the focal point serves a double expressive purpose, just as the circle in the portrait of St. Sebastian served as mouth and bull's eye. It is for the viewer to recognize these superimpositions and then to interpret them.

Lorca uses another device that we have studied already in poetry and drawings in a signature dated 1936. In this instance, a double portrait of a clown is accompanied by the signing of the poet's first name. The face's doubling is not unusual; Lorca consistently drew such faces throughout his career. What is striking is his name. He signs the first three letters of his name, *Fed*, then brings the line of the *d* down to the bottom of the page where he continues his name. Then, as if to highlight this move, he draws a crescent moon over the second part of his name, almost parallel with the first three letters. The juxtaposition of the two images suggests that the doubling of the face—one half-awake, the other asleep, and one half-crying—represents the same divisions of identity as the separated letters of the poet's name.

One final example of a signature is *Firma con motivos vegetales y*

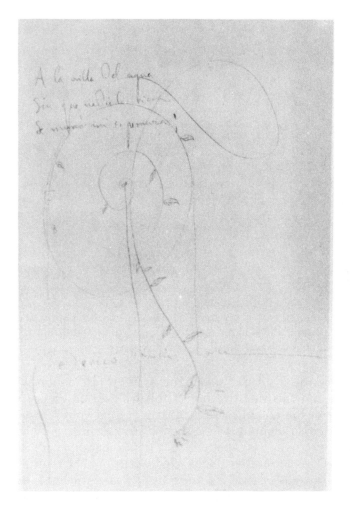

"**Firma con motivos vegetales y coplas**" © 1994 Artists Rights Society (ARS), New York/VEGAP, Madrid

copla, dated 1935, in which Lorca signs his name alongside some verses from his play *Mariana Pineda*. The line contained in the play reads "a la vera del agua;" in this drawing Lorca has used "la orilla." This signature is an excellent example of Lorca's sense of rhythm and how the drawn line can accompany the written verse almost musically. The verses read:

> A la orilla del agua
> Sin que nadie la viera
> se murió mi esperanza.

[At the edge of the water
without anyone seeing it,
my hope died.]

(*O.C.* 2:254)

Lorca's signature includes two circles drawn clockwise, the inner circle smaller than the second. The line then moves out of the circle to form another loop, counterclockwise and then dramatically drops down. The smaller circle growing into the larger repeats the growing expectation created by the first two lines while the third loop and descent echoes not only the rhythm and intonation of the third verse, but also its significance. Speaking of Lorca's use of this kind of line, Patrick Fourneret observes:

En las famosas firmas y dedicatorias de Lorca, este doble papel es patente: a la firma funcional se le añaden cascadas metafóricas-ornamentales de vegetales y flores.

[In the famous signatures and dedications of Lorca, this double role is patent: metaphoric ornamental cascades of plants and flowers are added to the functional signature.][4]

Caw's description of the arabesque as the "fascination with border ornament and this intertwining of foliage over an empty space . . . [the] play of the complicated against a central void"[5] resonates with the image of so many of Lorca's signatures against the blank page.

These observations about Lorca's fascination with the flower theme and his repetition in the signatures of that motif, as well as the actual images of swirling lines around straight lines, terminating in flowers that spill their contents lead us to consider their significance for his poetry. By signing his name, Lorca is claiming authorship. Most of the signatures to which this chapter refers are dedications and autographs of Lorca's own books. His care with the signatures suggests his reading of his *persona*, of the book he was dedicating or of the person to whom he was dedicating it. The variety of representation and the play of doubling, eye tricks, and the relationship between writing words and drawing images in these signatures suggest Lorca's awareness of how these two come together in his work. These signatures are not private drawings. They are intended to be seen, at least by the person to whom they are dedicated. One might interpret the phenomenon of such a blend of written and drawn elements as an acknowledgment on Lorca's part of the reader's role, seeing and interpreting at once.

Lines that Move into Metaphor:
Puta y luna and El marinero borracho

A similar treatment of images occurs in two drawings dated between 1929 and 1934 and in two poems found in the *Diván del Tamarit*. In both drawings and poems, Lorca creates and manipulates his material in a way that suggests the lines of an arabesque.

One significant function of the arabesque line is its patterning metaphorical structure. Lorca's observations regarding the components of metaphorical function that he made in his lecture on Góngora dovetail with R. Klein's description of the figure at work in arabesque and metaphor. Lorca states:

> Para que una metáfora tenga vida necesita dos condiciones esenciales: forma y radio de acción. Su núcleo central y una redonda perspectiva en torno de él. El núcleo se abre como una flor que nos sorprende por lo desconocido, pero en el radio de luz que lo rodea hallamos el nombre de la flor y conocemos su perfume.

> [In order for a metaphor to have life, it needs two essential conditions: form and a radius of action. Its central nucleus and a perspective that circles around it. The nucleus opens like a flower that surprises us by what is unknown about it, but in the radius of light that surrounds it we find the name of the flower and we know its perfume.] (*O.C.* 3:230)

Klein observes:

> The straight line surrounded by arabesques is a figure, but also a sign. What it signifies is correlative to the relation of its swirling periphery to its stable, vertical center. Or conversely, it enacts the relation that stands metaphorically for the way in which metaphor relates to its sense. In any case, the figure as sign signifies itself, itself standing as a metaphor for the movement of metaphor, for its own metaphoricity.[6]

This sense of the metaphor as a figure modeled after the arabesque can be traced in the development of images occurring in two drawings dated between 1929 and 1934 and in two poems found in the *Diván del Tamarit*. In both drawings and poems, Lorca creates and manipulates metaphors in a way that suggests the lines of an arabesque. He provides a nucleus, and then spins out his metaphor from that center.

The first drawing, is dated 1929–1931 and, because of the words included in the piece, has come to be referred to as *Puta y luna* [Whore and Moon]. In his editorial comments, Mario Hernández describes it as consisting of "un arabesco de delgadas líneas en tinta china" [an arabesque of thin lines in china ink]. As Hernández reads it, the drawing's lines originate in the word *puta* and then spread out in two directions. One line continues to spell out the words *y luna* at the top of its space, then descends to the bottom to end in a black crescent moon. The second line beginning with the word *puta* twirls around the drawing's surface, eventually spelling out the words *Pota, pita, peta, pata*.[7] Hernández's interpretation is most probably the result of reading the words written at the top of the drawing. However, my reading begins with the drawn image, and the first thing I see is an animal of the sort that appears frequently in the series of self-portraits drawn by Lorca during his stay in New York. Its body is drawn in red and a black paw and a black and red tail are very clearly distinguished from the rest of its body by a change of color. Directly below the black paw is the word *pata*, paw. What Hernández explains as Lorca's "haphazard" inventing of words (178), beginning with *puta*, is more logically seen as a transformation of the word *pata* by changing the vowel: *pata, peta, pita, pota, puta*. The *u–a* pattern would then be transformed into *luna*, by virtue of the vowels as well as the image associations the two words share. This establishes the drawn image as the beginning, as is, of course, the letter *a*, the beginning of the vowel chain.

Hernández accurately points out that the moon is represented three times in this drawing: through the word *luna*, written in black at the top of the drawing, in that same word written in red in the drawing's center, independent of the black curvy lines already discussed, and finally in the actual figure of the crescent moon at the bottom of the drawing, "establishing a circular relationship among them by means of a continuous line that ends in the drawn moon, *opposed*, *as a reflection*, to the verbal" [my italics] (178).

A careful firsthand look at the drawing, however, extends this basic connection of images. Certainly one must register the triple presence of the moon, in black letters, in red, and in black drawing. In addition, the color red of the word *luna* in the middleground of the drawing is linked chromatically with the red of the animal's body. The animal's black paw links the moon and its body by the line that connects it to the written black word *pata* to its lower left and chromatically with the black moon beneath it. The tail of the animal is drawn in black and red, the only place in the drawing where the two colors are superimposed. The word *puta* is also written in red in the drawing's right hand section. Like *luna* it is very difficult to see without good light. My theory is that Lorca added these two words in red after finishing the arabesque that began with *pata*. The position of the word *pata* at such close proximity to the drawing of the same appears to be no coincidence; neither does the position of both the word *pata* on the same visual level as the black moon. Thus a pattern emerges:

luna (black word).
luna (red word)   *puta* (red word)
paw (black) / *animal* (red) / *tail* (red and black)
puta (black word)   *pata* (black word)   *moon* (black crescent)

Finally, one adds the triple presence of three "tails" in the drawing: the tail of the animal itself, the lines at the drawing's end that terminate those lines that had wandered over the surface of the drawing, and the crescent moon that also serves as an end point to the line from which it had originated. Understanding this drawing as a manifestation of the arabesque as we are discussing it here, then, involves first accepting the interrelation among the drawing's components and reading those observations in light of the arabesque's dynamics.

Where are the metaphors in this drawing? The moon's cycles, expressed in circle and crescent shapes, link it to the feminine, to *puta*, as do its mythological and literary associations with the feminine. Throughout Lorca's poetry, the moon is portrayed as a feminine, sexual presence. In "Romance de la luna, luna" [Ballad of the moon, moon], for example, the moon seduces and then kills a Gypsy boy. The moon is also associated with blood and with death. We can recall the image of the moon as "un hocico de sangres derramadas" [a snout of spilt blood], in the "Llanto por Ignacio Sánchez Mejías." If the animal is read as masculine, then sexual opposition or completion must be read into the drawing. These associations do not explain the role of the animal's paw, clearly a key to the drawing, or the use of black.

The fact that this kind of animal is an intrinsic element of Lorca's self-portraits leads me to speculate on its significance in the drawing. If it represents Lorca, or at least some aspect of him, then it is intriguing to realize that it is found in between words and plastic lines, trapped by them, perhaps but also providing meaning. The black of the paw, the black of the lines and words, and the black of writer's ink affirm this interpretation. I read the drawing as a metaphor of the artistic process so often described by Lorca. Its spontaneity is evinced in the coincidental transformations along the vowel chain, in the meandering lines; its technique in Lorca's having worked parts of it over, adding red, deliberately placing the repeating words. The feeling evoked by the drawing of feeling overwhelmed by the twisting, turning, transforming lines is experienced by the artist who depicts, the animal depicted and the viewer who interprets.

The analysis of this drawing provides two important insights into the role of drawing in Lorca's writing process. First, it provides an example of how Lorca played with transformations along a continuing line. Secondly, I have shown here that the reading of the interrelations between words and drawn images need not, and in some instances should not, proceed from written word to drawn image. Seeing the drawn image as the nucleus of this text and allowing the transformation to open from there provides a reading that includes more than the "four elements" of which Hernández speaks. My reading sees the drawing of the animal as the beginning, around which the remainder of the text is constructed.

All of the elements of the arabesque cited by both Caws and Klein are contained in the drawing *Puta y luna*. The intertwining of the drawing's elements by means of arabesque lines, the geometric relationship among those elements maintained by a single, continuous line, even the presence of an element, the moon, and its reflected opposite all reinforce the dynamic exposed in other arabesque texts.

The second drawing, executed in 1934, portrays a frequent theme in Lorca's drawings, that of a sailor or sailors outside a tavern. Lorca himself titled this drawing *El marinero borracho* [The drunken sailor]. On the left is the figure of a standing sailor whose eyes are open and whose hands are empty, clearly the "sober side" of the representation. This figure is drawn a second time on the right, resembling the first, therefore suggesting a double of one sailor. Some differences in the way Lorca has drawn the two include: their hands (the number of fingers, the presence or absence of fingernails, and their positions), slight differences in the shirts they wear, and the presence of chest hair on the first and its absence on the second. This suggests a masculine/feminine opposition. The most significant differences between the two are that the second figure is sitting at a table, his eyes are closed, the ribbons of his cap droop (whereas those of the first turn upward), and his hand holds a bottle. The closed eyes of the second sailor, his lack of masculine chest hair, the crossing of his left hand over his right all suggest reading this drawing as a double portrait— a depiction of reason and intuition, a theme that we have already studied in Lorca, and which will be considered in a poem later in this chapter. This is not a rejection of the male/female dynamic. Such

"Marinero borracho" © 1994 Artists Rights Society (ARS), New York/ VEGAP, Madrid

polarity exists consistently throughout Lorca's work. We have seen it, for example in the ode to Dalí, in the joining of aesthetic positions represented by Apollo and Dionisius.

This drawing does not contain any sinewy or vinelike lines, but Lorca's treatment of three words, and the lines that connect them both suggest a superconscious effort on the part of the poet to play with what this motif might represent in his work, one might say a "meta-arabesque."[8] The word *ROMA* [Rome] is in the background immediately behind the second sailor's head, the word *AMOR* (Love), an inversion of *ROMA*, falls across the surface of the sailor's shirt, which serves in this instance as a mirror. The word *ROM*, not *ron* (rum), is on the bottle, ending, on the drawing's surface at least, the chain of word transformations. How it may be continued off the page will be discussed later. Connecting all three words is a series of straight, dotted lines that follow one of the angles created by the sailor's large triangular collar. These lines connect *ROMA*/his head to *AMOR*/his heart to *ROM*/the bottle in his hand. The straightness of these lines may seem to dissuade the viewer from including this drawing from those with an arabesque theme. It is the words themselves that both evolve or grow, *ROM* <> *ROMA*, then twist, *AMOR*

<> *ROMA*. At the *ROMA*<>*ROM* juncture, the reader naturally continues the transformation: *ROM*<*MOR*>*MORS*, death. This evolution begins on either end, at the top right of the drawing with the word *ROMA* or at its bottom right, with *ROM*, but it is the in twisting that the transformation occurs, midway between these two words, at the middle of the space occupied by the drunken sailor figure's heart where the word *AMOR* is located.[9] In addition, the word *ROMA* at the top, and the word *AMOR* are further connected by another pair of lines that curve around the sailor's head, thereby enclosing his face in a half-circle space that they and the straight lines already mentioned create. It is difficult to ascertain where the lines begin and where they end. This semicircle might also suggest a repetition of the figure of the moon behind the left-hand figure as well as its more deliberate repetition forming the crook of the right-hand sailor's arm. Both of these crescent moons are outlined in triplicate in black, white, and dotted texture. The motif of three is further found in the presence of three trees behind the first sailor.

I read the central position of the drawing—the sailor's chest where *AMOR* occurs as the nucleus of Lorca's metaphor in this text. If the poet has established the first sailor as a figure of consciousness, alertness, reason (associated with the head/intellect), then the second, drunk, asleep, represents unconsciousness (associated with the heart/body). As we shall see later in this chapter, Lorca has designed this drawing in order to suggest continuation. This would imply an off-the-page presence of a third sailor, somehow representing the third stage, the artistic expression latent in the *ROM/MORS/*hand location. In much of Lorca's work, love and death are intimately connected. He also speaks of his work in terms of love and discipline, so death here could represent the stifling of his artistic efforts. A logical association of imagery connects the hand with artistic expression.

The austerity of the lines in this drawing and the tranquility of its surface may tempt the viewer to dismiss it as not serving as an example of the arabesque dynamic. The metaphor at work in the arabesque, however, need not be characterized only by the sinewy swirls associated with Rococo. Even though Caws includes Góngora's work in her study as exemplary of the twisting, turning Rococo, one must bear in mind that for Lorca, Góngora's work represents precision, the achievement of architecture, a poetic control that is manifested even as it results in groundbreaking new imagery. In the lecture entitled "Imaginación, inspiración, evasión," Lorca writes:

La exaltación de Góngora que ha sentido toda la juventud poética española ha correspondido con la madurez del cubismo, pintura de raciocinio puro, austera de color y arabesco, que culminó en el castellanísimo Juan Gris.

[The exaltation of Góngora, which all the poetic Spanish youth have felt, has corresponded with the maturity of Cubism, painting of pure reason, austere of color and arabesque, which culminated with the most Castillian Juan Gris.] (*O.C.* 3:267)

The reason valued by Lorca in both Góngora's poetry as well as in Cubist painting is the maturity of the twisting of reality that characterizes the arabesque. The knot and its reflection, the use of positive and negative space, the gradual transformations of sliding metaphors can be assigned to the work of which Lorca speaks. This admiration for the rational, austere arabesque appears in Lorca's later works, including the *Diván del Tamarit,* described by Gallego as "ese exquisito *Diván del Tamarit,* que rehuye la opulencia de la Alhambra y se contenta con un huerto familiar" [that exquisite *Diván del Tamarit* which rejects the oppulence of the Alhambra and contents itself with a familiar garden].[10] This idea of mutation or transformation and its continuation is seen as well in two poems from the *Diván del Tamarit.*

"Gacela del mercado matutino"

The first poem to be discussed is the "Gacela del mercado matutino" [Gacela of the morning market]. This poem, by its very positioning on the page, the interaction of its components, and the transformations of its imagery suggest a comparison with the arabesque dynamic. One notices first that the odd numbered stanzas are written in italics, and the alternating stanzas in standard type. In addition, the second and fourth stanzas are characterized by the use of question marks and exclamations, whose presence at the beginning and end of each phrase adds texture to the poem on the page.

These visual differences and their impact on the reader are further delineated by the difference in the function of the odd and even verses. The italicized, odd verses serve the function of a refrain, and despite some changes, are largely repetitions of the same text. This repetitive, rote-like nature is reproduced visually by the smoothness of the italics. It is less easy to "slide" over the text in the even-numbered stanzas. The varied appearance created visually in the even verses is reinforced by the very nature of question and exclamation. The absence of any response in the poem heightens the sharpness of the poet's expressions. This sharpness, woven alternately with the more sedate refrain, creates the effect of a line rising away from more sedate, stable passages.

The twisting of the arabesque line occurs in the poem where changes occur. The changes from one repetition of the refrain to the next mark an augmentation from desire, "quiero" [I want], to intention, "voy a" [I am going to], as well as an increasing intimacy of goal, from a mental, more removed focus, "saber tu nombre" [to know your name], to physical and more familiar, even intrusive objectives, "beber tus ojos" [to drink your eyes] and "sentir tus muslos" [to feel your thighs]. The reader may deduce the unexpressed response to these statements by the change in tone portrayed in the other stanzas.

In contrast to the limited changes in the refrains, the language in the even-numbered verses is marked by striking transformations and connections. Chromatically, verse 2 presents contrasting images of white/gray and red, explicitly in luna gris/desangró, llamarada/nieve [gray moon/bled, flush/snow]; the red suggested in "asesina tu cristal" [kills your crystal]. The fourth verse offers images of height, depth, and distance—the voice raised in the market, mountains of wheat, the references to alienation, nearness and distance.

The agitation expressed in stanzas 2 and 4, and the enigmatic imagery contained therein are reminiscent of the dynamic observed by Klein:

> At the same time, the level of language within the poem is dramatically raised; the description of the thyrsus erupts in an unexpected frenzy. Words like "astonishing," "explosions of odor and color," mark the excitement which progressively seizes the language which describes the thyrsus. The frenzy of the language is correlative to the dance which the emblem has become, as the flowers and vines swirl around the rod, the spirals and arabesques spin around the straight lines.[11]

The refrain in this poem might serve as the "rod," stable yet climbing in intimate intensity while the other stanzas provide the swirling, elaborate movement described by Klein. Yet another way to understand Klein's observations in terms of this poem is to search for the "nucleus," the "straight rod" that gives the resultant imagery significance. Another drawing provides insight. In this poem, the image of drops of blood across a cheek is repeated as seeds across snow, needles against glass.

These images are also found in *Firma con luna reflejada*, a signature, which was discussed earlier in this chapter. Not only does this drawing contain the images mentioned of a crescent moon (a *9*?), a cheek, blood, and tears, but the "drops" drawn by Lorca are depicted in a way that also suggests seeds or needles. The elements of the metaphor are depicted in the drawing. If the moon is indeed a crescent as Lorca depicts it in the drawing, then it is almost completely waned and is ready to begin again its cycle. This reiterates the poem's tone of endings, of separation, of suffering. In the drawing, the dark sharpness of the lines falling across the moon's cheek are in contrast with the smooth, whiteness of the page. This depicts a disruption consonant with the feelings expressed in the poem.

In the poem, the roundness of the moon is repeated in the curve of the numeral *9*, in the cheek of the addressee, in the leaves of the cactus. The softness implied in the circular imagery is contrasted by both "semilla" and "alfiler" [seed and pin] that penetrate. These images of penetration, contrasted with smooth whiteness have clear sexual overtones. One notes the "sharpness" of the contrast of the last verse between far and near as well as the paradoxical "¡Qué lejos estoy contigo, qué cerca cuando te vas!" [How faraway I am with you, how close when you go!] This reflects the poet's conflictive feelings, longing for intimacy to be restored, resorting to seeing the beloved in the market.

"Casida de las palomas oscuras"

The second poem to be analyzed, "Casida de las palomas oscuras" [Casida of the dark doves], is presented as one stanza with no division into smaller units. The length of the lines permits the poem to assume the appearance of a column. As we shall later see, this column-like appearance is reinforced by the creation of descending movement achieved through an ongoing process of negation or devalorization. The use of enjambement throughout the poem as well as the transformations in imagery suggest the pattern of a Solomonic column, in which the lines of the column wrap themselves around its surface rather than repeat its upward movement. An analogous image is expressed as a "thrysus" by Richard Klein who, in describing it, also states its significance:

> The straight line surrounded by arabesques is a figure, but also a sign. What it signifies is correlative to the relation of its swirling periphery to its stable, vertical center. (66)

In this poem, the narrative element is the "stable vertical center" of which Klein speaks. This use of narration on the part of Lorca is defended by the poet in terms that link his poetics to those described by Klein. Lorca articulates the role of narration when he states:

La narración es como un esqueleto del poema envuelto en la carne magní-
fica de las imágenes. Todos los momentos tienen idéntica intensidad y
valor plástico, y la anécdota no tiene ninguna importancia, pero da con
su hilo invisible unidad al poema.

[Narration is like a skeleton of the poem wrapped in the magnificent flesh
of the images. Every moment has an identical intensity and plastic value,
and the anecdote has no importance, but with its invisible thread, gives
the poem unity.] (*O.C.* 3:243–44)

In "Casida de las palomas oscuras," narration is achieved through the
contrasting elements of repetition and change. The pattern of seeing,
describing, questioning, and answering is repeated completely twice
and begun again at the poem's end. The questioner, the poetic "I;"
the question, "¿dónde está mi sepultura?" [Where is my tomb?]; the
responses, "en mi garganta," "en mi cola" [in my throat, in my tail];
and the respondents, the sun and moon, never vary in the poem.
These consistent elements are highlighted by those that vary from
one line to the next. Thus, the consistent repeated elements permit
escapes into more complicated imagery. Klein has described this dynamic in other texts: "The movement must seem to stop in order that
it continue. The condition of the metaphor's continued spinning, and
hence of its self-reflection, is the fictional projection of its repose."[12]
   The spinning out of metaphor is seen in this poem through the
transformation from one image to the next. First, in chromatic terms,
there is a fading process. In the initial verse the two birds are dark
doves, in the second round they become snowy eagles, and finally
in the third are doves again, but this time, nude doves. Apart from
the semantic interchanges effected by Lorca (dark to snowy to nude),
there is another, more stealthy exchange of characteristics at work.
One usually associates the characteristic of darkness with the eagle
and that of being snow-white with the dove. This interchange or
con-fusion [my emphasis] may serve, ironically, as another unifying
element in the poem, another place where movement appears more
stable, which makes other less conventional transformations less
threatening to the poem's coherence. The changes are so gradual
and subtle that the reader does not become put off or confused.
   The progress from black to white to naked is paralleled by a progression toward nothingness realized by Lorca's identifying of the
characters in his poem. In the first movement of the poem, the two
doves are identified, respectively, as the sun and the moon. In the
second passage, the two eagles exchange less striking identities; that
is, they are merely presented as "la una era la otra" [One was the
other]. One of the characters in this segment of the poem, the girl,

is negated: "la muchacha era ninguna" [the girl was neither]. In the final passage, the two doves are completely negated. Not only are they naked, but, Lorca tells us: "y las dos eran ninguna" [and the two were neither].

Lorca's placing of himself in the poem's middle, in the central position of the poem, is striking for a number of reasons. First, it coincides with his use of the word *cintura* [waist]. In both the drawing *El marinero borracho* and in this poem, this middle place is where change occurs. Even more striking is the image of the poet wandering. This resonates with that of the function of drawing lines. Seemingly aimless, the meandering path followed by pencil or feet leads to transformation. It is in the wandering that the poem is realized, and so, in my view, it is no coincidence that this image is placed immediately before the change from a conventional imagery to a more adventuresome one. (Recall the changes wrought along the lines of *Puta y luna*). The sight of two doves in a laurel is more likely than that which follows this passage, that is of two eagles with a nude girl.

The central metaphors of the poem are linked to one another, almost forming a chain. The doves first mentioned are the sun and the moon. The poet's tomb is to be, not in the earth as we might suspect, but in the sun's tail and in the moon's throat.[13] The earth, yet unseen, but invoked both by the reference to a tomb, as well as by its absence in the unexpected responses, appears metaphorically as a person; the poet is walking "con la tierra por la cintura" [up to his waist in earth]. Perhaps in the next stanza the level of the earth would rise or fall. The phrase might also be read "with the earth by the waist," sugggesting the image of a companion, which takes shape next in the nude girl who is with the eagles. Finally, her nudity is imposed on the birds. The images in the poem, then, both anticipate and continue adjacent images, swirling, in Klein's terms, away from the central narration, yet always returning to it.

Other analogies with visual art in the poem exist in the treatment of space as well as in the existence of contrasts. Space is established by direct references to the earth itself, to the space between earth and sky in the branches of the laurel tree, and indirectly to the sky in the invocation of the eagles. The constant use of the vowel sounds of *o* and *a* throughout the poem suggests openness and space. Other sounds serve as borders and lines that give shape, changing the open sounds into intelligible words.

Contrast, or the presence of opposites—light and dark, masculine and feminine, sun and moon, throat and tail, eagle and dove—is not static but rather interactive, reinforced by the repetition that "la una era la otra." Such an exchange might be seen as a cross-fertilization of sorts, for after each such statement, a transformation or a transmutation occurs. Dark doves become snowy eagles; the nudity of the girl in the central passage, as well as her state of being "ninguna," is taken on by the doves at the poem's end. This "light and witty struggle of opposing forces,"[14] in addition to creating the descending motion already described, maintains interest (there is no victor in this struggle) and balances the heaviness of the poet's repeated question.

Lines and Words Together

The transformations or mutations observed in the *Puta y luna* drawing occur in a confined space, since the very lines that both construct and connect the words also enclose them. The pattern of repetition present in the second drawing, and in the two poems analyzed, is reminiscent of the arabesque braid that shares an end point with the surface it covers, but whose very design suggests unlimited potential for continuity, for ongoing spinning out. The effect of such an ongoing sequence, be it in a visual context (a braid down a column, for example) or in a literary one (the consistent repetition of a pattern or refrain) is the experience of the text not ending or returning to the beginning. Do the metamorphoses represented in the drawings terminate at their border, or do they continue off the page? The fact that the original verses are not repeated in either poem, but that the pattern of change is continued, implies an open-endedness. The presence of three trees in the *El marinero borracho,* as contrasted with only two moons and two sailors, could suggest the presence of a third in that space that extends beyond the limits of the drawing. Even the word transformation implies a continuation. Hernández observes:

> In one of his works, "The Drunken Sailor," Lorca will uncover the anagramatic reversal of Rome: Love (playing intentionally with the name of liquor "Rum").[15]

Of course, Hernández is referring to the transformation from *ROM* to *MOR, MORS,* death.

Candelas Newton analyzes the role of Granada as a backdrop to the *Diván del Tamarit,* a place where Lorca experienced the meeting of his Western Christian background with the Arab culture. She cites as well its "identidad agónica" [agonic identity], which Lorca sees concretized in the enclosed gardens of the homes, microcosms of landlocked Granada.[16] For Lorca, of course, the theme of restriction is not new; Newton cites his poetry as a "locus de la dialéctica existencial" [locus of the existential dialectic] (122). Finally, she discusses this *locus*, "a circumscribed spatial-temporal locus" since in the *Diván* both images of enclosure occur: the enclosed garden, and the day-into-night cycle (130). I would add that the combination of verbal repetition, heard or read over time and the placement of the poems on the page, or their space, also suggests a time-space configuration. Newton studies these paradigms as manifestations of the uroboros figure (150–64).

Specifically, in her analysis of the "Casida de las palomas oscuras," Newton observes that this poem leads (as I have noted as well) to annihilation, to nothingness (164). Newton's reading of the *Diván del Tamarit* is strong and convincing. The very elements on which she bases her reading—the Granadan theme and the uroboros figure—invite a continued reading. I have shown throughout this study that Lorca begins many of his poems with precisely such an image of nothingness. Silence, whiteness, death, are equatable to the blank page, the beginning of the poetic/artistic process. So, the nothingness encountered at the end of the poem might be read as a readiness to begin a new stanza. When he introduced the *Diván del Tamarit* in 1944, Honig stressed the openness that Lorca had inherited from Arab culture in its themes and in its forms.

> Lorca had learned from the Arabs and from his own experience the rich capabilities of poetry built with a few symbols in which all desire could be poured, as into a bottomless sea, because no cessation and no fulfillment were ever expected. Lorca leaves the entrances and exits open. This, however, is intentional and should not suggest simply incompleteness about the poems; rather a condition of the soul which has been seeped in the truth of its perceptions and which can never again lie about the beginning and end of things.[17]

Lorca's openness, the consistency of his symbols and the guiding force of poetic logic (which I have read as metaphoric), are all present in these final drawings and poems.

Each of the images mentioned earlier in Lorca's signatures—the moon, lemons, and flowers—have elements in common with the uroboros paradigm. Northrop Frye links the uroboros with the moon in its cycle of death and rebirth, as well as with the hermaphrodite, and sees all as redemptive signs (157).[18] All three images, then, have a double significance, each of which is appropriate to Lorca. These images are present throughout his work. In many of Lorca's poems and plays, the moon represents death. The image of pollen falling into the ground instead of into a female receptacle may symbolize loss, sterility, and inability to reproduce—frequent themes in his writing. In much of his work he expresses bitterness, associated with lemons. Thus, the presence of these three elements strongly suggest that the transformations depicted will end in annihilation.

However, the moon's cycles also represent rebirth. In only four of Lorca's drawings is the moon waning. In the vast majority it is a waxing crescent and in many others it is full. And when Lorca was asked why lemons were such a consistent motif in his drawings, especially in his signature, he said that the lemons were there so that the recipient of the autograph (in this case La Argentinita) could make lemonade as a proof of the poet's love.[19] This is evocative of his earlier assertion that the poet must draw a cloud over his work so that after it is finished, from time to time the rain will fall on it, provoking new growth.[20] The granules falling from Lorca's flowers could be unfertilized pollen, but they could also be seed, the fruit of a fertilization process. With few exceptions, these flowers occur only when their lines/stems have crossed, usually a round, curved line (feminine) crosses a straight vertical line (masculine). Assigning traditional male/rational and female/intuitive values to these lines resumes earlier discussion of Lorca's work as "offspring of reason and intuition."

These two lines of interpretation are not mutually exclusive. The richness of Lorca's genius resulted in a body of works that hold many possibilities of interpretation. In keeping with the basic structure of significance that I have just explored, the cross-fertilization between poetry and drawing results in new life for the reading and viewing of Lorca's texts.

5

Conclusion

I have studied Lorca's drawings and their significance in the reading of his poetry. By first reading the drawings, by asking, in Fish's words, "what they do," I have discerned structures by which the reader may derive meaning and then sought those structures in other texts.[1] I have brought together the texts of Lorca's drawings and of his poetry, and have read the two with "one eye," claiming what Caws calls the "beholder's share" of their significance, "a constructive creation and recreation of the texts," in this case, of the poetry through the drawings.[2] I have consistently referred to Lorca's concept of the poem and drawing as the surface where the meeting of the artist's inner and outer world occurs or the place where the poet/artist meets the reader/viewer, or where the reader/viewer encounters his or her own inner reality.

The fact that familiarity with the drawings is not essential to understanding Lorca's poetry is proven by the insightful work done by many Lorca scholars over the years before the drawings were accessible. But once they become known, the reading of Lorca's work must be affected. The study of the the drawings contaminates the eye of the reader in a process described by Louis Renza:

> But what happens, as must happen, when one leaves a particular painting behind? The necessary afterimage of a painting, of course, exists in time—in a medium of memory akin to the comparatively insubstantial medium of literary or textual imagery. Painting here willy-nilly becomes a kind of literature, just as literature, at least in its less iconoclastic moments, would become a kind of painting.[3]

For Lorca, the images he captured in his drawings surely became such an afterimage, and eventually, as Renza describes, a kind of literature that showed its presence in his writing. So for the reader who has become familiar with the drawings, they become this same kind of afterimage, leaving not just the impression of their appearance, but a deeper sense of their inner structure, the poetic logic which supports and controls them as well. Knowing them as a body of work further enriches this process. Readers then approach the poetry with inner eyes full of the drawings and Lorca's poetry will never be the same again. A correspondence or a mutual illumination arises between the two that informs the reading of both, resulting in a cyclical dynamic like that seen in the last chapter. This is the end result of which Fish speaks, an accumulation of meaning gathered as the reader proceeds through the text(s) (24).

I have shown that the drawings are rooted in a system of significance that Lorca derived from his life experience, his reading, his impressive knowledge of Spanish literature, and his openness to the literary and artistic movements of his day. The drawings, from 1923 on, were his constant companions. We have read that he felt comforted, like a child, when he did them.

In the fall of 1928, Lorca wrote to Jorge Zalamea. From Lorca's letter, it would appear that Zalamea had confided difficulties to him; Lorca's response is affectionate and wise. But more than its expression of human warmth and wisdom, the letter offers another entry into Lorca's sense of equilibrium. Having himself experienced a difficult time emotionally that summer, Lorca speaks out of his own experience. His advice to Zalamea is:

> Dibuja un plano de tu deseo y vive en ese plano dentro siempre de una norma de belleza. Yo lo hago así, querido amigo . . . ¡y qué difícil me es! pero lo vivo.

> [Draw a map of your desire, and live on that plane always within a norm of beauty. I do it this way, dear friend, and how difficult it is for me! but I live it.] (3:981)

It is no surprise that Lorca should employ the metaphor of drawing to speak to his friend. He often speaks in figurative terms using such words as *dibujar* [to draw], *perfil* [profile], and so on. I have discussed Lorca's sensitivity to the dynamic between inner and outer space; the idea then, of creating a plane on which one can live one's inner life fits this notion, apparent in so many of his drawings and poems. Reading *plano* in another sense, also used by Lorca, I understand that he advises Zalamea to make a map, a guide to help him withstand all that surrounds him, much as Lorca's poet in the Góngora lecture. Either reading confirms these concepts as intrinsic to Lorca's vision.

In the next paragraph, Lorca tells Zalamea:

> Estoy un poco en contra de todos, pero la belleza viva que pulsan mis manos me conforta de todos los sinsabores.

[I'm a bit against everyone, but the living beauty that my hands feel comforts me from all displeasures.] (*O.C.* 3:981)

He does not use the word drawings, but the use of the word *conforta* [comforts] and his speaking (in the letters to Gasch the summer before) of his hand entering the "tierra virgen" [virgin land] from which the drawings arise both suggest that he is expressing how important drawing and the drawings themselves were for him. This fulfills the expectancy created by the use of the word "dibuja" in the first paragraph. The drawings are an anchor for the poet, a constant reminder of the beauty that he claims as the norm for his living. They remind him of what he knows, of what he has seen and felt, of what he will say.

What are the implications of these words for the reader? The images formed by the reading of Lorca's drawings become what Arnheim calls "products of active exploration and search for meaningful form."[4] Lorca says that drawing provides a way for him to escape poetic staleness. They also provide us with new insights into the poems, releasing them and us from the stale cycles of interpretation and analysis, a reading that is a "refreshing of the literary eye."[5] In my reading I have striven to be faithful to what is present in Lorca's work and rely less on outside instruments or superimpositions of meaning. The analyses contained here are consistent with the imagery found in Lorca's poetry and drawing.

There are additional, more tangible results of this reading. First, I have set Lorca's drawings in the context and of the artistic debates of the mid-twenties and have applied the criteria arising from those debates to his work. This artistic background has been discussed in terms of Lorca's poetry. By reading Lorca in light of this context and by studying his reading of the work of others as well as his reading of his own drawings and poems, I have integrated these criteria and specific drawings.

Second, I have read the poetry in light of the drawings and in light of what Lorca says he was trying to accomplish in them. As a result, specific literary texts—such as "Santa Lucía y San Lázaro," for example—become more crucial for Lorca's poetics than has been suspected in the past. Still other texts, when read in light of the drawings, offer important insight into his creative process. Images become less enigmatic, and what has previously been seen as a gap in Lorca's production—the summer of 1927—is now considered to be not so much fallow as simply productive in other media.

The use of one approach, in this case, the dynamic of the arabesque, when applied to Lorca's poetry and drawings proves that it is possible to discuss the texts together, providing a common space in which to study them without depriving either text of its intrinsic characteristics. Not only does such a discussion bring texts together for reading, but it also reveals a basic construct to Lorca's system of meaning, the cyclic, regenerative nature of images and lines in poetry and art itself. Over all, the reading of drawings and poems together affirms the coherence of Lorca's artistic system, providing the connective threads that link his work, the recurrent dynamics and images, which explain both the changes in his work as well as its consistencies.

Finally, I have studied the effect of Lorca's drawings on the reader and the consequences of my study on the reading of his poetry. My text is a product of reading, in Lorca's words, "una narración del viaje" [a narration of the voyage] that can effect (as well as affect) further readings of Lorca. New discoveries and other correspondences between drawings and poems remain unexplored. Theater in Lorca is intrinsically related to the visual and to drawing and painting. Work in this field has only begun. Different creative approaches to Lorca's visual and verbal texts may yet be applied to their analysis. What I offer here is a beginning, a map of my first venture into this world and a chart to help realize the exciting possibilities of future excursions.

Notes

The following abbreviations are used to identify frequently cited works:

Dibujos Federico García Lorca. *Dibujos*, Edited by Mario Hernández. Madrid: Ministerio de Cultura, 1986.
GL *La Gaceta Literaria* 1 (1927–1929).
LLS Mario Hernández. *Line of Light and Shadow: The Drawings of Federico García Lorca.* Translated by Christopher Maurer. Durham, N.C.: Duke University Press, 1991.
O.C. Federico García Lorca. *Obras Completas.* 3 vols. Edited by Arturio Del Hoyo. Madrid: Aguilar, 1989.

Introduction

1. Among these critics is Lucía García de Carpi, who states: "What in the beginning was no more than mere party entertainment, in time was transformed into a form of personal expression as important as literature, music or recital, that is, into one more river bed through which to channel, in a new way, the poetic torrent which García Lorca carried within himself." "Bajo el astro de la noche." *Dibujos*, 33.
2. See Eugenio Carmona, "<<Sin Tortura ni sueño>> La Renovación plástica española de los años 20 y García Lorca, dibujante," in *Homenaje a Federico García Lorca*, ed. Manuel Alvar (Málaga: Ayuntamiento de Málaga, 1988), 114.

Chapter 1. The Place of the Drawings in Reading Lorca

1. Manuel Fernández-Montesinos García, "Variantes significativas en algunos borradores de Federico García Lorca," in *L'"imposible/posible" di Federico García Lorca*, Atti del convegno de studi, ed. Laura Doldi (Napoli: Scientifiche Italiane, 1989), 22.
2. Kurt Hanks and Larry Belliston, *Draw! A Visual Approach to Thinking, Learning and Communicating* (Los Angeles: Kaufman, 1977), 11.
3. All references to Lorca's writing are taken from the Aguilar edition of his complete works: *Obras Completas*, (Madrid: Aguilar, 1989).
4. Philip Rawson, *The Art of Drawing* (Englewood Cliffs, N.J.: Prentice-Hall, 1984), 7.
5. Mario Hernández, *LLS*, 15.
6. Kimon Nicolaïdes, *The Natural Way to Draw* (Boston: Houghton Mifflin, 1969), xiii.
7. Rawson, *Art of Drawing*, 37.
8. Rawson, *Art of Drawing*, 7.
9. Professor Snitzer's review of Lorca's drawings may be found in the 3 Decem-

ber 1990 edition of the *Barnard Bulletin*, 17. She also shared her reflections with me in a personal interview.

10. Hernández, *LLS*, 87.

11. From "Some Comments on García Lorca's Aesthetics," a conference given at the opening of the exhibition of Lorca's drawings at Duke University Museum of Art, Durham, N.C., 1 March 1991. Mr. Fernández Montesinos graciously provided me with a copy of his remarks.

12. In a 1948 interview, Joan Miró, speaking of his own work, said, "We Catalans believe you must always plant your feet firmly on the ground if you want to be able to jump up in the air. The fact that I come down to earth from time to time makes it possible for me to jump all the higher." Joan Miró, *Selected Writings and Interviews*, ed. Margit Rowell (Boston: G. K. Hall, 1986), 211. Lorca's drawings are often compared to Miro's, and there existed a mutual admiration between the two artists.

13. Hernández, *LLS*, 11.

14. Mario Hernández cites this influence in "Ronda de los autorretratos con animal fabuloso y análisis de dos dibujos neoyorquinos," *Dibujos*, 112.

15. Tim Mathews, "Figure/Text," *Paragraph: The Journal of the Modern Critical Theory Group* 6 (1985): 28.

16. See Jean Gebser, *Lorca: poète-dessinateur*, (Paris: GLM, 1949); Gregorio Prieto, *Dibujos de Garcia Lorca* (Madrid: Aguado, 1949), *Garcia Lorca as a Painter* (London: De La More, 1946); and Helen Oppenheimer, *Lorca: The Drawings: Their Relation to the Poet's Life and Work* (London: Herbert, 1986).

17. Prieto, *Dibujos de Garcia Lorca*, 22.

18. Loughran states that "the difficulty with this (Gebser's) approach is its very modestly substantiated and overly biographical nature, which relies on a supposed mother fixation and father rejection." Loughran also quotes Joseph Gorman that each of the drawings presented by Gebser is "given an appropriately mysterious and imposing interpretation which, while interesting, does not seem at all definitive or conclusive." *Federico García Lorca: The Poetry of Limits* (London: Tamesis, 1978), 198. See also "Impressions of Lorca," *Book Review, Times Literary Supplement*, 11 May 1951, 294.

19. See Ian Gibson, *Federico García Lorca: A Life* (New York: Pantheon, 1989).

20. In 1984, six years after Loughran's book, Estelle Irizarry concurred, "this aspect of his [Lorca's] creativity has attracted limited critical attention and is seldom treated in relation to his literature." *Writer-Painters of Contemporary Spain* (Boston: Twayne, 1984), 55.

21. For example, Loughran observes, "One must always bear in mind the discussion of the following recurrent symbols or images that has taken place in preceding chapters: roots, hands, arrows, sailors, the circle, Love, vines/grass/weeds, the moon, the balcony, and the general interior-exterior or upward-downward tension that has been dealt with at length in Lorca's work as a whole." *Poetry of Limits*, 199.

22. Ibid., 199.

23. Felicia Londré Hardison, *Federico García Lorca* (New York: Frederick Ungar, 1984).

24. Londré, *Federico García Lorca*, 90.

25. Estelle Irizarry, *Painter-Poets of Contemporary Spain* (Boston: Twayne, 1984).

26. See Federico García Lorca, *Dibujos*, ed. Mario Hernández (Madrid: Ministerio de Cultura, 1986).

27. Rudolf Arnheim, "The Reading of Images and the Images of Reading," in *Space, Time, Image, Sign: Essays on Literature and the Visual Arts*, ed. James A. W. Heffernan (New York: Peter Lang, 1987), 84.

28. See Susanne Langer, "Deceptive Analogies: Specious and Real Relationships among the Arts," in *Modern Culture and the Arts*, ed. James B. Hall and Barry Ulanov (New York: McGraw-Hill, 1987), 27.

29. Langer, "Deceptive Analogies," 25.

30. Lucia García de Carpi affirms, "In spite of this simplicity of means, the plastic work of Federico García Lorca demonstrates the assimilation of the most advanced formulations of the painting of the moment. García Lorca did not ever possess the same recourses of an academic formation, but his drawings are infantile only when he wants them to be. He knew how to articulate distinct planes by means of lines, he had an acknowledged precision in drafting, as the ovals of his faces and the arabesques of his initials attest, and he possessed an exquisite sense of proportion, evident in the stylized designs of his signatures and in the distribution of figures over the surface of the paper, something which, unfortunately only a few times has been respected at the moment of reproducing his drawings] "Bajo el astro," *Dibujos*, 34.

Chapter 2. Reading Poetry and Plasticity

1. Lorca's exposure to the artistic currents of his day in both the Residencia de estudiantes in Madrid and in Catalonia are reported by Eugenio Carmona, "<<Sin Tortura ni sueño>> La Renovación plástica española de los años 20 y García Lorca, dibujante," in *Homenaje a Federico García Lorca*, ed. Manuel Alvar (Málaga: Ayuntamiento de Málaga, 1988), 113, 117, and by Andrés Soria Olmedo in "Federico García Lorca y el arte," in *Lecciones sobre Federico García Lorca* (Granada: Comisión Nacional del Cincuentenario, 1986), 59, among others.

2. Soria Olmedo, "Lorca y el arte," 62.

3. Carmona, "Sin Tortura ni sueño," 114.

4. This intertextuality is mutual. It is analyzed by Rafael Santos Torroella, "Barradas—Lorca—Dali: Temas compartidos," *Dibujos*, 39–53, and by Antonina Rodrigo, *Lorca-Dalí Una amistad traicionada* (Barcelona: Planeta, 1981).

5. See, for example, Andrés Soria Olmedo, "Federico García Lorca y el arte;" Cecilia Castro Lee, "La Oda a Salvador Dalí: Significación y trascendencia en la vida y creación de Lorca y Dalí," *Anales de Literature Española Contemporanea* 11 (1986): 61–78; Paul Ilie, *The Surrealist Mode in Spanish Literature* (Ann Arbor: University of Michigan, 1968); Mario Hernández, *LLS*, for analysis of the poem along these lines. My observations do not represent a rejection of their analysis, but rather the position that another reading is possible.

6. *LLS*, 21, 27.

7. Dalí is quoted by Robert Descharnes in his book *The World of Salvador Dalí* (New York: Viking, 1962), 21.

8. *LLS*, 19.

9. *LLS*, 129.

10. See James Hall, *Dictionary of Symbols and Subjects in Art* (New York: Harper and Row, 1974), 58.

11. See Terence McMullan, "Federico García Lorca's 'Santa Lucía y San Lázaro' and the Aesthetics of Transition," *Bulletin of Hispanic Studies* 67 (1990): 1–20. As examples, McMullan cites an article in *Verso y prosa*, which in January of 1927 introduced Lorca as an up-and-coming author but mentioned only *Impresiones y paisajes* (published in 1918) as his literary production and described him as a Gypsy. Although McMullan shows that the article was meant to be "a witty display of teasing

banter," Lorca complained in several letters about the restrictive impression it created at a time when he wished to be recognized for a "mature creative personality" (1–2).

12. See Patrick Fourneret, "Dibujos de Lorca: Soportes, técnicas, y epocas," *Dibujos*, 72. Fourneret's article offers an in-depth analysis of these drawings.

13. Mario Hernández, "El Arte del dibujo en la creación de García Lorca," in *Federico García Lorca Saggi critici nel cinquantenario della morte*, ed. Gabrielle Morelli (Rome: Schena, 1988), 121.

14. Gibson, *A Life*, 190–1.

15. Carmona, "Sin Tortura ni sueño," 115.

16. Carmona observes, "In the articles he publishes in *L'Amic* [*des Arts*] as well as in *La Gaceta [Literaria]*, from the beginning of 1927 to the end of 1928, the references to Totalism are constant." ("Sin Tortura ni sueño," 118).

17. See Carmona: "He explains continually the sense that he himself finds in his drawings, he asks Gasch's opinion courteously, takes in many of these valuations, even entire sentences when he writes about the "new" drawer." ("Sin Tortura ni · sueño, 119).

18. Gasch, "Pintura y cinema," GL, 272.

19. In this same article, a review of Dalí's work published in *La Gaceta Literaria in April of 1927*, Gasch writes: "The regenerative pictoric movement that has been named Cubism—purely instinctive in its beginnings—once a unified, reconstructive period, became the easy prey of the profiteers and of the ambitious, of the cerebral and theoretitians, who seized it completely and did not delay in imprisioning it behind the grill of precise formulas mathematically fixed, converting it into a collection of coldly engendered postulates. This eagerness to explain the inexplicable, to reason that which does not admit reasoning, to encode a thing so little inclined to being encoded as is the artistic deed, did not delay in producing its fruits." ("Salvador Dalí," *GL*, 84).

20. Gasch, "El pintor Joan Miró," *GL*, 45.

21. Gasch, "La Exposición en Dalmau," *GL*, 168.

22. See Gasch, "Salvador Dalí," *GL*, 84.

23. See Gasch, "El arte poético y plástico del pintor Domingo," *GL*, 310.

24. Gasch, "Del cubismo al superrealismo," *GL*, 121

25. These critics include Soria Olmedo, "Lorca y el arte," 67; Francisco Cao, "Tradición y originalidad en la iconografía lorquiana," *Lecturas del texto dramático: Variaciones sobre la obra de Lorca* (Oviedo: Universidad de Oviedo, 1990): 21, and García de Carpi: "Despite all that he (Lorca) declared, he conformed to the plastic formulations of surrealism. . . . the processes employed by García Lorca in the realization of the drawings to which he alludes in a letter directed to the same Catalan critic could not be more conclusive. Here appear annotated the two options that permit the abandon of the artist to the dictates of automatism, the basis of Surrealism, on one hand allow the hand to operate under the impulses of the subconscious without any kind of control, although later the painter might be able to add to the design thus birthed, sketches that contribute to the standing out of the suggestions that such a design provoke in him; on the other hand, in a faithful manner to give concrete form to the images that flowered already formed by the subconscious" ("Bajo el astro," *Dibujos*, 35).

26. Gasch quotes Bretón: "The marvellous is always beautiful, whatever marvellous thing is beautiful, there is no marvellous thing that is not beautiful." "Del cubismo al superrealismo," (*Gl*, 121).

27. Fourneret, "Dibujos de Lorca," 70.

28. Carmona, "Sin Tortura ni sueño," 124.

29. See Carl G. Jung, "On the Relation of Analytical Psychology to Poetry," in *The Spirit in Man, Art, and Literature*, trans. R.F.C. Hull, vol. 15 of *The Collected Works of C. G. Jung* (New York: Bollingen, 1966), 73.

30. Dalí, "Realidad y Sobrerrealidad," *GL*, 283.

31. See C. B. Morris, *Surrealism and Spain* (Cambridge: Cambridge University Press, 1972), 6.

32. McMullan, "The Aesthetics of Transition," 4.

33. Describing Domingos's painting, Gasch wrote in 1928: "These words can summarize perfectly the spiritual role of art. In the first place, to extract the hidden substance of things that the majority of persons does not see and that only the artist knows how to discern. That is, to discover the deep reality, the superreality the lyricism of reality, the substance of things, or however it might be named, that all these words are good to signify the spirit that lives in the material" ("El arte poético y plástico del pintor Domingo," *GL*, 310).

34. See Gasch: "Finally, let us summarize: Surrealism in its absolutely pueril nature, is no more than the imagination taken to its ultimate consequences. Untiring seekers in the world of the unknown, the Surrealists desire to reach the super-reality, that is, the reality sublimated, exceeded, and over-refined by fantasy and imagination. This doctrine does not standout because of its novelty. Its very promoters do not exalt themselves for having invented something new. According to Breton, Dante, Shakespeare, Chateaubriand, Hugo, Poe, Baudelaire, all the artists of imagination, were in fact more or less Surrealists." ("Del cubismo al superrealismo," *GL*, 121).

35. Fourneret, "Dibujos de Lorca," 80.

36. See J. H. Matthews, *Eight Painters: the Surrealist Context* (Syracuse, N.Y.: Syracuse University Press, 1982), 3.

37. Ibid., 123.

38. Gasch, "Salvador Dalí," *GL*, 84.

39. Gasch, "La Exposición en Dalmau," *GL*, 168.

40. Gibson, *A Life*, 190.

41. Hernández, "El Arte del dibujo," 125.

42. Fourneret, "Dibujos de Lorca," 80.

43. R. Santos Torroella copied the letter from the original [now lost] and published it in *ABC* 2 October 1990.

44. See Gasch, "Lorca, dibujante," *GL*, 4.

45. Carmona, "Sin Tortura ni sueño," 123.

46. Soria Olmedo, "Lorca y el arte," 64.

47. This comment raises another possibility for the reading of Lorca in terms of his "re-humanizing" his art. Both Guillermo Díaz Plaja (*Federico García Lorca: Su obra e influencia en la poesía española* [Buenos Aires: Kraft, 1954], 157) and Gil Casado (*La novela social española* [Barcelona: Seix Barral, 1975], 101) have counterpoised the aesthetics of New Romanticism alongside those of Surrealism in Lorca's work.

48. Soria Olmedo "Lorca y el arte," 64.

49. *LLS*, 21.

50. See McMullan, "The Aesthetics of Transition," 2.

51. Gibson, *A Life*, 192.

52. Morris, *Surrealism and Spain*, 50.

53. Conversation, March 1992.

54. See Edwin Honig, "Santa Lucía y San Lázaro," *New Directions* 8 (1944): 381.

55. Michael Riffaterre, *Semiotics of Poetry* (Bloomington: Indiana University Press, 1978), 185.

56. Ibid., 63.

57. Gibson, *A Life*, 191.

58. This is not Lorca's invention. The legend surrounding the martyrdom of St. Lucy includes this detail.

59. Riffaterre, *Semiotics of Poetry*, 8–9.

60. Writing about Lorca's work in general, Rafael Alberti described the transition in Lorca's aesthetics this way: "He has passed from the direct to the indirect, from the seen to the glimpsed, from the real to the dreamed, but not as nebulous, because there is always a handle, a guiding thread that gives to the mystery a greater and more attractive depth." ("Líneas y colores," *Trece de Nieve* 1–2 (1976): 154–55).

61. McMullan explains much of the enigmatic imagery in this piece as references to the city of Barcelona and especially its cathedral, where there is a chapel of St. Lucy, an image of the saint, and where devotion to her continues to this day. See "The Aesthetics of Transition," 9–11.

62. Candelas Newton observes that "The senses, especially sight with the eyes and sound in general all the sensorial elements, possess in the author's poetic world an essentially vital value. Besides conducting life and flourishing, the senses are the door of access to the precinct of the ideal. Its possession brings with it the light of orientaion in the chaos of the world and the possibility of penetrating and capturing the esssence of Total Being." (*Lorca: Libro de Poemas*, [Salamanca: Universidad de Salamanca, 1986], 138–39).

63. McMullan reads this entire section as a statement of their blindness: "Suspicions of visual handicap, aroused when their muffled voices, 'como dos topos huidos, tropezaban con las paredes' [like two fleeing moles, were banging into the walls] are confirmed by an involuntary failure of normal eye contact between them: 'se miraron . . .' [they looked at one another]." "The Aesthetics of Transition," 10.

64. One interesting example of the dynamic of Lorca's observation and transformation of what he observes involves his use of the image of the crocodile in his book *Poeta en Nueva York*. Much speculation has occurred surrounding possible explanations of this image; a basic one is that many streets of New York in 1929 were cobblestoned, bearing a resemblance to the reptile's skin. This man is removing man-hole covers with a crowbar. (Conversation with Robert C. Manteiga, 12 October 1990.

65. Mary Ann Caws, *The Eye in the Text* (Princeton: Princeton University Press, 1981), 17.

66. McMullan, "The Aesthetics of Transition," 8.

67. McMullan, "The Aesthetics of Transition." See note 12 of McMullan's article for more connections between the Lazarus figure of Lorca's text and that of Christ.

68. Fourneret summarizes the effect of such treatment of images: ""The drawing delivers in its entirety a union of elements reduced in number, but by means of its great stylization and emotional and evocative power, perception is immediate." ("Dibujos de Lorca," 80).

69. Honig, "Santa Lucía y San Lázaro," 381.

70. McMullan, "The Aesthetics of Transition," 14.

71. Gasch, "El arte poético y plástico del pintor Domingo," *GL*, 310.

72. Fourneret observes, "The line seems to acquire a complete plastic autonomy, free, but only in appearance, from any intention of representation or figuration. The wandering (lines) construct in reality, markedly abstract human figures in the lyric

mode, but easily identifiable; the pair of lovers and, throwing herself head first, the swimmer of the corresponding poem." ("Dibujos de Lorca," 79).

73. See Loughran, *Poetry of Limits*, 200–201. These poems are also analyzed by Moraima Semprún in *Las narraciones de Federico García Lorca: Un franco enfoque* (Barcelona: Hispam, 1975).

74. This same image is repeated in "La Vista y el tacto" [Sight and touch] in which all the lines proceed from a similar rectangle.

75. This resembles Lorca's drawing of body hair in other drawings, such as "Aleluya del Marinero y su novia" [Alleluia of the sailor and his bride].

76. Among them is Fourneret, "Dibujos de Lorca," 79.

77. "Carefully elected, some elements submit in these 'abstractions' to the real, . . . 'magic keys' of the drawings that anchor them in reality" (Fourneret, "Dibujos de Lorca," 79).

78. Loughran, *Poetry of Limits*, 200.

79. For a reading of all the homosexual imagery present in the text, see Semprún. The number nine carries homosexual connotations. *Las narraciones de Lorca*, 46.

80. Hernández, "El Arte del dibujo," 128.

81. These expressions also are in keeping with the poem's having been dedicated to the musician Manuel de Falla.

82. Marie Laffranque provides this reading of the poem's dynamic: "He (God) only knows impurity or tearing in order to bring them a symbolic redemption: to unite under one same sign that which is opposed" (*Les Idées esthétiques de Federico García Lorca* (Paris: Institut d'Etudes Hispaniques, 1968), 205).

83. See Christopher Eich, *Federico García Lorca, poeta de la intensidad*, trans. Gonzalo Sobejano (Madrid: Gredos, 1970), 119. Eich concludes: "The poet desires to possess Christ in like manner. Not as a rigid, far-off effigy, which a supplication can hardly reach, not as incomprehensible dogma, nor as an abstract and inoperative article of faith, but as a present, outlined figure, close to the senses. Not projected into a vague infinity, but limited in form and time, in the moment of encounter; concrete, approachable, nameable, uncontradictibly real, as when He sojourned on earth. Not in an inanimate imitation, but in the very moment of his bodily presentation. As a brief form is how Lorca desires to possess Christ."

84. Gibson observes: "It is significant that, in the extract which Lorca included with the letter, from the section 'The Devil, Second Enemy of the Soul,' the emphasis is on sexuality without love, on the Devil's resplendent beauty 'without nostalgia or dream' (a phrase reminiscent of Dalí) on his concern of present ecstasy, with no personal allegiance or responsibility." *A Life*, 215. The faithfulness embodied in the Eucharist serves as an example of what Lorca is seeking in both his personal life and his artistic expression.

85. Laffranque believes that this paradigm is identified with Impressionism: "The devil is the semblance and the mutilated form of love. A game of wounded edges, of splinters and of reflections, of strips and of cold rays. One thinks of a cruel Impressionism, reduced to a type of mineral light or of certain of Carra's paintings" (Les Idées esthétiques, 206).

86. It is then no coincidence that the homosexual then, enters here as well: Hernández notes that "It is inevitable that one should mention to this end the burlesque and delicately dramatic representation of another homosexual couple in the New York work. "Man and young sailor," as well as to remember the pressure of the theme in poems of the period, from the unfinished "Ode to Sesostris" to the ode dedicated to Walt Whitman in *Poet in New York*. Presently, in "Flesh," the last section of the quoted "Ode to the Holy Sacrament," Lorca writes,

Come, come! The veins extend their points
to bite the comb of the mooned cayman
while the blood of Sodom glistens
through the hall of a rigid aluminum heart."

Dibujos, 95

87. García de Carpi notes his "proclivity toward the enigmatic, the dark and the lethal" ("Bajo el astro," 36).

88. "Perhaps one has never seen aesthethic concerns and a metaphysic and moral anxiety for the fate of humanity so intimately joined in his work. One has never been able to ascertain to what degree all abstract and conventional solution remains powerless and more or less illusory in the face of his personal drama" (Laffranque, Les Idées esthétiques, 205–6).

Chapter 3. Reading Space and Subject

1. See Dennis, "Lorca in the Looking Glass: On Mirrors and Self-Contemplation," in *Cuando yo me muera: Essays in Memory of Federico García Lorca*, ed. C. Brian Morris (Lanham, Md.: University Press of America, 1988), 41–42.

2. Specifically, in this chapter, I shall refer to Nigel Dennis's article (see note above), to Christopher Flint, "Flesh of the Body: Representations of the Body in *Romancero gitano* and *Poeta en Nueva York*," *Papers on Language and Literature* 24 (1988): 177–211, and Harriet Turner, "Lorquian Reflections: 'Romance del emplazado,'" *Hispania* 70 (1987): 447–56. Although Turner's article focuses on one specific poem, the "Romance del emplazado," her observations aptly convey many dynamics generally present in Lorca's poetry.

3. See Maurice Blanchot, "Mallarmé and Literary Space," in *The Siren's Song: Selected essays by Maurice Blanchot*, ed. Gabriel Josipovici (Bloomington: Indiana University Press, 1982), 110.

4. Recall Gasch's insistence that "What is essential for the artist are the resonances of his interior world upon colliding with the exterior world." "Lorca, dibujante." (*GL*, 4).

5. See Arnheim, "Space as an Image of Time," in *Images of Romanticism: Verbal and Visual Affinities*, ed. Karl Kroeber and William Walling (New Haven: Yale University Press, 1978), 7.

6. See Edward Casey, "Imagination and Repetition in Literature: A Reassessment," *Yale French Studies* 52 (1975): 255, and Louis Renza, "Response to W.J.T. Mitchell," in *Space, Time, Image, Sign: Essays on Literature and the Visual Arts*, ed. James A. W. Heffernan (New York: Peter Lang, 1987), 11–14.

7. Michael Cohen cites "the twentieth century's more revolutionary attempts to deal with space and time, such as Duchamp's *Nude Descending a Staircase* and Picasso's faces combining front view and profile." See "Lessing on Time and Space in the Sister Arts: The Artist's Refutation," in *Lessing and the Enlightenment*, ed. Alexej Ugrinsky (New York: Greenwood, 1986), 15.

8. Carlos Bousoño, *Teoría de la expresión poética* (Madrid: Gredos, 1976).

9. Cohen, "Time and Space in the Sister Arts," 14.

10. See Lawrence Klibbe's important study of this text, *Lorca's Impresiones y paisajes: The Young Artist* (Madrid: Porrúa Turanzas, 1983), 29.

11. "Without the shaping force of repetition, this imagination is tempted to wander aimlessly beyond the bounds of the work and the world" (Casey, "Imagination and Repetition," 255).

12. Francisco Cao notes that: "Federico never re-creates free-flowing water, he employs it as a dominated force, which returns our gaze once more to that great cultural magma of the Mediterranean world which, since antiquity, and especially with the Roman Empire uses water daily and defines urban life, in relation with "otium" in themes and fountains. The arab world, from which Federico was also nurtured, would also employ water within these same architectural premises, but in a more intimate and less turbulent tone" (Tradición y originalidad en la iconografía lorquiana.) (37).

13. Hernández, *Dibujos*, 93.

14. Prieto, *García Lorca as a Painter*, 7.

15. Oppenheimer identifies these values in *Lorca: The Drawings*, 86.

16. Hernández, *LLS*, 66.

17. Gasch described such art and its artists as: "Characterized from the plastic point of view by a renaissance of color, a color rich in dramatic expression and from the lyrical point of view, by an exaltation of the tragic—they did not tire of preaching the excellences of an emotive art, to the detriment of a cerebral plasticity" ("Salvador Dalí," *GL*, 84).

18. See Candelas Newton's discussion of this theme in *Lorca: Una escritura en trance* (Amsterdam: Benjamins, 1992), 122.

19. Bousoño, *Teoría de la expresión poética*, 406.

20. Lorca's use of terminology provides yet another layer to the reading of this poem, if one recalls that he subtitled the play "Romance popular en tres estampas" [Popular ballad in three engravings], indicating in the prologue that the play's setting was to provide the sensation or appearance of "una vieja estampa iluminada . . . una de las casas que se ven pintada con escenas marinas" [an old illuminated engraving . . . one of the houses seen painted with marine scenes] *O.C.* 2:165.

21. Turner, "Lorquian Reflections," 448.

22. Rafael Santos Torroella, "Barradas—Lorca—Dalí: Temas compartidos," *Dibujos*, 51.

23. Hernández, *Dibujos*, 150.

24. Andrés Soria Olmedo, "Federico García Lorca y el arte," 69.

25. Caws, *Eye in the Text*, 88.

26. Bousoño, *Teoría de la expresión poética*, 428.

27. My study of Lorca's original manuscripts was made possible by photocopies graciously provided by Manuel Fernández Montesinos of the Fundación García Lorca.

28. In addition to his study of Góngora and his familiarity with the artistic currents of his own time, Lorca watched with interest the evolving field of film and its potential. Sebastià Gasch, speaking of film, reiterated this multiperspective character delineation. While acknowledging the cinematic image's capability of giving the viewer a rounded view of the subject, Gasch reminds his readers that even the camera cannot offer such an image instantaneously: "with the juxtaposition of images, it comes to give us a complete idea of the persons and things represented. An identical juxtaposition of images is observed in the Cubist canvasses of the first period. It is what has been called optical synthesis. That is, the total figuration of the objects, or the simultaneous representation of different aspects of things, this is, the same object seen from the front, back, and in profile." ("Pintura y cinema, *GL*, 272).

29. See John Crosbie, "Structure and Counter-Structure in Lorca's *Romancero gitano*," *Modern Language Review* 77 (1982): 76.

30. Turner, "Lorquian Reflections," 449.

31. See Robert G. Havard, introduction and commentary in *Gypsy Ballads*, by Federico García Lorca (Warminster: Aris and Phillips, 1990), 16.

32. Dennis, "Lorca in the Looking Glass," 46.

33. Havard, *Gypsy Ballads*, 134.

34. Flint, "Flesh of the Body," 204.

35. See Karl Lugwig Selig, "Lorca's Santa Olalla and the Problems of the Text," *Teaching Language through Literature* 24 (1985): 46.

36. H. Ramsden, introduction to *Romancero gitano*, by Federico García Lorca (Manchester: Manchester, 1988), 67.

37. Selig notes the choice of tense and its function: "The text/story is set in Hispano-Roman times, but one should note a dominant present tense: the temporal sphere emphasizes presentness and an evocation of presentness, and in this way the "story" is brought to the present" ("Lorca's Santa Olalla," 45).

38. Havard states that "The relevance of the poem to the volume as a whole clearly centers on the issue of oppression by force, while there is too a strong sense of sexual innocence being abused or perverted by an unjust authority" (*Gypsy Ballads*, 157).

39. Flint concludes that, in *Romancero gitano* and in *Poeta en Nueva York*, "The suffering body does not exclusively signal in Lorca's poetry the experience of marginal individuals or groups. It also comes to represent the human condition in a more general sense since it is consistently linked to the surface of the world itself. As microcosm, the anguished body connotes a world in the throes of pain" ("Flesh of the Body," 199).

40. Selig, "Lorca's Santa Olalla," 46.

41. Flint, "Flesh of the Body," 199.

42. Havard, *Gypsy Ballads*, 158.

43. See Ramsden: "Apotheosis, with a monstrance that shines amidst a world reborn, with stream gorges where there was frozen water, nightingales in branches where there were 'brazos sin hojas' [arms without leaves] and leaping colours where there was inert whiteness, Olalla's elevation is finally confirmed by association with Catholic liturgy and direct quotation from it" (*Romancero gitano*, 160).

44. Hernánadez, LLS, 29.

45. See Andrew Anderson, *Lorca's Late Poetry: A Critical Study* (Leeds: Francis Cairns, 1990), 8.

46. García de Carpi, "Bajo el astro de la noche," *Dibujos*, 36.

47. García de Carpi, "Bajo el astro de la noche," *Dibujos*, 37; J. H.Matthews, *Eight Painters*, 71; and Cecilia Castro Lee, "La 'Oda a Salvador Dalí:' Significación y trascendencia en la vida y creación de Lorca y Dalí," *Anales de Literatura Española Contemporanea* 11 (1986): 73.

48. Oppenheimer, *Lorca: The Drawings*, 91.

49. Flint, "Flesh of the Body," 202.

50. Flint notes this dynamic in Poeta en Nueva York: "This bodilessness or absence becomes a kind of keynote. One encounters in almost every poem some reference to 'huecos,''obscuros,' 'huellas,' 'vacío,' [holes, dark, footprints, empty], etc." ("Flesh of the Body," 186).

51. Hernández, *Dibujos*, 88, 91.

52. Dennis, "Lorca in the Looking Glass," 46.

53. Hernández, *Dibujos*, 96.

54. Flint, "Flesh of the Body," 202.

55. Caws, *Eye in the Text*, 89.

56. Paul Ilie, *Surrealist Mode in Spanish Literature*, 77.

57. Caws, *Eye in the Text*, 92.

58. These details are documented and illuminated by Andrew Anderson in his chapter on the "Llanto" in *Lorca's Late Poetry*.

59. See Andrew Anderson, ed., *Diván del Tamarit, Seis poemas gallegos, Llanto por Ignacio Sánchez Mejías*, by Federico García Lorca (Madrid: Espasa Calpe, 1988), 285.

60. Anderson documents this fact, as well as the information that the phrase "a las cinco de la tarde" [at five in the afternoon] was a catch phrase used by the press at the time to write of the bullfighter's demise. *Diván del Tamarit*, 285.

61. Anderson, *Lorca's Late Poetry*, 177.

62. Anderson, *Diván del Tamarit*, 290.

63. Anderson, *Diván del Tamarit*, 295–96.

Chapter 4. Reading Arabesques: Lines and Words Together

1. Mary Ann Caws and Richard Klein have studied the arabesque in both Baroque or Rococo artistic expression as well as in modern work. See Mary Ann Caws, "Reflections in a Rococo Eye: Arabesques and Serpentines," chap. 5 of *The Eye in the Text* (Princeton: Princeton University Press, 1981), and Richard Klein, "Straight Lines and Arabesques: Metaphors of Metaphor," *Yale French Studies* 45 (1970): 64–86.

2. Fourneret explains: "This fondness for the line, usually thin and sinuous, could be related to writing and calligraphy, and, why not, could have its source of inspiration in the Koranic versicles that adorn the Alhambra of Granada" ("Dibujos de Lorca," 78).

3. Bousoño, *Teoría de la expresión poética*, 428.

4. Fourneret, "Dibujos de Lorca," 79.

5. Caws, *Eye in the Text*, 71.

6. Klein, "Straight lines and arabesques," 66.

7. For Hernández's description of this drawing, see *Dibujos*, 178.

8. As we have seen, this is not the first appearance of words in Lorca's drawings. They are present in at least two previous drawings, in a manner resembling those to be discussed here, but their use is not so complicated. In *Muchacha granadina en un jardín*, dated 1925 (not the drawing analyzed in an earlier chapter), for example, the word *AMOR* is written on a wall behind the central figure, much in the way *ROMA* appears in this drawing. In drawings of sailors, the word *AMOR* is written on a sailor's cap. Both instances bear similarity in both the word used, its position and the sailor motif, with the drawing under discussion here.

9. For Mario Hernández, the reference to Rome relates to the reference to the city represented in *Poeta en Nueva York*: ". . . One of the roots of "Shout toward Rome" and of the same "Dance of Death" is surely in the condemnation and threat of destruction of Babylon produced in Isaiah, Jeremiah, and St. John, although the point of view adopted by the modern poet, which puts nature and civilization face to face, is very different" ("Ronda de autorretratos," *Dibujos*, 94).

10. Gallego, Julián, "Arabescas," *Dibujos*, 31.

11. Klein, "Straight Lines and Arabesques," 81.

12. Ibid., 75.

13. See Candelas Newton, *Escritura en trance*, for discussion of the sexual imagery at work in the poem.

14. Caws, *Eye in the Text*, 77.

15. Hernández, *Dibujos*, 94.

16. See Candelas Newton, *Escritura en trance*, 122.

17. Honig, "The Diván at the Tamarit," *New Directions* 8 (1944): 361.

18. The Oxford English Dictionary cites Jabir, an Arabian alchemist who used the sign to indicate either a closed system or any eternal process (19:34). I have not been able to substantiate Lorca's direct knowledge of this figure, but the Arab context and the double significance of the image are both appropriate, given his aesthetics.

19. Diener, Pablo, "Lichtlos ist der Horizont" *du* 11 (1986): 78.

20. Christopher Maurer quoted this line from an unpublished manuscript "Twelve Rules for the Poet," which he read on 3 December 1990 at New York University at the symposium held during the exhibition of Lorca's drawings in New York. Maurer later repeated this same rule to me in a conversation on 23 March 1991 at the symposium held during the exhibition of Lorca's drawings at the Duke University Museum of Art, Durham, N.C.

Chapter 5. Conclusion

1. See Stanley Fish, *Is There a Text in This Class?* (Cambridge: Harvard University Press, 1980), 23.

2. Caws, *Eye in the Text*, 4.

3. Renza, "Response to W.J.T. Mitchell," 14.

4. Arnheim, "Images of Reading," 83–87.

5. Mary Ann Caws coins this phrase in *Eye in the Text*, 4. This notion is not new; it reflects the nature and role of poetry espoused by Russian Formalism, Shklovsky among them. Just as these theorists asserted that the defamiliarizing nature of poetic language had aesthetic motives and potential, so I have shown Lorca's position that his "drawn poems" could suggest new interpretation of meaning.

Bibliography

Primary Sources

García Lorca, Federico. *Dibujos*. Edited by Mario Hernández. Madrid: Ministerio de Cultura, 1986.

———. *Obras Completas*. Madrid: Aguilar, 1989.

Studies

Alberti, Rafael. "Líneas y colores." *Trece de Nieve* 1–2 (1976): 153–55.

Anderson, Andrew. *Lorca's Late Poetry: A Critical Study*. Leeds: Francis Cairns, 1990.

Anderson, Andrew, ed. *Diván del Tamarit, Seis poemas gallegos, Llanto por Ignacio Sánchez Mejías*, by Federico García Lorca. Madrid: Espasa Calpe, 1988.

Arnheim, Rudolf. "A Plea for Visual Thinking." In *The Language of Images*, edited by W. J. T. Mitchell. Chicago: University of Chicago Press, 1980.

———. "The Reading of Images and the Images of Reading." In *Space, Time, Image, Sign: Essays on Literature and the Visual Arts*, edited by James A. W. Heffernan. New York: Peter Lang, 1987.

———. "Space as an Image of Time." In *Images of Romanticism: Verbal and Visual Affinities*, edited by Karl Kroeber and William Walling. New Haven: Yale University Press, 1978.

Barricelli, Jean-Pierre, and Joseph Gibaldi, eds. *Interrelations of Literature*. New York: Modern Language Association, 1982.

Berroa, Rei. "Manos y ojos: Dos símbolos clave de la poesía y la pintura de García Lorca." *Mundo* [Mexico] 1 (1987): 110–22.

Blanchot, Maurice. "Mallarmé and Literary Space." *The Siren's Song: Selected Essays by Maurice Blanchot*. Edited by Gabriel Josipovici. Bloomington: Indiana University Press, 1982.

Bousoño, Carlos. *Teoría de la expresión poética*. Madrid: Gredos, 1976.

Cao, Francisco. "Tradición y originalidad en la iconografía lorquiana." *Lecturas del texto dramático: Variaciones sobre la obra de Lorca*. Oviedo: Universidad de Oviedo, 1990.

Carmona, Eugenio. "<<Sin Tortura ni sueño>> La Renovación plástica española de los años 20 y García Lorca, dibujante." In *Homenaje a Federico García Lorca*, edited by Manuel Alvar. Málaga: Ayuntamiento de Málaga, 1988.

Casey, Edward. "Imagination and Repetition in Literature: A Reassessment." *Yale French Studies* 52 (1975): 249–67.

Castro Lee, Cecilia. "La 'Oda a Salvador Dalí': Significación y trascendencia en la vida y creación de Lorca y Dalí." *Anales de Literature Española Contemporanea* 11 (1986): 61–78.

Caws, Mary Ann. *The Eye in the Text.* Princeton: Princeton University Press, 1981.

Cheney, Seldon. *A Primer of Modern Art.* New York: Liveright, 1966.

Cohen, Michael. "Lessing on Time and Space in the Sister Arts: The Artist's Refutation." In *Lessing and the Enlightenment,* edited by Alexej Ugrinsky, 13–23. New York: Greenwood, 1986.

Crosbie, John. "Structure and Counter-Structure in Lorca's *Romancero gitano.*" *Modern Language Review* 77 (1982): 74–88.

Dalí, Salvador. "Realidad y Sobrerrealidad." *La Gaceta Literaria* 1 (1927–29): 283.

Dennis, Nigel. "Lorca in the Looking Glass: On Mirrors and Self-Contemplation." In *Cuando yo me muera: Essays in Memory of Federico García Lorca,* edited by C. Brian Morris. Lanham, Md.: University Press of America, 1988.

Descharnes, Robert. *The World of Salvador Dalí.* New York: Viking, 1962.

Díaz Plaja, Guillermo. *Federico García Lorca: Su obra e influencia en la poesía española.* Buenos Aires: Kraft, 1954.

Diener, Pablo. "Lichtlos ist der Horizont" *du* 11 (1986): 76–83.

Eich, Christopher. *Federico García Lorca, poeta de la intensidad.* Translated by Gonzalo Sobejano. Madrid: Gredos, 1970.

Eisenburg, Daniel. "A Catalogue of Lorca's Drawings: Additions and Corrections to Musical Settings of Lorca's Texts." *García Lorca Review* 4 (1976): 13–31.

Fernández-Montesinos García, Manuel. "Some Comments on García Lorca's Aesthetics." Paper presented at Duke University Museum of Art, Durham, N.C., 1 March 1991.

———. "Variantes significativas en algunos borradores de Federico García Lorca." In *L' "imposible/posible" di Federico García Lorca, Atti del convegno de studi,* edited by Laura Doldi. Napoli: Scientifiche Italiane, 1989.

Fish, Stanley. *Is There a Text in this Class?* Cambridge: Harvard University Press, 1980.

Flint, Christopher. "Flesh of the Body: Representations of the Body in *Romancero gitano and Poeta en Nueva York.*" *Papers on Language and Literature* 24 (1988): 177–211.

Fourneret, Patrick. "Dibujos de Lorca: Soportes, técnicas, y epocas." *Dibujos.* 69–84.

Friedman, Norman. "Symbol." *Princeton Encyclopedia of Poetry and Poetics.* Princeton: Princeton University Press, 1965.

Gallego, Julián. "Arabescas." *Dibujos.* 27–32.

Garcia de Carpi, Lucia. "Bajo el astro de la noche." *Dibujos.* 33–58.

Gardner, Howard. *Art, Mind and Brain: A Cognitive Approach to Creativity.* Chicago: Basic Books, 1982.

Gasch, Sebastià. "Del cubismo al superrealismo." *La Gaceta Literaria* 1 (1927–29): 121.

———. "El arte poético y plástico del pintor Domingo." *La Gaceta Literaria* 1 (1927–1929): 310.

———. "La Exposición en Dalmau" *La Gaceta Literaria* 1 (1927–1929): 168.

———. "Lorca, dibujante." *La Gaceta Literaria* 1 (1927–1929): 4.

———. "Obras recientes de Dalí." *La Gaceta Literaria* 1 (1927–29): 335.

———. "El pintor Joan Miró." *La Gaceta Literaria* 1 (1927–1929): 45.

———. "Pintura y cinema." *La Gaceta Literaria* 1 (1927–1929): 272.

———. "Salvador Dalí." *La Gaceta Literaria* 1 (1927–1929): 84.

Gebser, Jean. *Lorca: Poéte-dessinateur.* Paris: GLM, 1949.

Gibson, Ian. *Federico García Lorca: A Life.* New York: Pantheon, 1989.

Gil Casado, Pablo. *La novela social española.* Barcelona: Seix Barral, 1975.

Hall, James. *Dictionary of Symbols and Subjects in Art.* New York: Harper and Row, 1974.

Hanks, Kurt, and Larry Belliston. *Draw! A Visual Approach to Thinking, Learning and Communicating.* Los Angeles: Kaufman, 1977.

Havard, Robert G. Introduction and Commentary to *Gypsy Ballads,* by Federico García Lorca. Warminster: Aris and Phillips, 1990.

Heffernan, James A. W. Preface to *Space, Time, Image, Sign: Essays on Literature and the Visual Arts.* New York: Peter Lang, 1987.

Hernández, Mario. "El Arte del dibujo en la creación de García Lorca." In *Federico García Lorca Saggi critici nel cinquantenario della morte,* edited by Gabrielle Morelli, 119–34. Rome: Schena, 1988.

———. "Catalogación y comentario." *Dibujos.* 117–251.

———. *Line of Light and Shadow: The Drawings of Federico García Lorca,* translated by Christopher Maurer. Durham, N.C.: Duke University Press, 1991.

———. "Ronda de los autorretratos con animal fabuloso y análisis de dos dibujos neoyorquinos." *Dibujos.* 85–116.

Honig, Edwin. "The Diván at the Tamarit and Other Poems." *New Directions* 8 (1944): 360–79.

———. "Santa Lucía y San Lázaro" *New Directions* 8 (1944): 380–90.

Ilie, Paul. *The Surrealist Mode in Spanish Literature.* Ann Arbor: University of Michigan, 1968.

"Impressions of Lorca." *Book Review, Times Literary Supplement,* 11 May 1951, 294.

Irizarry, Estelle. *Writer-Painters of Contemporary Spain.* Boston: Twayne, 1984.

Jung. Carl G. "On the Relation of Analytical Psychology to Poetry." In *The Spirit in Man, Art, and Literature,* trans. R. F. C. Hull, 65–83. Vol. 15 of *The Collected Works of C. G. Jung.* New York: Bollingen, 1966.

Klein, Richard. "Straight Lines and Arabesques: Metaphors of Metaphor." *Yale French Studies* 45 (1970): 64–86.

Klibbe, Lawrence. *Lorca's Impresiones y paisajes: The Young Artist.* Madrid: Porrúa Turanzas, 1983.

Laffranque, Marie. *Les Idées esthétiques de Federico García Lorca.* Paris: Institut d'Etudes Hispaniques, 1968.

Langer, Susanne. "Deceptive Analogies: Specious and Real Relationships among the Arts." In *Modern Culture and the Arts,* edited by James B. Hall and Barry Ulanov, 22–31. New York: McGraw-Hill, 1987.

Londré, Felicia Hardison. *Federico García Lorca.* New York: Frederick Ungar, 1984.

Loughran, David K. *Federico García Lorca: The Poetry of Limits.* London: Tamesis, 1978.

Manteiga, Robert C. Personal Interview, 12 October 1990.

Mathews, Tim. "Figure/Text." *Paragraph: The Journal of the Modern Critical Theory Group* 6 (1985): 28–42.

Matthews, J. H. *Eight Painters: The Surrealist Context*. Syracuse, N.Y.: Syracuse University Press, 1982.

Maurer, Christopher. "Opening Remarks." Panel Commemorating the Fiftieth Anniversary of Federico García Lorca's *Poeta en Nueva York*. New York University, 3 December 1990.

———. Personal Interview, 23 March 1991.

McMullan, Terence. "Federico García Lorca's 'Santa Lucía y San Lázaro' and the Aesthetics of Transition." *Bulletin of Hispanic Studies* 67 (1990): 1–20.

Morris, C. B. *Surrealism and Spain*. Cambridge: Cambridge University Press, 1972.

Newton, Candelas. *Lorca: Libro de poemas*. Salamanca: Universidad de Salamanca, 1986.

———. *Lorca: Una escritura en trance*. Amsterdam: Benjamins, 1992.

———. Personal Interview, 23 March 1991.

Nicolaïdes, Kimon. *The Natural Way to Draw*. Boston: Houghton Mifflin, 1969.

Oppenheimer, Helen. *Lorca: The Drawings: Their Relation to the Poet's Life and Work*. London: Herbert, 1986.

Pratt, Heather. "Place and Displacement in Lorca's *Poeta en Nueva York*." *Forum for Modern Language Studies* 22 (1986): 248–63.

Prieto, Gregorio. *Dibujos de Garcia Lorca*. Madrid: Aguado,1949.

———. *Garcia Lorca as a Painter*. London: De La More, 1946.

Ramsden, H. Introduction. *Romancero gitano*, by Federico García Lorca. Manchester: Manchester, 1988.

Rawson, Philip. *The Art of Drawing*. Englewood Cliffs, N.J.: Prentice-Hall, 1984.

Renza, Louis. "Response to W.J.T. Mithcell." In *Space, Time, Image, Sign: Essays on Literature and the Visual Arts*, edited by James A. W. Heffernan. New York: Peter Lang, 1987.

Riffaterre, Michael. *Semiotics of Poetry*. Bloomington: Indiana University Press, 1978.

Rodrigo, Antonina. *Lorca-Dalí: Una amistad traicionada*. Barcelona: Planeta, 1981.

Rowell, Margit. *The Captured Imagination: Drawings by Joan Miró*. New York: American Foundation of the Arts, 1987.

Rowell, Margit, ed. *Joan Miró: Selected Writings and Interviews*. Boston: G. K. Hall, 1986.

Santos Torroella, Rafael. "Barradas—Lorca—Dali: Temas compartidos." *Dibujos*. 39–53.

Selic, Karl-Lugwig. "Lorca's Santa Olalla and the Problems of the Text." *Teaching Language through Literature* 24 (1985): 45–49.

Semprún. Moraima. *Las narraciones de Federico García Lorca: Un franco enfoque*. Barcelona: Hispam, 1975.

Shklovsky, Victor. "Art as Technique." In *Russian Formalist Criticism: Four Essays*, translated and edited by Lee T. Lemon and Marion J. Reis. Omaha: University of Nebraska Press, 1965.

Signorile, Vito. "Capitulating to Captions: The Verbal Transformation of Visual Images." *Human Studies* 10 (1987): 281–310.

"Sketches of the Banned." Time, 20 August 1965, 50.

Soria Olmedo, Andrés. *Lecciones sobre Federico García Lorca*. Granada: Comisión Nacional del Cincuentenario, 1986.

Turner, Harriet S. "Lorquian Reflections: 'Romance del emplazado.'" *Hispania* 70 (1987): 447–56.

Weisstein, Ulrich. "Comparing Literature and Art: Current Trends and Prospects in Critical Theory and Methodology." *Proceedings ICLA Innsbruck* 3 (1979): 19–30.

———. "Literature and the Visual Arts." In Barricelli and Gibaldi, *Interrelations of Literature.*

Zardoya, Concha. "La técnica metafórica de Federico García Lorca." In *Poesía española contemporánea.* Madrid: Guardarrama, 1961.

Index

Drawing titles in bold italics indicate color reproductions. Page numbers in italics indicate black and white reproduction of drawings.

199